Introduction to PCI Express[†]

A Hardware and Software Developer's Guide

Adam H. Wilen
Justin P. Schade
Ron Thornburg

Intel
PRESS

ISBN 0-9702846-9-1

This book is printed on acid-free paper. ∞

Publisher: Richard Bowles
Editor: David J. Clark
Managing Editor: David B. Spencer
Content Manager: Matt Wangler
Text Design: Marianne Phelps
Composition: WASSER Studios
Graphic Art: Donna Lawless (illustrations), Ted Cyrek (cover)

Library of Congress Cataloging in Publication Data:

Printed in the United States of America
10 9 8 7 6 5 4 3 2
Second printing, September 2009

IMPORTANT

You can access the companion Web site for this book on the Internet at:

www.intel.com/intelpress/pciexpress

Use the serial number located in the upper-right hand corner of the last page in the book to register your book and access additional material, including the Digital Edition version.

Contents

Chapter 10 PCI Express Software Overview   201

Chapter 11 Power Management   227

Acknowledgements

*When something can be read without effort, great effort has
gone into its writing.*

—Enrique Jardiel Poncela

Trying to take a complicated technology and explain it in an understandable format requires a great amount of effort. Throw on top of that the (well deserved) reputation that engineers have for poor communication skills, and it becomes a virtual miracle if the industry can avoid tripping all over itself anytime a new technology emerges. Those daunting issues are what led to the creation of this book.

The authors realize that this book is far from perfect in clearly explaining all the complexities of PCI Express. Nonetheless, we hope that this book presents the technology in a format that is easy to read and adds to your understanding of PCI Express. If the book is at all successful in accomplishing that goal, it is due to the help of numerous folks. Special thanks to Shiva Aditham and Steve Krig for creating the Appendix that provides excellent insight into compliance and interoperability concepts and issues.

Many thanks to Matt Wangler who helped guide this book through the long, long journey from its original inception to its actual publication. Additional thanks go to David Clark and Ed Solari for all of their help during the editing and review process. Donna Lawless also deserves credit for her assitance with all of the book's internal artwork. There are numerous folks (too many to mention, unfortunately), both within Intel and in the industry as a whole, who were kind enough to volunteer their feedback and technical knowledge throughout the book's development.

The authors would like to extend a special thank you to Jasmin Ajanovic, co-author of PCI Express specifications and Chairman of PCI Express Protocol and PCI Express Bridge workgroups within the PCI-SIG for his comprehensive review of this manuscript.

The authors would also like to acknowledge the PCI-SIG, the industry organization chartered to develop and manage the PCI standards. The PCI Express 1.0a specifications were used as the basic reference in preparing this manuscript.

Since this book was written outside the scope of our "real" jobs, we would like to thank our managers and advisors as well for providing us the flexibility to work on this project. Thanks to Tony Shaberman, Logan Smith, Bob Gregory, Lee Hayashida, Scott Janus, and Steve Bacchini.

Finally, we would like to acknowledge our friends and family for the support that they provided. We appreciate your patience and encouragement during the late nights and lost weekends when this book was written. In particular we'd like to thank Michelle, Jeanette, Courtney, and Alex.

Chapter **1**

Introduction

Every great advance in science has issued from a new audacity of imagination.

—John Dewey

There are certain times in the evolution of technology that serve as inflection points that forever change the course of events. For the computing sector and communications, the adoption of PCI Express will serve as one of these inflection points. PCI Express, a groundbreaking new general input/output architecture, allows computers to evolve far beyond the limitations imposed by their current infrastructure. In addition to this, PCI Express provides many new and exciting features such as Active State Power Management, Quality of Service, Hot Plug and Hot Swap support, and true isochronous capabilities.

Throughout this book there are references to three separate general I/O technologies. These technologies include: PCI (Peripheral Component Interconnect), PCI-X (a derivative of PCI), and the new architecture PCI Express. PCI-X is not an abbreviation for PCI Express. PCI-X evolved from PCI and is backward-compatible with PCI from a hardware and software perspective. PCI Express is neither an evolved nor an enhanced form of PCI or PCI-X, but does preserve the configuration, programming, and ordering models that PCI has established over the last ten years. At the physical level there are many differences between PCI/PCI-X and PCI Express. These differences are justifiable since they address many of the challenges that general I/O faces today, such as bandwidth limitations, physical space constraints, quality of service issues, and the inability to address immediate and future usage models. These differences are also equally justified through the new abilities and opportunities they bring to the platform such as evolutionary and revolutionary design opportunities. Aside from the opportunity of introducing a brand new general I/O architecture, there are several motivations for writing this book. One of the primary motivations is to give the reader an easy-to-follow, introductory overview of PCI Express technology. This book is not a replacement for reading the *PCI Express Base Specification*. The opinion of the authors is that this book makes the *PCI Express Base Specification* easier to comprehend by giving it a context with extra background and insights into many areas of the technology. The second motivation is to prepare the industry for a transition to PCI Express architecture by discussing system-level impact, application-specific transitions, and the general timeline for consumer market introduction.

A Quick Overview

PCI Express is a high-performance interconnect that gives more for less, meaning more bandwidth with fewer pins. PCI Express is designed to leverage the strengths of yesterday's and current general I/O architectures while addressing immediate and future I/O architectural and mechanical issues with current technologies. A few examples of these issues are bandwidth constraints, protocol limitations, and high pin count. More technically speaking, PCI Express is a high speed, low voltage, differential serial pathway for two devices to communicate with each other. PCI Express uses a protocol that allows devices to communicate simultaneously by implementing dual uni-directional paths between two devices, as shown in Figure 1.1.

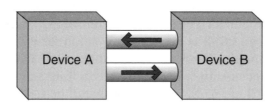

Figure 1.1   Dual Uni-directional Path Concept

For PCI Express, high speed equates to a bit rate of 2,500,000,000 bits per second (2.5 gigabits per second). Low voltage equates to a differential signaling environment of between 0.8 and 1.2 volts. The theoretical bandwidth of PCI Express nearly doubles the theoretical bandwidth of PCI with approximately one tenth the number of pins.

Aside from connecting two devices, PCI Express provides two methods to satisfy the growing bandwidth, or data-throughput capacity, requirements between two devices. Much like a rubber band, PCI Express can be stretched to meet the demands of general I/O, which eliminates the need to support multiple I/O technologies within a system. As an example, PCI Express can replace AGP, PCI/PCI-X, and the proprietary interconnect between chips. PCI Express can be scaled in a linear manner by adding additional serial lanes that work together to meet the bandwidth objectives of a device. Additionally, PCI Express provides hooks for expanding the bus frequency beyond what is currently defined today in order to maximize the use of this architecture and reduce the chance of having to define a new technology every few years. A key advantage of PCI Express scalability is that it can be scaled on a device-to-device basis within a system of multiple PCI Express connections. For instance, if one system device-to-device interconnect requires PCI Express to be scaled to meet its bandwidth objectives, the rest of the PCI Express system device-to-device interconnects are not affected.

The *PCI Express Base Specification* defines the following configuration of serial links: x1, x2, x4, x8, x12, x16, and x32 (read as "by one, by two," and so on). For example, a x1 configuration indicates a single serial path to and from a device. A x2 configuration indicates two serial paths to and from a device, as shown in Figure 1.2.

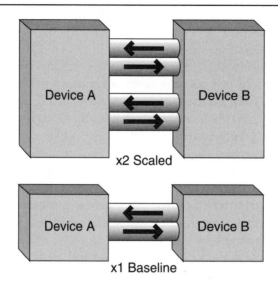

Figure 1.2   Scaling Example (x1 Link Compared to x2 Link)

Why Develop a New I/O Technology?

When first introduced in the early 1990s, the PCI Bus played a unifying role for multiple I/O elements. It was first adopted as a chip-to-chip interconnect and a replacement for the somewhat fragmented ISA technologies. During the early years the 33 megahertz PCI Bus was a good match for the I/O bandwidth requirements of the mainstream PC platform. Today the story is quite different. Processor and memory frequencies have been increasing frequently with the system processor increasing in frequency at the most aggressive rate. Over the last ten years the PCI bus has increased in frequency (from 33 megahertz to 66 megahertz in 1995) while processor frequencies have increased from 33 megahertz to just over 3 gigahertz. Interestingly, nearly 80 percent of the computer systems sold today are still trying utilizing the 33 megahertz PCI bus introduced almost a decade ago. The emerging I/O devices of today, such as Gigabit Ethernet and 1394b monopolize nearly all of the bandwidth of the PCI bus as single devices on the bus. There is a strong need to close the gap again between the processor's capability and the general I/O's capability.

In addition to bringing the I/O bandwidth capacity in line with system processor capabilities, the I/O architecture needs to address the bandwidth requirements of current and future I/O devices. During the last few years I/O bandwidth demands have increased beyond what PCI architecture can sustain. As a result the I/O has once again become fragmented with singular function architectures (such as the AGP, USB2, ATA100, SATA, and more) to fill the bandwidth gaps. Systems designed with fragmented architectures require many different types of connectors, test tools, designer expertise, and a variety of other things that increase not only the complexity of the system but the cost to the user as well. A strong need exists for an architecture that will reunite the general I/O, simplify the design, reduce overall system costs, and address the current and future bandwidth requirements and usage models.

PCI architecture is based upon parallel bus signaling at 33 megahertz and more recently 66 megahertz. A close inspection of parallel bus signaling technology in general reveals that the practical limits (1 gigahertz) of performance are not far off. Since PCI is nowhere near the 1 gigahertz frequency it could be argued that there is some room for PCI to grow. An argument against that line of thinking is the return on investment for making such advances. Parallel bus signaling technologies that operate at bus frequencies of 250 megahertz and higher are plagued with electrical challenges and a limited set of routing solutions. Advancing the bus frequency beyond 500 megahertz will require massive efforts and yield less than friendly results, if those results are useable at all. There is no question that something beyond PCI is required going forward. This is the opportunity to go beyond the stopgap approach of trying to squeeze more life out of PCI by simply bumping up the frequency. This is the chance to make changes that will carry general I/O architecture comfortably into the next decade.

PCI is based on a protocol that is nearly a decade old. As usage models change, the protocol must adapt to deal with new models. The aggressive multimedia nature of today's applications such as streaming audio and video require the ability to guarantee certain amounts of bandwidth. The PCI protocol does not have the ability to deal appropriately with these types of deterministic transactions. There is a need to define an architecture that is equipped to deal with these multimedia usage models.

Who Should Read This Book

This book is an introduction to PCI Express, its motivations, applications, technology, and timeline. As such it is written for anyone with a desire to understand PCI Express at a baseline technical level. Many of the concepts and ideas introduced in this book are easier to understand with some basic knowledge of computer architecture, the PCI protocol, and electric circuits; however, there are many analogies and illustrations in this book to assist the reader in understanding the key points and ideas presented. Specifically this book is written with the system integrator, hardware developer, software developer, product marketing engineer and application engineer in mind. Others may also find this information insightful and useful.

System Integrators

System integrators will benefit from the system level information that is discussed in many sections of this book. Of particular interest is the impact to the current infrastructure, cost structure, flexibility, applications, and technology timelines. System integrators can take advantage of this information for developing strategic short-range and long-range goals for incorporating PCI Express into current and future designs.

Hardware Developers

Hardware developers can use the information in this book to assist in interpreting the *PCI Express Base Specification*. The technology sections of this book are written to address and answer many of the "why" questions that the specification does not clearly articulate. This book can be used to bring hardware developers up to speed quickly on key PCI Express concepts before and while reading through the *PCI Express Base Specification*.

Software Developers

Software developers can use the information in this book to understand what must be done by BIOS code and drivers to take advantage of PCI Express features. Software developers should focus on which features can take advantage of the existing PCI configuration model and which features cannot. The information in the technology section of the book is helpful in outlining the general flow of software routines in setting up the advanced features.

Product Marketing Engineers

Product marketing engineers will find the information very useful for advocating and selling PCI Express-based designs and applications to their customer base. Product marketing engineers should focus on the general goals and requirements of PCI Express, actual PCI Express applications, and the general product definition and timetables.

Application Engineers

Applications engineers will find the entire book useful to support and drive their customer base through the transition to this new technology. As with silicon designers, application engineers can use this book to provide insight and additional understanding to many key areas of the *PCI Base Express Specification.*

The Organization of This Book

This book is organized into three key sections. Each section has been shaped to provide the necessary insights and information to lead the reader through an informative journey. While each section has some sense of independence and can be studied separate from the rest, the reader can gain a better understanding if the sections are investigated in the order they are placed in this book, Beyond PCI, The Technology, and Adopting PCI Express.

Beyond PCI

The first section of this book sets the stage for understanding the motivations, goals and applications of PCI Express. As a baseline, a brief history of PCI is explored in Chapter 2, as are the successes and challenges PCI has encountered during its lifetime. The successes of PCI are discussed as a foundation for PCI Express, while the challenges PCI faces are disclosed to reveal areas that need to be addressed by a next generation technology.

Chapter 3 includes an investigation of the goals and requirements of PCI Express. This section explores the metrics and criteria for PCI Express adoption, with a focus on preserving key commonalities such as infrastructure, manufacturing, multi-segment support, and cost. In addition to this, many new capabilities are discussed.

The first section ends with a discussion of next generation applications in Chapter 4, looking closely at the applications for which PCI Express offers significant benefits beyond existing I/O architectures. This discussion takes into account the various segments such as desktop, mobile, server, and communications. New and revolutionary usage models are also discussed as a natural solution to evolving system and I/O requirements.

The Technology

The second section of this book is the general hardware and software architecture of PCI Express. This section examines what it means to have a layered architecture, how those layers interact with each other, with software, and with the outside world. This section also introduces and explains the advantages of the PCI Express transaction flow control mechanisms, closing with a look at PCI Express power management.

Chapter 5 introduces PCI Express as an advanced layered architecture. It includes an introduction to the three key PCI Express architectural layers and their interaction with each other, with software, and with the outside world. A top-down description follows where the uppermost layer (the Transaction Layer), which interacts directly with application software and hardware, is discussed first, followed by the intermediate (Data Link Layer), and final layer (Physical Layer). Chapters 6, 7, and 8 examine each of the three architectural layers in detail. Following the discussion of the individual PCI Express layers is a discussion in Chapter 9 on the various transaction flow control mechanisms within PCI Express. This section describes the ordering requirements for the various PCI Express transaction types. The bulk of this section, however, focuses on the newer flow control mechanisms that PCI Express utilizes such as virtual channels, traffic classes, and flow control credits.

Chapter 10 presents insights into PCI Express software architecture. This section focuses on identifying the PCI Express features available in a legacy software environment. It also includes a discussion of software configuration stacks for control of advanced features.

Chapter 11 concludes this section with a discussion on PCI Express power management. This chapter discusses the existing PCI power management model as a base for PCI Express power management. This base is used to discuss PCI Express system-level, device-level, and bus/link power management states.

Adopting PCI Express

The final section of this book is what system integrators and designers must consider in implementing PCI Express. This section is subdivided into three categories that focus on different elements of the design or project lifecycle. The discussion begins with an exploration of the implementation-specific details of PCI Express, is followed by a general timetable for PCI Express and concludes with a specific definition and planning discussion that takes an informative look at several different PCI Express products.

PCI Express implementation in Chapter 12 outlines various design and infrastructure specific details that must be considered. In the design-specific arena of PCI Express, general chipset partitioning is discussed as it relates to the general architecture of PCI Express. While actual partitioning will vary from chipset vendor to chipset vendor, there are some general commonalities that are discussed at a high level. This chapter also examines generic PCI Express routing recommendations and legacy and evolving form factor infrastructure. This discussion outlines new form factor opportunities and mechanical considerations such as cards and connectors and their impact to the system.

The general timetable for PCI Express in Chapter 13 includes the planning and preparation-specific details that system designers and integrators must consider. This chapter also discusses the challenges and benefits of early adoption, especially factors that can affect the adoption and schedule of PCI Express. In addition to this a general profile of an early and late adopter will be examined. This allows companies to assess what type of adopter they are and what opportunities, challenges, and tools are available to them.

Chapter 14 closes the book with a case study of several different PCI Express-based products. The development phase of each product is examined along with a discussion of some of the challenges of implementing PCI Express technology.

Chapter 2

The PCI Legacy, Successes, and Challenges

We live in a moment of history where change is so speeded up that we begin to see the present only when it is already disappearing.

—R. D. Laing

This chapter looks at the legacy of the Peripheral Component Interconnect commonly called PCI, identifying what PCI does well and where it has become inadequate. The chapter outlines the introduction of PCI and the evolution of the architecture up to the present, explaining the need for a new I/O architecture.

The Introduction of PCI

The concept of PCI was originally developed in the early 1990s by Intel Corporation as a general I/O architecture that could theoretically transfer four times more data than the fastest I/O buses at the time, as shown in Table 2.1. Intel developed the architecture to address the problem of data bottlenecks resulting from new graphics-based operating systems such as Microsoft Windows[†] 3.1. Additionally, the bandwidth capacity of PCI was an ideal match for the new Intel® Pentium® brand of processors that Intel was preparing to market. PCI was viewed as the vehicle that would fully exploit the processing capabilities of the new brand of processors.

Table 2.1   I/O Bus Bandwidth Comparison

I/O Bus	MHz	Bus Width (Bits)	Megabytes Per Second (MB/s)
Industry Standard Architecture (ISA)	8.3	16	8.3
Extended Industry Standard Architecture (EISA)	8.3	32	33
Peripheral Component Interconnect (PCI)	33	32	132

Up to this point in the computing industry, technology patents were used as a means to secure cash flows by leaders in the technology sector (to some extent this is still common practice today). Access to technology was available through the purchasing of costly licenses. Violators who infringed on patent rights without purchasing the proper license rights were often punished through a painful and costly litigation process. While revenues could be enjoyed by technology patent holders for a time, they were generally short lived because of patent wars between competing architectures. This era of patent wars was a time of constant change and massive industry segregation that resulted in little flexibility for the consumer and higher system costs overall.

In 1992 Intel took steps to help change the PC industry into what it is today. In an effort to unite the computing industry around a core architecture, Intel and several other key industry players organized the Peripheral Component Interconnect Special Interest Group. Membership in the group was given to all those willing to participate, sign a PCI license agreement, and pay a small fee. This license in essence was a give-and-take agreement between group members that required current and future PCI-related patent claims to be licensed royalty-free to other PCI-SIG members. Unfortunately, very few companies ever signed the original license agreement, which would have made the specification truly royalty free. The Peripheral Component Interconnect Special Interest Group was eventually reorganized as a non-profit corporation named the PCI-SIG. With that reorganization, the license agreement was changed to be reasonable and nondiscriminatory instead of royalty free. Reasonable and nondiscriminatory is defined by the following paragraph as documented under Section 15.3 of the PCI-SIG bylaws.

Member and its Affiliates hereby agree to grant to other Members and their Affiliates under reasonable terms and conditions that are demonstrably free of any unfair discrimination, a nonexclusive, nontransferable, worldwide license under its Necessary Claims to allow such Members to make, have made, use, import, offer to sell, lease and sell and otherwise distribute Compliant Portions, provided that such agreement to license shall not extend to any part or function of a product in which a Compliant Portion is incorporated that is not itself part of the Compliant Portion.

The PCI-SIG was given the charter to manage, develop, and promote PCI. Over the last ten years the PCI-SIG has done exactly that. The PCI specification is currently in its third major revision and many other PCI-related technologies and concepts have evolved at the hands of this group. The founding of the PCI-SIG has done more to unify and shape general I/O in the computing industry than any other forum. Currently there are more than 800 member companies of the PCI-SIG. PCI Express will use the influence of this group to assist in its adoption as the next I/O standard.

PCI Successes

As fast as technology has evolved and advanced over the last ten years, it is amazing how long PCI has remained a viable piece of the computing platform. The original architects of PCI had no idea that this architecture would still be integral to the computing platform ten years later. PCI has survived and thrived as long as it has because of the successes it has enjoyed. The most noted success of PCI is the wide industry and segment acceptance achieved through the promotion and evolution of the technology. This is followed by general compatibility as defined by the *PCI Local Bus Specification*. Combine the above with processor architecture independence, full-bus mastering, Plug and Play operation, and high performance low cost implementation, and you have a recipe for success.

Industry Acceptance

Few technologies have influenced general PC architecture as much as PCI has. The way in which this influence can be gauged is by analyzing segment acceptance and technology lifespan. PCI has forged its way into the three computing segments (desktop, server, and mobile), as well as communications, and has become the I/O standard for the last ten years. The primary force that has made this possible is the PCI-SIG. The PCI-SIG placed ownership of PCI in the hands of its member companies. These member companies banded together to drive standardization of I/O into the market through the promotion of PCI. A list of current PCI-SIG members can be found on the PCI-SIG web site at *http://www.pcisig.com*.

There are two ways in which PCI is sufficiently flexible that member companies banded together under the PCI-SIG. The first is that PCI is processor-agnostic (both its frequency and its voltage). This allows PCI to function in the server market, mobile market, and desktop market with little to no change. Each of these markets supports various processors that operate at different voltages and frequencies. This allows members to standardize their I/O across multiple product groups and generations. The net effect to the vendor is lower system cost through the use of common elements that can be secured at lower pricing through higher volume contracts. For example, a system integrator can use the same PCI based networking card in all of their product lines for three to four generations. Along the same line of thought, multiple segments can use the same I/O product that invokes the economic concept of reduced pricing through economy of scale.

The second way that PCI is flexible is in its ability to support multiple form factors. The PCI-SIG members defined connectors, add-in cards, and I/O brackets to standardize the I/O back panel and form factors for the server, desktop, and mobile markets. The standardization of add-in cards, I/O brackets, and form factors in particular has had a massive impact to cost structure of PCI from not only a system integrator's perspective, but from a consumer perspective as well. This standardization made the distribution of PCI-based add-in cards and form-factor-based computer chassis possible through the consumer channel. For a product to be successful in the consumer market it must be standardized in order to sustain sufficient volumes to meet general consumer price targets.

Defined Specifications

PCI add-in cards and discrete silicon are available from hundreds of different vendors fulfilling just about every conceivable I/O application. For example, consumers can choose from over thirty brands of PCI add-in modem cards alone ranging from several dollars to several hundred dollars in cost. These PCI add-in solutions can function in systems that feature chipsets from multiple vendors like Intel and others.

It is no mere coincidence that PCI is very successful from a vendor compatibility standpoint. This success can be attributed to the electrical, protocol, mechanical, and software requirements that are clearly documented within the various PCI specifications:

1. *PCI Local Bus, 2.3*
2. *Mini PCI, 1.0*
3. *PCI-to-PCI Bridge Architecture, 1,1*
4. *PCI Hot Plug, 1.1*
5. *PCI Standard Hot-Plug Controller Subsystem, 1.0*
6. *PCI Bus Power Management Interface, 1.1*
7. *PCI BIOS, 2.1*

These specifications define how a generic PCI device should function at every level. This level of definition makes it possible for vendors to build generic models with which they can test for protocol and electrical compatibility prior to manufacturing. As vendors design their devices to meet these guidelines, they can be assured that their devices are compatible with devices from other vendors that also meet these specification guidelines.

In addition to the various PCI specifications that outline device requirements, the PCI-SIG has also developed a compliance program. The program has a compliance checklist that vendors can use to verify the compliance of their devices and motherboards. In addition to the checklist, compliance workshops, also referred to as plug-fests, are held to allow vendors to check the interoperability of their devices. Upon completing the checklist and compliance workshop, vendors can move to have their devices and/or motherboards added to an integrators list kept by the PCI-SIG. This list of integrators is available online through the PCI-SIG website at *http://www.pcisig.com*. System integrators use this list to verify that their preferred hardware complies with the applicable PCI specification. If their preferred hardware is not listed on the integrators list the system integrator can quickly choose a compatible piece of hardware that is. Refer to Appendix A for more on compliance.

Processor Architecture Independence

Prior to PCI, the architecture of computers was expanded to place high speed peripherals and devices on the CPU local bus, which provided quick access to main memory, as shown in Figure 2.1. This topology allowed systems to increase overall performance of the computer while still maintaining backward compatibility with legacy ISA- and EISA-based devices and peripherals that existed on the expansion bus. While this architectural concept did increase the overall system performance of the personal computer, it was not a long-term solution. In a world of increasing CPU speeds this presented a major problem. As bus speeds increased, the number of loads (devices) that could be supported on the CPU local bus decreased. Additionally, the CPU local bus operated on a single clock, which meant that the CPU performance was no faster than the slowest device on the bus. Even if device loading was not an issue, the fact that all system peripherals and devices would have to match the frequency of the CPU to realize actual CPU performance was hard to balance. Under this type of architecture computer system integrators were faced with the fact that they would either have to live with a greatly increased cost or come up with a different architectural solution to address the problem.

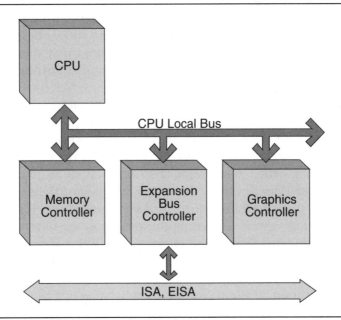

Figure 2.1   CPU Local Bus Architecture

PCI was incredibly successful at increasing the number of high speed peripherals and devices that could be supported by electrically isolating and frequency isolating those peripherals and devices from the CPU local bus, as shown in Figure 2.2. This is referred to as *buffered isolation.* There are two other key benefits to buffered isolation. The first is the ability to run concurrent cycles on both the PCI bus and the CPU local bus, thus increasing overall system efficiency. The second benefit is the ability to increase the CPU local bus frequency independent of the PCI bus speed and device loading. In this way PCI was designed to be a long-term solution.

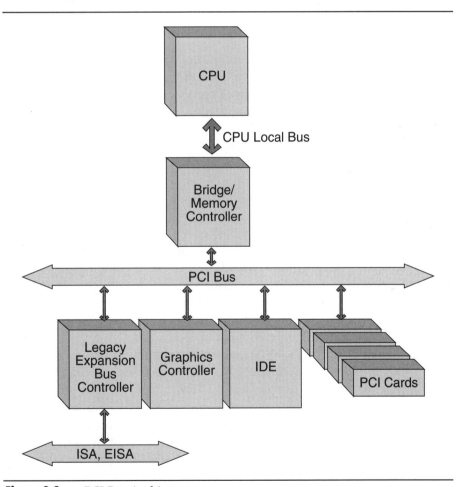

Figure 2.2   PCI Bus Architecture

Full Bus Mastering

PCI architecture allows any capable PCI device on the bus to become the bus master. The concept of *bus mastering* predates PCI; however, PCI is the first architecture to put all the necessary pieces together, software and hardware, to bring the benefits of full bus mastering to the PC. PCI bus mastering allows peripherals and devices requiring service to gain immediate and direct control of the bus through an arbitration process. This allows individual devices to master a transaction directly instead of waiting for the host CPU to service the device. The net effect to the system is a reduction of overall latency in servicing I/O transactions.

Plug and Play Operation

PCI changed the personal computing industry forever with the introduction of PCI Plug and Play. Prior to PCI Plug and Play, the configuration of add-in peripherals and devices such as ISA and EISA cards was very cumbersome. Users were required to navigate through a web of jumpers and software configuration screens with knowledge of every other peripheral in their system in order to hit the right combination that would make the peripheral or device function. In many cases, a user ended up taking his or her computer to a computer shop to get the hardware installed and configured properly. Since peripherals and devices were difficult to install, the number of users making hardware purchases was limited.

PCI Plug and Play established cooperation between hardware and software to allow peripherals and devices to become automatically detected and configured. This allowed users to easily upgrade their systems by simply plugging the peripheral or device into the slot and powering the system back up. Upon power-up the hardware would be identified, resources allocated, and the proper driver would be invoked through a series of easy to follow configuration screens.

The first PCI-based Plug and Play computer systems did not appear in the marketplace until late 1994. However, due to Plug and Play dependence on both hardware and software mechanisms, full Plug and Play functionality was not in place until 1996. PCI Plug and Play required a new operating system, a new BIOS architecture, and changes in both chipset and add-in card hardware. In the context of this chapter PCI Plug and Play is considered a success because of the positive impact it had on bringing more novice users into the computer realm. As a side note, getting PCI Plug and Play to work properly was a massive challenge due to the dependencies on software communities, chipset hardware communities, and PCI add-in card device communities.

High Performance Low Cost Implementation

PCI architecture hit the proverbial technology sweet spot that is very important to device and motherboard manufacturers. The sweet spot is defined as the most for the least. PCI offered the highest performance at the lowest cost. The technology could be realized and manufactured on the common processes and fabrication technologies available at that time. Additionally, since PCI could consolidate nearly all I/O into a single architecture, system vendors could get away with building fewer motherboard variations. A single variation could support different features depending on the add-in device installed in the PCI slot. Many of the details around high performance and low cost are addressed in much more detail in Chapter 3.

PCI Challenges

Equal to the successes that PCI has enjoyed are the challenges it now faces. These challenges pave the way for defining a new architecture. The challenges that PCI faces are, in essence, areas where it has become inadequate. The primary inadequacies are bandwidth limitations, host pin limitations, the inability to support differentiated services such as real time (isochronous) data transfers, and the inability to address future I/O requirements such as security and I/O virtualization.

Bandwidth Limitations

PCI transfers data at a frequency of 33 megahertz across either a 32-bit or 64-bit bus. This results in a theoretical bandwidth of 132 megabytes per second (MB/s) for a 32-bit bus and a theoretical bandwidth of 264 megabytes per second for a 64-bit bus. In 1995 the PCI-SIG added support for 66 megahertz PCI to the *PCI Local Bus Specification*. This support is backward-compatible with 33 megahertz PCI in a 32- or 64-bit bus configuration. Currently, the server market has been the only market to make use of 66 megahertz PCI and 64-bit PCI, as shown in Table 2.2. This server market only adoption is probably because 64-bit PCI requires so much space on the platform due to the connector size and signal routing space. The server market is much less sensitive to physical space constraints than the desktop and mobile market.

Table 2.2   PCI Bandwidth and Market Use

PCI Bus Width in bits	Bus Frequency in Megahertz	Bandwidth in MB/s	Market
32	33	132	Desktop/Mobile
32	66	264	Server
64	33	264	Server
64	66	512	Server

The introduction of PCI-X in 1999, which operates at 66 megahertz and higher and has 32-bit and 64-bit bus support, essentially slowed any momentum in the server market for PCI. The desktop and mobile markets continue to use only 33 megahertz PCI in the 32-bit bus form. In light of this, when PCI is mentioned in this book it is in reference to 33 megahertz, 32-bit PCI, which is used exclusively in the mobile and desktop systems that account for over 85 percent of the total computer market.

The usable bandwidth (approximately 90 megabytes per second) of the PCI bus is much less than the theoretical bandwidth due to protocol overhead and general bus topology issues, such as shared bandwidth, that are discussed in more detail in Chapter 3. Since PCI is a shared bus, the available bandwidth decreases as number of users increase. When PCI was introduced, 90 megabytes per second was more than adequate for the I/O usage models and applications that had been defined. Today's I/O usage models and applications have grown to require far more bandwidth than can be supplied by PCI (take Gigabit Ethernet, for example, that requires 125 megabytes per second). While PCI has been improved over the years (the current *PCI Local Bus Specification* is version 2.3, however, it is currently being revised to a version 3.0), the operational frequency of PCI has only been increased once. Comparatively, CPU frequencies have increased dramatically. Ten years ago 66 megahertz was a pretty fast CPU speed, but today's CPU speeds are two orders of magnitude larger, already passing the 3000 megahertz (or 3 gigahertz) mark, as shown in Figure 2.3. PCI bandwidth hardly dents the I/O processing capability of today's CPUs.

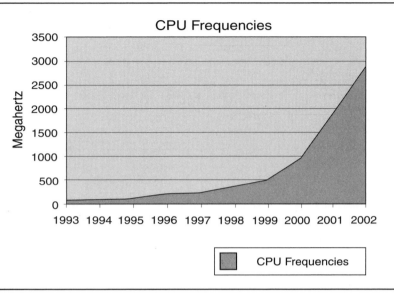

Figure 2.3   CPU Frequency History

Host Pin Limitations

At 33 megahertz, PCI is ideal as a multipoint solution for slot-based add-in cards. The benefit of operating at frequencies of 33 megahertz and slower is the ability to support multiple devices on the same bus. At these frequencies, impedance mismatches due to multiple connectors and various topologies are not as dominant in determining signal integrity. Many systems today have as many as six PCI connectors that connect to the same 33 megahertz PCI bus. This gives an advantage to the hardware developer who desires to support multiple devices. Looking at the pin-to-device ratio, parallel busses such as PCI require quite a few pins to support a single bus. Without the ability to support multiple devices per bus, silicon devices become heavily burdened with pins.

As PCI frequencies have become inadequate in certain environments, the PCI derivative PCI-X has sought to provide some bandwidth relief by increasing the bus frequency. PCI-X supports the following bus frequencies: 33 megahertz (using conventional PCI protocol instead of PCI-X protocol), 66 megahertz, 100 megahertz, 133 megahertz, 266 megahertz, and 533 megahertz, and is backward compatible with PCI. Not surprisingly, there is a correlation between the number of connectors that can be supported on a bus and the operating frequency of the bus. For example, PCI-X running at 66 megahertz can support no more than four connectors reliably. As the frequency is increased to 100 megahertz, the number of connectors that can be reliably supported is two. At 133 megahertz and above, only one PCI-X connector can be supported. Increasing the frequency to 266 megahertz or 533 megahertz reduces the routing length from the host silicon to a single connector and makes the design extremely difficult and very expensive by requiring an increase in number of printed circuit board (PCB) layers. This presents a challenge for system designers who require more bandwidth and extra connectors on the platform.

The 64-bit PCI-X specification requires approximately 150 pins on the host silicon per bus segment. The average host silicon device for I/O has nearly 600 pins and supports various types of I/O in addition to PCI or PCI-X. If each PCI-X segment supports only one connector at high frequencies and requires nearly 25 percent of the available chip pins, then supporting two segments would require 50 percent and three segments would require 75 percent of the available chip pins, as shown in Figure 2.4. As a baseline most systems require at least four connectors for flexibility and upgradeability. As mentioned earlier, PCI-X is used exclusively in servers, which do not have the same constraints as desktop and mobile systems. Servers can tolerate the addition of extra host silicon devices to a system in order to support additional PCI-X bus segments, partly because their system budgets (cost, power, and real estate) are much higher and partly because their form factors are much larger. Desktop and mobile budgets can neither bear the cost nor the system space to add additional host devices to support multiple PCI-X segments. This is one of the primary reasons why PCI-X is not used in desktop or mobile systems. Desktop and mobile systems are constrained to use PCI to maintain upgradeability through available connectors.

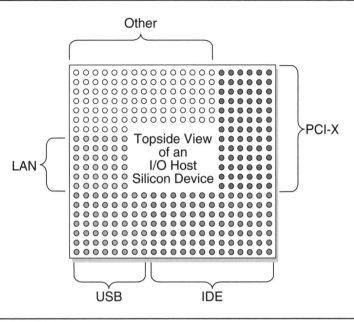

Figure 2.4   Pin-limited I/O Example

Inability to Support Real-Time (Isochronous) Data Transfers

Applications, such as streaming audio and video, require guaranteed bandwidth and deterministic transaction latency. Without these guarantees users can experience glitches in audio and video. This is the result of lost data due excessive latency or delays due to bandwidth conflicts. When PCI was first introduced the number of real-time (*isochronous*) I/O applications was limited and the bandwidth of those applications was relatively narrow compared to the overall bandwidth that PCI offered. As a result, PCI architecture did not define a mechanism to support isochronous data transfers. Isochronous data transfers consist of data that must be given dedicated bandwidth and deterministic latency since it is time-sensitive. In a PCI-based system where arbitration must be fair between all devices, dedicated bandwidth and deterministic latency cannot take the form of more than a priority scheme.

It can be argued that PCI supports isochronous data transfers. There are many PCI-based audio and video application add-in cards available on the market today. A clarification needs to be made here. Some of those applications may appear to be isochronous, but they are not. Low bandwidth feeds over a high-speed interface can look isochronous to some extent. Given that PCI does not support true isochronous transactions, it becomes a relationship of device requirements to overall bus bandwidth and loading. Today's isochronous data transfers, such as high-definition uncompressed video and audio, are anything but low-speed (as an example consider host controllers for USB2 and 1394B that need in excess of 60–80 megabytes per second and trending up) and reveal quite rapidly through system glitches and audio pops that PCI is not designed to deal with isochronous data transfers.

Inability to Address Future I/O Requirements

PCI was never intended to last beyond the 1990s and as such is not well equipped to deal with I/O requirements of the future. User applications have evolved dramatically from what they were ten years ago and are expected to continue to evolve through the next ten years (many of these applications are discussed in Chapter 4). During the era in which PCI was first introduced I/O bandwidth was well matched to the processing power of the system CPU. As CPU frequencies have quickly scaled, an invitation has been given to I/O vendors to develop applications that can take advantage of today's and tomorrows processing power. From a design perspective, PCI is not well positioned to be defined on the next generation silicon processes. These new processes do not easily support PCI signaling voltages. With some degree of difficulty these voltages can still be supported today. However, this is not the case for future processes.

The very direction of the computing industry is dependent upon addressing, designing for, and certainly delivering on future I/O requirements. CPU vendors such as Intel are not designing 3 gigahertz CPUs to run word processing applications. These powerful CPUs are being designed to address the types of I/O applications that will put the computer at the center of the digital world with I/O extensions connecting to every conceivable digital device.

PCI Moving Forward

Since the conception of PCI several splinter technologies and specifications have been created while the PCI-SIG moved to advance the frequency, bus width, voltage support, and special features of PCI. The name of these technologies and specifications usually bears PCI as some portion of its designation. A few commonly known PCI based technologies are Mini-PCI and PCI-X. Both of these technologies are based on PCI and use a subset of the same signal protocol, electrical definitions, and configuration definitions as PCI. Mini-PCI defines an alternate implementation for small form factor PCI cards. PCI-X was designed with the goal of increasing the overall clock speed of the bus and improving bus efficiencies while maintaining backward compatibility with conventional PCI devices. PCI-X is used exclusively in server-class systems that require extra bandwidth and can tolerate the PCI-X bus width, connector lengths, and card lengths as well as associated system design complexity and cost.

The PCI SIG will continue to work on enhancements to the existing base of standards (like the 533 megahertz PCI-X). However, the future of PCI is PCI Express. PCI Express is not the next stretch of PCI architecture, but rather an architectural leap that keeps the core of PCI's software infrastructure to minimize the delays to adoption that were experienced with PCI. PCI Express completely replaces the hardware infrastructure with a radically new forward-looking architecture. The goal of this leap is to hit the technology sweet-spot like PCI did nearly a decade ago.

Chapter 3

Goals and Requirements

---

*I don't know the key to success, but the key to failure is to
try and please everyone.*

—Dr. William Cosby

This chapter explores key goals and requirements for smooth migration of systems and designs to PCI Express architecture. A basic as-
sumption is that PCI Express must be stable and scalable for the next
decade and longer. This chapter discusses the need for PCI Express scalability and pin link usage efficiency. Another primary requirement is
market segment support, focusing on the four primary market segments,
desktop PCs, servers, mobile PCs, and communications. Following the
discussion on market segment support, the chapter explores system level
cost parity with PCI as a key requirement for technology migration. Af-
terwards, I/O simplification goals are explored with an emphasis on consolidation of general I/O. Finally, the chapter investigates backward
compatibility as it relates to current software environments and form
factors.

Scalability, Stability, and Performance

The direction of the personal computing market and the focus of many
large players in the computer industry is to make the PC the center of the
digital world. Over a period of a few years the implementations and
requirements of I/O have changed dramatically. The usage models for

general I/O have grown to include not only streaming audio and video, but the entire array of digital devices such as PDAs, MP3 players, cameras, and more. At first introduction PCI Express will have sufficient bandwidth to support the existing applications. However, evolving applications and future applications will require PCI Express to be scalable, as seen in Figure 3.1.

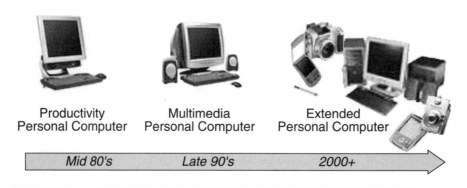

Productivity   Multimedia   Extended
Personal Computer   Personal Computer   Personal Computer

Mid 80's   Late 90's   2000+

Figure 3.1   Evolving I/O Implementation

Stability Requirement: Stability for the Next Decade

Scalability has stability as a byproduct. This is accomplished by removing the need to change the architecture dramatically every few years. Designs that still use conventional PCI today are considered to be very stable because they have been around for so long. PCI Express architecture is designed to allow maximum reuse of the existing PCI infrastructure such as software and form factors while establishing new architectural capabilities that propel system performance beyond what it is today. Each piece of PCI Express architecture is designed and organized with the future in mind. The goal of PCI Express is to minimize the risk of advancing the technology while preserving stability of the local environment. Features and applications that transition to PCI Express architecture can continue to leverage the stability of PCI while capitalizing on the benefits of PCI Express.

Scalability Requirement: Growth Options for the Future

For many years conventional PCI defined scalability as having the ability to populate more PCI slots on the platform to take advantage of the bandwidth (133 megabytes per second theoretical maximum) conventional PCI offers. Initially, there were not many usage models that could take advantage of all the bandwidth that the conventional PCI bus could supply. PCI Express looks at scalability a bit differently.

The most generic definition that can be extracted from the word "scalable" is "the ability to increase." With this definition in mind, there are two ways in which an electrical connection can be made scalable. The first deals with increasing the number of logical signal lines and the second deals with clock speed or operational frequency. PCI Express makes use of both methods of scaling.

The first scaling requirement for PCI Express is the ability to scale the number of logical signal lines. Unlike conventional PCI, PCI Express has the ability to add or reduce the number of logical signal lines to meet bandwidth objectives. As mentioned in previous chapters, PCI Express defines the following logical line widths also referred to as a link width: x1, x2, x4, x8, x12, x16, and x32. Consider PCI Express to be very similar to a highway. When a city builds a highway it must consider the amount of traffic that will use the highway. If a single lane is understood to support 2000 cars per hour, and the projected need is 4000 cars per hour, the city will lay asphalt for two lanes to support the projected traffic. When the city grows and traffic becomes congested, as 8000 cars per hour try to use the two lanes, the city adds additional traffic lanes to support the need. This is similar to how PCI Express can scale its logical signal lines. The approach is quite different from conventional PCI, which requires 32 logical signal lines regardless of the actual bandwidth requirement.

The second scaling requirement for PCI Express is the ability to scale the clock speed or operational frequency. One concept that the past ten years has made incredibly clear is that there is a point where making a bus wider and wider becomes undesirable due to challenging routing requirements and constraints. As a result PCI Express has defined a method to support the scaling of operational frequencies beyond the initial 2.5 gigahertz. Since PCI Express uses a layered architecture, frequency scaling only affects the Physical Layer. This allows the core layers (Transaction and Data Link Layers) to remain unchanged, thus preserving compatibility. The next generation frequencies have not been specifically documented yet. However, they are expected to be more than 5 gigahertz and up to 10 gigahertz as shown in Figure 3.2.

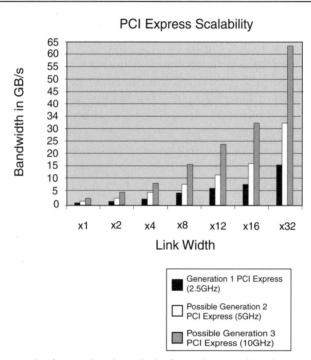

The next generation frequencies shown in the figure above are based upon current speculation.

Figure 3.2   PCI Express Scalability

Performance Requirement: Pin and Link Efficiency

The market craves technological advances that can dwarf the preceding year's technology in not only performance, but in size. This presents a very interesting challenge to architects, system designers, and silicon designers. To address market cravings, PCI Express seeks to be the most pin-efficient and link-usage-efficient interface available. An examination of the per-pin performance and bus/link usage efficiency of conventional PCI, PCI-X, and PCI Express follows.

Pin Efficiency

First consider conventional PCI, which uses a 32-bit wide (4 byte) bi-directional bus at an operational frequency of 33.3 megahertz. In addition to the 32 data pins, there are typically 42 side band and power and ground pins.

$$33.3\,megahertz * 4\,bytes \cong 133\,megabytes\ per\ second\ TX\ and\ RX$$

$$\frac{133\,megabytes\ per\ second}{74\,pins} \cong 1.80\,megabytes\ per\ pin$$

Note: In conventional PCI, 32 pins are used for signaling. The remaining 42 pins are typically used for side band signals, power and ground. The actual number of side band and power and ground pins depends on the package technology and the aggressiveness of electrical design.

Equation 3.1   Conventional PCI Peak Bandwidth-per-Pin Calculation

Next examine the pin efficiency of PCI-X. The equation assumes that PCI-X 2.0 is being investigated, which operates at 533 megahertz and has a 64-bit wide (8-byte) bi-directional bus typically requiring 150 total signal, sideband, and power/ground pins.

$$533\, megahertz * 8\, bytes \cong 4264\, megabytes\; per\; second\; TX\; and\; RX$$

$$\frac{4264\, megabytes\; per\; second}{150\; pins} \cong 28.4\, megabytes\; per\; pin$$

Note: In PCI-X, 64 pins are used for signaling. The remaining 86 pins are used for side band signals, power and ground. The actual number of side band and power and ground pins depends on the package technology and the aggressiveness of electrical design.

Equation 3.2   PCI-X 2.0 Peak Bandwidth-per-Pin Calculation

Considering the per-pin performance of PCI Express requires some additional information that has not been discussed up to this point. Both prior examples consider busses that utilize a bi-directional topology. PCI Express forms a dual uni-directional link that has bandwidth traveling in both directions simultaneously. As such the (TX) transmit and (RX) receive bandwidth must be added together.

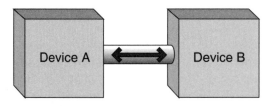

Shared Bi-Directional Topology

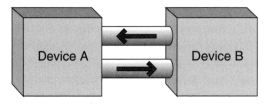

Dual Uni-directional Topology

These topologies are for illustration purposes only. Conventional PCI and PCI-X are not generally point-to-point solutions (at high frequencies PCI-X does become a point-to-point solution). However, for bandwidth purposes the topologies above are sufficient.

Figure 3.3   Bi-directional/Uni-directional Bus Concept

The calculation of PCI Express bandwidth per-pin is a little bit different from the comparison calculations above. For starters, PCI Express does not share a single link. Instead it has two uni-directional links that operate independently of one another. In addition to this PCI Express encodes every byte of data it sends out on the link with an additional two bits (referred to as 8-bit/10-bit encoding, which is discussed in detail in Chapter 8). Taking these details into consideration the following calculations can be made.

$$2500\,megahertz * 1\,bit * \frac{1\,byte}{10\,bits} \cong 250\,megabytes\,per\,second\,TX$$

$$2500\,megahertz * 1\,bit * \frac{1\,byte}{10\,bits} \cong 250\,megabytes\,per\,second\,RX$$

$$\frac{500\,megabytes\,per\,second}{8\,pins} \cong 62.5\,megabytes\,per\,pin$$

Note: In PCI Express 10 bits are equated to a single byte due to 8-bit/10-bit encoding, needed with embedded clock serial links. In PCI Express (x1), four pins are used for signaling. The remaining four pins are used for power and ground. A link that has multiple transmit and receive pairs is actually more pin-efficient with regards to power and ground pins. As link width increases the theoretical bandwidth per pin increases to 100 megabytes per second.

Equation 3.3   PCI Express Peak Bandwidth-per-Pin Calculation

When compared to past and present general I/O architecture technologies, PCI Express has the highest peak bandwidth per pin. This is not to say that other technologies are poor performers, but rather that when performance per pin is a requirement, PCI Express has a real advantage.

Link Efficiency

To foster link efficiency, PCI Express uses a split transaction protocol that benefits from the adoption of advanced flow control mechanisms. This allows PCI Express to maximize the bandwidth capability of the architecture by minimizing the possibility of bottleneck contentions and link inactivity. This type of efficiency is extremely critical when dealing with a serial architecture such as PCI Express.

Within any architecture there are devices that exhibit *latencies* that do not allow a transaction to complete immediately (considered a latent transaction). This requires mechanisms to be defined to handle these types of transactions. As an example of a PCI configuration, consider two devices, A and B, which are interconnected and defined to have multiple functions. Devices A and B could represent a real world chip-to-chip connection where Device A is a host bridge and Device B is a PCI-to-PCI bridge to other bus segments supporting multiple devices. Similarly Devices A and B could represent a host/PCI bridge communicating to a slot-based device that has multiple functions, as shown in Figure 3.4.

If Device A desires to receive some data from Function 1 on Device B, it is likely that Device B will require time to obtain the requested information since Function 1 exists outside of Device B. The delay from the time the request is comprehended in Device B until it can be serviced to Device A is considered the latency period. If no further transactions are allowed until the outstanding transaction is finished, system efficiency is reduced severely. Take the case where Device A also requires information from Function 2 of Device B. Without an intelligent mechanism for maximizing the efficiency of the system, Device A would have to wait for Device B to complete the first request before beginning the next transaction, which will most likely have a latency associated with it.

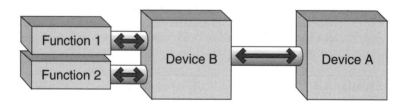

Figure 3.4   Device Function Requests that Can Result in Latencies

Conventional PCI defined the concept of a delayed transaction between a master and a target device to address this kind of issue. The concept of master and target is derived from the fact that multiple devices share the same bus, which is bi-directional in the case of conventional PCI, as shown earlier in Figure 3.3. This requires devices on the bus to arbitrate for control of the bus, or in other words, compete to become the master. Consequently, the arbitration algorithm for bus control must be fair for all devices. This technique of competing for control of the bus, along with some other inadequacies, limits the ability of conventional

PCI to support devices that require guaranteed bandwidth such as the isochronous data transfers that are discussed in Chapter 4.

To begin a conventional PCI transaction, the master, Device A in this case, must arbitrate for control of the bus. In this simple example Device A is arbitrating for control of the bus with only one other device, Device B. (Conventional PCI systems can have multiple devices competing to become the bus master at any given time.) Once Device A wins control of the bus it generates a transaction on the bus in which Device B is the target. Device B decodes the transaction and determines that Device A is requesting information stored in Function 1. Since Device B does not have the requested information readily available, as defined by the *PCI Local Bus Specification*, it terminates the transaction with a retry response, which buys extra time to retrieve the data and complete the original request. Terminating the transaction also allows the bus to become available for other devices to arbitrate for control and complete other transactions. The delayed transaction protocol requires Device A to again arbitrate for control of the bus, win control, and send the original request to Device B. This process can repeat multiple times and takes place until Device B can service the request within the minimum specified time, thereby completing the transaction.

PCI-X adopts a split transaction protocol, which offers advantages over the delayed transaction protocol of conventional PCI. The arbitration technique of PCI-X for control of the bus is reflective of conventional PCI since PCI-X is also a bi-directional and shared bus architecture, as shown earlier in Figure 3.3. The main difference between the delayed completion protocol of conventional PCI and the split transaction protocol of PCI-X is the way in which latent transactions are handled. Split transactions do not require the master device to continually retry transactions that cannot be completed immediately by the target device. Referring back to the example based on Figure 3.4, Device A is desiring to access another Device B, Function 1. When Device A successfully arbitrates for control of the bus, a transaction is sent to Device B, Function 1. It is assumed that the information being requested from Function 1 of Device B is not readily available. The retry response does not exist in the split transaction protocol, so instead of terminating the transaction with a retry response as in conventional PCI, Device B, terminates the transaction with a split response. The split response lets the device master know that the transaction will be completed some time in the future. Since the split response also terminates the original transaction, the bus becomes available for other devices to arbitrate to become the master. In the meantime Device B completes the original request by obtaining the requested information from Function 1. As soon as Device B can complete the transaction, it arbitrates to become the bus master. Once Device B successfully arbitrates for control of the bus it sends a Split Completion Packet to Device A, which is now the target. In essence the split transaction protocol eliminates the need for redundant requests to service latent transactions. As a side note, PCI-X still supports immediate transactions (not a true split transaction) that due to hesitation (initial access wait states) can make overall protocol less efficient due to higher average latency.

PCI Express adopts a split transaction protocol that is improved over that of PCI-X. PCI Express replaces the device-based arbitration process of conventional PCI and PCI-X with flow-control-based link arbitration that allows data to pass up and down the link based upon traffic class priority. High priority is given to traffic classes that require guaranteed bandwidth such as isochronous transactions while room is simultaneously made for lower priority transactions to avoid bottlenecks. The best way to understand how PCI Express flow control works is to consider another traffic analogy.

First consider a small bridge that must service cars in both directions. To get access to the road, a driver must arbitrate for control of the road with other drivers going both the same direction and the opposite direction. This is a good representation of how conventional PCI and PCI-X flow control works. Now consider that the road is changed into a highway with four lanes in both directions. This four lane highway has a carpool lane that allows carpoolers an easier path to travel during rush hour traffic congestion. There are also fast lanes for swifter moving traffic and slow lanes for big trucks and other slow traffic. Drivers can use different lanes in either direction to get to a particular destination. Each driver occupies a lane based upon the type of driver he or she is. Carpoolers take the carpool lane while fast drivers and slow drivers occupy the fast and slow lanes respectively. The different lanes in this highway example represent what are referred to in PCI Express as *virtual channels*. In general, the highway example may suggest that every virtual channel has the same amount of bandwidth. As a clarification, this is not true, since PCI Express defines a virtual channel arbitration model that allows budgeting of the bandwidth per virtual channel. As an additional note, in this example the traffic lanes are not associated with PCI Express lanes, but rather virtual connections that can occupy a single PCI Express lane.

Virtual channels are virtual wires between two devices. The finite physical link bandwidth is divided up amongst the supported virtual channels as appropriate. Each virtual channel has its own set of queues and buffers, control logic, and a credit-based mechanism to track how full or empty those buffers are on each side of the link. Thinking back to the highway example, in the real world those four lanes can become congested and blocked. The advancement of cars on the highway is in direct proportion to the amount of road available in front of each vehicle. Some lanes may have more space for traffic to move then others. Likewise, if the receive queues and buffers for a virtual channel on one side of the link or the other are full, then no further transactions can be sent until they are freed up by completing outstanding transactions. Additionally, on the transmit side, if the transmit queues and buffers become full, no further transactions are accepted until they are freed up by completing outstanding transactions. The benefit that virtual channels offer to PCI Express is that each virtual channel will support certain types of traffic. Bottlenecked transactions on one virtual channel do not cause bottlenecks on another virtual channel since each virtual channel has its own set of queues and buffers.

System traffic is broken down into classes that are based on device class and negotiation with the operating system. In the traffic example above, the *traffic classes* would consist of carpoolers, fast drivers, and slow drivers. PCI Express supports up to eight different traffic classes and hence, eight different virtual channels. Each traffic class may be mapped to a unique virtual channel; however, this is not a requirement. Unlike drivers on a four lane highway who may continually change lanes, once a packet is assigned a traffic class it cannot change to another traffic class.

Figure 3.5 illustrates how PCI Express links can support multiple virtual channels. Each virtual channel can support one or multiple traffic classes; however, a single traffic class may not be mapped to multiple virtual channels. Again recall that virtual channels are in fact virtual. You cannot infer simply because a PCI Express link is defined as a x2 link that there are two virtual channels. A x1 PCI Express link can have as many as eight virtual channels and a x32 link can have as few as one virtual channel. Additional details of PCI Express flow control are examined in Chapter 9.

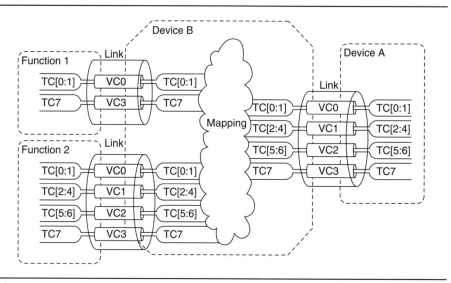

Figure 3.5   PCI Express Flow Control through Virtual Channels and Traffic Classes

In addition to PCI Express split transactions and enhanced flow control there are other differences from PCI and PCI-X to consider that optimize the link efficiency. The first main difference is that PCI Express is always a point-to-point solution. The second main difference is the link topology, which is composed of two uni-directional links that operate independently of one another. This allows transactions to flow to and from a device simultaneously. Since the master/target relationship is removed in PCI Express, transactions are no longer identified by who mastered the transaction. Instead PCI Express identifies transactions by specific identifiers that contain details as to which transaction is being serviced, who initiated the transaction and who serviced it as well.

PCI Express achieves link efficiency by using a split transaction protocol and adopting a dual uni-directional link topology to allow simultaneous traffic in both directions. In addition, PCI Express defines multiple traffic classes and virtual channels to eliminate single transaction bottlenecks by allowing a variety of different transaction types to become multiplexed and flow across the link. The combination of these techniques gives PCI Express a technical advantage over both conventional PCI and PCI-X from a protocol level.

Market Segment Support

PCI Express must support multiple market segments. An architectural change this large requires integration into multiple market segments to gain the appropriate momentum for mass acceptance. In addition to this, it has become apparent that the various market segments are becoming more unified as time goes on. Mobile and desktop segments have been merging for years. Many corporate stable systems have now shifted to become desktop/mobile hybrids that also require manageability features found primarily in the server market. Leveraging the mass adoption and economy of scale in the computing sectors, PCI has also been adopted as a control mechanism in the communications sector. To this end PCI Express has been defined to support the primary feature requirements of the desktop, server, mobile, and communications segments.

Market Segment Requirement: Mobile

Particular to the mobile segment is the ability to remove or replace (hot-plug) system devices while the system is running. Some commonly hot-plugged devices in mobile systems today include PCMCIA cards (which have features that range from audio to LAN and modem functions), CD/DVD-ROM drives, and docking connections. Today's mobile designs, which support the capability to hot-plug features (aside from PC cards, which use a staggered pin height mechanism), require additional circuitry on the board to support the hot-plug mechanism. These circuits are required to manage the hot-plug event and protect the devices and the system host from becoming damaged during device insertion and removal. In particular, the damage that these circuits try to prevent is electrical overstress conditions caused by backfeeding current into an unpowered buffer. When buffers are electrically stressed they risk becoming weakened or completely burned out.

PCI Express defines buffers that are capable of dealing with the circumstances that are typical during a hot-plug event or surprise insertion/removal. Surprise insertion/removal events happen when devices are inserted or removed from a system unexpectedly. Hot-plug events are defined as being known to the system before they happen. PCI Express transmit and receive buffers have been designed to withstand sustained shorts to ground of the actual data lines. Additionally receive buffers remain in high impedance whenever power is not present to protect the device from circuit damage. This allows PCI Express to support hot plug/hot swap without as much additional circuitry on the board.

Market Segment Requirement: Desktop

Desktop requirements can be summarized in a few words, cheap bandwidth and more cheap bandwidth. This requirement is driven by bandwidth-intensive multimedia applications that are becoming more and more prevalent for the desktop-based personal computer. These applications have grown as a result of the shifting market focus for desktop-based personal computers in the last few years. The desktop computer is not just a productivity device anymore. It is now a gaming console, a video editing studio, an entertainment system, and a digital photography station. Supporting these types of features requires massive amounts of bandwidth, which PCI Express is able to deliver.

During the 1990s desktop I/O bandwidth requirements were based upon bulk or occasional data transfers from an I/O device to some memory location. In most cases there was not a time-based dependency on the arrival of data to its location. This "occasional need" usage model required much less bandwidth overall because data transfers were bursty in nature. If bottlenecks occurred on the bus they could be overcome in time by waiting or trying the transaction again without too many consequences.

Today's desktop usage models are based upon the need for isochronous data transfers. Isochronous data transfers are typically based on multimedia applications such as audio and video, where timing is just as important as data integrity. If an audio stream is fed into a system at the same time a video stream is sent, the data must be synchronized to make much sense to the user. If the audio stream becomes bottlenecked behind another transaction, the audio stream becomes out of sync with the video data and must therefore be dropped. The result of the dropped audio frame results in glitches and pops out of the system speakers. PCI Express defines a mechanism to support isochronous data transfers in which bandwidth can be guaranteed and data loss can be avoided.

Market Segment Requirement: Servers

One major difference that has separated the technologies used in the server segment from the desktop and mobile segments is hardware-based error-checking and retry mechanisms. One of the key goals of the server segment is to avoid having to shut down servers. The consequence of having to shut down a server because of data corruption or hardware failure is the loss of hundreds or even thousands of hours of productivity, assuming that many users are relying on the services of a particular server. As such, the ability to replace hardware (hot-plug) while the system is running and have mechanisms that check data integrity and allow recovery in some error cases is a primary requirement. PCI Express defines an extensive mechanism for hardware-based data integrity verification and retry mechanisms in the case that data has been lost or corrupted. Also, similar to mobile, PCI Express simplifies the hardware requirements for hot-plug functionality while retaining the same ability to replace damaged system devices, such as networking components and storage controllers, without shutting down the system.

Market Segment Requirement: Communications

Although not originally intended for such uses, PCI has been widely accepted in communications equipment from embedded applications to chassis-based switching systems. Communications adopted the PCI protocol due to the wide availability of building blocks and economies of scale from adoption in the desktop, mobile, and server markets. Providing a solution for communications is also critical.

In addition, the adoption of advanced switching establishes mechanisms to send PCI Express packets peer-to-peer through the switch fabric gaining wide acceptance in the communications sector. PCI Express is a natural solution for connecting embedded and communications devices because of its high-speed differential serial interconnect. These markets also benefit from the server class hardware-based error detection that comes free with PCI Express.

System-Level Cost Parity

It is understood that acceptance of this new architecture is in direct proportion to the system-level cost parity shared with conventional PCI. History has shown that cost parity can dramatically affect the acceptance of new technologies. As an example, Digital Video Disc (DVD) technology took many years to become widely adopted. One of the primary reasons that it took so long to adopt was the fact that DVD players cost far more to manufacture than video cassette players. As a result, they were sold for nearly four and five times the cost of a good quality video cassette player. DVDs have much higher quality than video tapes. However, if the cost is inhibitive for the market in question, adoption will be incredibly slow or will fail altogether. As a consequence, PCI Express is designed to keep costs at parity with PCI by using current fabrication technologies in four key areas: printed circuit board fabrication technology, four-layer routability, connector manufacturing technology, and silicon design process technology.

Cost Requirement: Ability to Use Common Printed Circuit Board Fabrication Technology

Advances in computer-based electronics, especially cutting edge advances, generally require the advancement of PCB (printed circuit board) manufacturing capabilities. The printed circuit board industry uses a variety of glass laminates to manufacture PCBs for various industries. Each laminate exhibits different electrical characteristics or properties. The most common glass laminate used in the computer industry is FR4. This glass laminate is preferred because it has good electrical characteristics and can be used in a wide variety of manufacturing processes.

In addition to its versatility, FR4 gives the ability to control the impedance of a trace on a PCB within a specific tolerance due to the characteristics of the glass laminate. Processes that use FR4 have relatively uniform control of trace impedance, which allows it to be used in systems that support high speed. PCI Express electrical requirements were developed to allow system designers to use commonly available glass laminates to build printed circuit boards that feature PCI Express. PCI Express does not have a significant cost burden beyond what is already being spent to manufacture conventional PCI PCBs.

Cost Requirement: Common Connector Manufacturing Technology

PCI Express defines connectors that are very similar to those used in conventional PCI, as shown in Figure 3.6. By using the same contact style and through-hole design, the manufacturing costs can be reduced. Additionally, the same processes for securing connectors to the printed circuit board can be reused. It is expected that PCI Express connectors will cost slightly more in the beginning due to supply and demand. However, given the fact that PCI Express connectors are much smaller than conventional PCI connectors, there are some material savings realized from a manufacturing standpoint that may balance out the cost.

Figure 3.6   Mid-size (x8) PCI Express Connector

Cost Requirement: Routing in Four-Layer Motherboards

The majority of conventional PCI-based motherboard designs are based on a desktop four-layer stackup to save money on system fabrication costs. A traditional four-layer stackup consists of a signal layer, a power layer, a ground layer, and another signal layer, as illustrated in Figure 3.7. The cost associated with adding more signal layers (two layers to maintain symmetry) is roughly $4.00 per platform given the extra materials and manufacturing costs. When compared to the overall system cost of a typical four-layer design, the cost of adding two additional layers is burdensome and highly undesirable. PCI Express benefits from pin efficiency, which translates into fewer signal pins to route, the ability to repurpose pins, and simplified power delivery solutions. Since additional bandwidth can be had with less pins and routing congestion, future designs can continue to use a cost effective four-layer stackup motherboard.

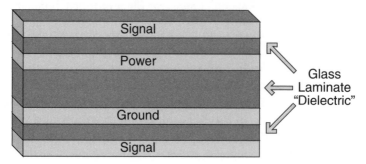

Four-layer stackups are used primarily in the desktop computer market, which makes up approximately 70 percent of overall computer sales.

Figure 3.7   Four-Layer Stackup Example

Cost Requirement: Usability on Multiple Silicon Process Technology

PCI Express defines this new architecture to be transparent to the silicon process. Silicon designers use different processes dependent upon the technology in question and process access. Silicon process relates to the minimum dimension of the circuit elements and the voltage tolerance of these devices. A general rule of thumb is that the smaller the dimensions, the more devices per silicon wafer, the faster the circuit elements, and the lower the voltage tolerance of the circuits. Silicon device vendors are constantly trying to move their designs to tighter dimension processes to get a higher device yield per silicon wafer. The decision to move to smaller processes must be balanced against the cost elements associated with moving to the newer processes. New processes are early in their manufacturing learning curve and therefore are higher cost until the process matures.

When considering the silicon process there are two constraints. Larger dimension processes are harder to use because they require extraordinary circuit methods to handle PCI Express frequencies, if they can be handled at all. On the other hand, the smaller, faster processes cannot tolerate high voltages on the core devices. At present, 3.3 volt PCI signaling is beyond the tolerance of many new processes. High-voltage tolerance devices are available with some newer processes to allow handling of legacy voltages. Since PCI Express circuits must be capable of functioning at 2.5 gigahertz, processes larger than 0.25 micron are not recommended. Fortunately, most vendors today have the 0.25 micron process or smaller for their devices.

Voltage constraints also exist. PCI Express was designed to operate at I/O voltage levels compatible with 0.25 micron and future low voltage processes. Since PCI Express uses AC coupling to decouple the common mode DC element between devices, devices manufactured on different processes can be connected to one another. In short PCI Express has some design flexibility in that it can be designed on multiple silicon processes. For additional consideration and insights into manufacturing choices see Chapter 14.

I/O Simplification

PCI Express seeks to simplify general I/O by consolidating the I/O strategy for the desktop, mobile, and server segments. I/O consolidation gives a sense of validity to the architecture by removing technological constraints and architectural constraints that have generally separated the segments. PCI Express is defined as an open specification and will allow all hardware vendors alike to adopt the technology without the burden of paying royalties. PCI Express is not currently defined to replace all I/O that currently exists across the multiple segments. However, it is expected that as time passes, the I/O that was not originally consolidated will soon become so.

Simplification Requirement: I/O Consolidation

When conventional PCI was first introduced in the early 1990s it fulfilled the role of a high performance bus that consolidated chip-to-chip interconnect and expansion board architecture of the personal computer, as shown in Figure 3.8.

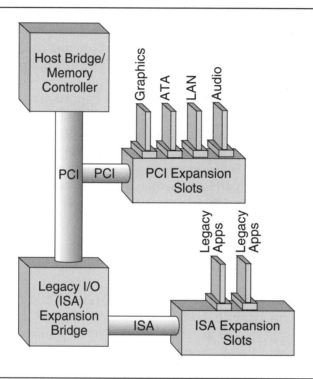

Figure 3.8   Early PCI Architecture

Within a few years, however, the architectural picture was quite different. In a relatively short period of time the demand for bandwidth increased beyond what conventional PCI could deliver. Since conventional PCI was not designed to be scalable, chipset manufacturers had to explore other options, resulting in the integration of high bandwidth I/O elements such as graphics and ATA into the memory and I/O controller respectively. While the integration of high bandwidth I/O gave some bandwidth relief to the expansion slots portion of the platform, it made the PCI-based chip-to-chip interconnect bandwidth problems even worse. The natural result of feature integration into the I/O controller was the simultaneous development of proprietary high-bandwidth chip-to-chip solutions. The end result was segmentation of a once consolidated I/O, as illustrated in Figure 3.9.

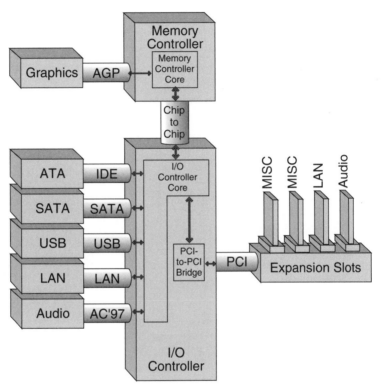

In many systems audio and LAN still exist as expansion cards on the PCI Bus

Figure 3.9   Segmented PCI Architecture

PCI Express gives chipset designers the ability to reconsolidate graphics and the chip-to-chip interconnect. Features that still remain on conventional PCI will be transitioned over a period of time to PCI Express, as shown in Figure 3.10. Most importantly, the scalability infrastructure of PCI Express provides a framework for growth based upon scalable clock frequencies and logical signal lines. Conventional PCI has remained an important part of the computing platform for the last ten years despite its lack of scalability. PCI Express is expected to be a key part of the platform for the next decade and beyond.

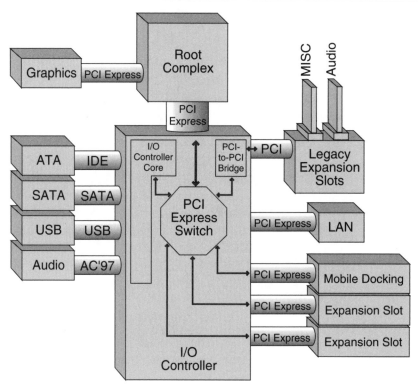

Conventional PCI may coexist with PCI Express as an I/O controller feature during the transition phase. The system level architecture will be PCI Express-based.

Figure 3.10   PCI Express Initial I/O Consolidation

Backward Compatibility

PCI has developed an extensive infrastructure that ranges from operating system support to chassis form-factor solutions. This infrastructure is the result of many years of coordinated efforts between hardware vendors and software vendors. The infrastructure established through the adoption of PCI has been the springboard of success for the personal computing platform. The most significant requirement for smooth migration of PCI Express architecture is the level of backward compatibility it has with the existing infrastructure.

Compatibility Requirement: Legacy Operating System Support

PCI Express has been defined to be 100-percent compatible with conventional PCI compliant operating systems and their corresponding bus enumeration and configuration software. All PCI Express hardware elements have been defined with a PCI-compatible configuration space representation. This gives the architecture a sort of transparency to the operating system. In other words, a system with PCI Express architecture looks to software exactly like a conventional PCI-based system. As a side note, PCI Express adds extended device configuration space and advanced features such as isochrony for future operating systems and configuration software to take advantage of. PCI Express also defines an enhanced access mechanism by mapping configuration space into a memory region.

The adoption of PCI Express architecture is highly accelerated by specifying PCI Express to be backward compatible with existing PCI compliant operating systems. The typical design cycle of a computing platform involves multiple hardware iterations coupled with operating system beta releases. The ability to ship a product to market is dependent on the ultimate success of both the hardware vendor and the operating system vendor. By minimizing operating system risk, hardware design cycle time decreases considerably. This results in PCI Express-based systems on the shelf in a shorter period of time.

Compatibility Requirement: Existing System Form Factor Support

PCI Express has been defined to support existing ATX and server form factors. PCI Express defines connectors that are similar to conventional PCI connectors, as shown in Figure 3.6. This allows PCI Express connectors to occupy the same space once occupied by traditional PCI connectors. PCI Express add-in cards follow the same height and length requirements that are defined for conventional PCI. Additionally PCI Express-based add-in cards use the same I/O bracket to secure cards to the chassis as conventional PCI. Specific details of PCI Express cards and connectors are discussed in more detail in Chapter 12.

Compatibility Requirement: Allowing Coexistence During Transition

PCI Express is designed to replace conventional PCI over time as the key architecture of the computing platform. Since PCI Express architecture has been defined to support the existing PCI software model unchanged, PCI and PCI Express can coexist on the same platform for as long as needed. This allows devices a smooth migration path to PCI Express over time. Devices that require the benefits of PCI Express can transition to the architecture quickly, whereas devices that do not require the benefits of PCI Express (56K PCI modem cards for example) can make the change slowly.

Chapter **4**

PCI Express
Applications

The best way to predict the future is to invent it.

—Alan Kay

This chapter looks more closely at the applications where PCI Express offers significant benefits beyond existing interconnect technologies. PCI Express is a unique technology in that it provides immediate benefits across multiple market segments from desktop PCs, mobile PCs, enterprise servers, to communications switches and routers. This chapter starts with a brief overview of the key benefits of PCI Express and then covers the applications where PCI Express is a natural solution due to evolving requirements. Finally this chapter reviews some of the applications where PCI Express provides a new and revolutionary usage model.

Benefits of PCI Express

PCI Express provides benefits across five main vectors: high performance, I/O simplification, layered architecture improving serviceability and scalability, next generation multimedia, and ease of use. These benefits come at a very small impact to software. The software driver model of PCI Express is backward compatible to the PCI software infrastructure. Unlike parallel bus architectures such as AGP8x and PCI-X, future scalability to higher bandwidth can be achieved due to the layered architecture without compromising the software compatibility. For example, future speed upgrades are possible through a change in the Physical

Layer while not impacting the Data Link Layer or Transaction Layer. A full discussion on the various layers can be found in chapters 5 through 8. This section briefly discusses the benefits for each topic in Figure 4.1.

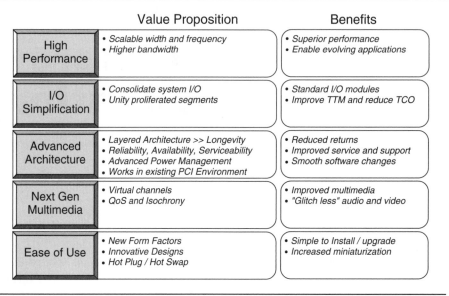

	Value Proposition	Benefits
High Performance	• *Scalable width and frequency* • *Higher bandwidth*	• *Superior performance* • *Enable evolving applications*
I/O Simplification	• *Consolidate system I/O* • *Unity proliferated segments*	• *Standard I/O modules* • *Improve TTM and reduce TCO*
Advanced Architecture	• *Layered Architecture >> Longevity* • *Reliability, Availability, Serviceability* • *Advanced Power Management* • *Works in existing PCI Environment*	• *Reduced returns* • *Improved service and support* • *Smooth software changes*
Next Gen Multimedia	• *Virtual channels* • *QoS and Isochrony*	• *Improved multimedia* • *"Glitch less" audio and video*
Ease of Use	• *New Form Factors* • *Innovative Designs* • *Hot Plug / Hot Swap*	• *Simple to Install / upgrade* • *Increased miniaturization*

Figure 4.1   PCI Express Benefits

High Performance

A key metric of performance is bandwidth, or the amount of data that can be transferred in a given time. True usable bandwidth, typically measured in millions of bytes or megabytes per second is the result of total theoretical peak bandwidth multiplied by efficiency. For example, recall PCI is a 32-bit bus running at 33 megahertz, which is 132 megabytes per second. Although the PCI specification evolved to a 64-bit bus running at 66 megahertz for a total of 533 megabytes per second, approximately 85 percent of the computing industry continues to use the 33-megahertz version. However, the PCI bus cannot actually transfer data at these rates due to overhead required for commands as well as the inability to perform reads and writes at the same time. To determine the actual data transfer capability requires an understanding of the bus efficiency. The bus efficiency is determined by several factors such as protocol and design limitations and is beyond the scope of this chapter.

Maximum theoretical bandwidth is used in this chapter for the purpose of comparing various applications.

PCI Express provides an immediate boost in performance and close to twice the amount of data per second due to the tremendous increase in bandwidth over PCI. Recall from Chapter 3 that the PCI Express interface can be scaled in a linear manner by simply adding additional differential pairs to create more lanes. The specification supports x1, x2, x4, x8, x12, x16, and x32 configurations. In addition to adding more lanes, the architecture supports the ability increase the signaling rate of the Physical Layer attributes for future scaling possibilities. The initial implementations utilize a 2.5 gigabit per second encoded differential pair, but the capability of the bus has the potential for growth to 10 gigabit per second differential pairs pushing the limit of low cost PCB manufacturing capability. PCI Express provides the bandwidth scalability of 250 megabytes per second per direction for initial x1 lanes to 32,000 megabytes per second for 10 gigabits per second per direction signaling across 32 lanes.

I/O Simplification

A look inside several computing platforms today illustrates that there is an overabundance of I/O technologies. Today's platforms have PCI-X for servers, Cardbus (PCMCIA slot for expansion) on mobile PCs, and PCI for desktop PCs. In addition, several I/O technologies have evolved to application-specific usage models such as IDE and SCSI for disk drives, USB or IEEE 1394 for PC peripherals, AGP for graphics cards, and proprietary chip-to-chip interconnects such as Intel's Hub Interface. Although many of these technologies will continue to coexist moving forward, PCI Express provides a unique interface technology serving multiple market segments. For example, a PC chipset designer may implement a x16 PCI Express configuration for graphics, a x1 configuration for general purpose I/O, and a x4 configuration as a high-speed chip-to-chip interconnect. Notice the platform of the future consolidates the design and development effort to a single PCI Express core away from three separate and distinct I/O technologies (AGP, PCI, and Hub Interface respectively). Refer to Figure 12.2 and Figure 4.11 for examples of what a future desktop PC and server platform could look like.

Layered Architecture

PCI Express establishes a unique divergence from historical PCI evolutions through a layered architecture improving serviceability and scalability as well as easing software transitions through backward compatibility. Figure 4.2 shows the various layers within the PCI Express architecture.

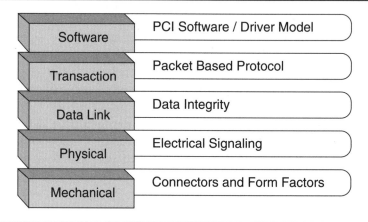

Figure 4.2   PCI Express Layered Architecture

The software layer contains two critical aspects to maintain software compatibility with PCI to ease migration: initialization operations and run-time operations. PCI implements a time-proven initialization routine for configuration. The initialization, or enumeration, remains unchanged in PCI Express architecture, easing software migration. In fact, existing operating systems are expected to boot with PCI Express without modifications. The run-time software model also remains unchanged with the exception that future software enhancements will be able to take advantage of the new capabilities PCI Express provides. For new software development, PCI Express provides a standard register and programming interface to ease migration to new capabilities, such as next generation multimedia.

The PCI Express layered architecture improves serviceability through server-class error detection, correction, and reporting. The PCI Express Data Link Layer detects as well as corrects several types of data integrity errors by interacting with both the Physical Layer and the Transaction Layer. Some of the key capabilities introduced in the Data Link Layer are the packet and link error detection for a reliable connection. This will be described in more detail in Chapter 7. In addition to the error reporting capability, PCI Express has native support for hot plug insertion, easing serviceability.

The layered architecture is critical to enabling the scalability of PCI Express. Future performance enhancements to the signaling rate will likely only affect the Physical Layer. For the next generation speed bump from 2.5 gigabits per second to probably more than 5.0 gigabits per second, only the Physical Layer needs to evolve. The remaining layers can continue to operate flawlessly, reducing development cost and time for each incremental evolution of PCI Express.

Next Generation Multimedia

PCI Express provides new capabilities for multimedia not available in the platform today—namely isochronous support. Isochronous support is a specific type of QoS (Quality of Service) guarantee that data is delivered using a deterministic and time-dependent method.

Platform-based isochronous support relies on a documented system design methodology that allows an application that requires a constant or dedicated level of access to system resources to gain the required bandwidth at a given time interval. PCI Express isochrony starts with attributing virtual channels and traffic classes to data as a foundation (Refer to Chapter 9 for more information). Unlike other QoS implementations that provide priority only, isochrony goes one step further to actively manage the admission to the virtual channels and balance the available resources such as latency (time through the fabric) and total available bandwidth. Additional factors include traffic regulation and policing. PCI Express provides the interconnect portion between devices for a complete isochrony solution.

Compare today's example of watching an employee broadcast from the company's CEO on your desktop while working on a report as shown in Figure 4.3. Data is routed from the intranet into main memory where the application utilizes the data to create an audio stream sent to the user's headphones via a PCI add-in card and a video stream sent to the display via a graphics controller. If simultaneous operations are occurring within the PC, such as disk reads, data coming off the Internet, word processing, e-mail, and so on, there is no guarantee that the audio and video stream will be truly glitchless. Data is delivered on a "best effort" method only. The user may experience skips or stalls as applications compete for the same resources. Isochrony in PCI Express solves this problem moving forward by establishing a mechanism to guarantee that time-sensitive applications are able to secure adequate system resources.

For example in Figure 4.3, the video time sensitive data would be guaranteed adequate bandwidth to prevent skips at the expense of noncritical data such as e-mail.

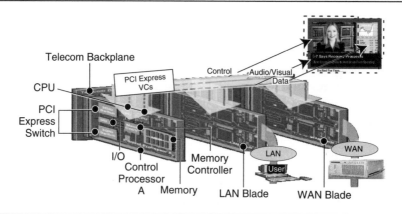

Figure 4.3 Isochronous Example

Ease of Use

PCI Express will revolutionize the way users install upgrades and repair failures. PCI Express natively supports hot swap and hot plug. *Hot swap* is the ability to swap I/O cards without software interaction where as *hot plug* may require operating system interaction. PCI Express as a hardware specification defines the capability to support both hot swap and hot plug, but hot plug support depends on the operating system. In the future, systems will not need to be powered down to replace faulty equipment or install upgrades. In conjunction with the PCMCIA and PCI-SIG industry groups defining standard plug-in modules for mobile, desktop PCs, and servers, the PCI Express interconnect enables systems to be easier to configure and use.

For example, compare the events following the failure of a PCI Ethernet controller in the office today with what the future could look like. If a PCI card fails today, a technician is dispatched to the location of the PC. The PC must be powered down, opened up, and the card must be physically removed. Opening the PC chassis can be cumbersome, as screws need to be removed, cables disconnected and pushed out of the way, and the card unseated from the motherboard. Once the faulty card is replaced with an identical unit, the system is then reassembled, reconnected, and powered back on. Hopefully all goes well and the PC is up and running after a short two-hour delay. In the future, PCI Express modules could be plugged into the external slot on the PC without powering down, disassembling, and disconnecting the PC. Refer to Figure 4.4 for a picture of the modules. In the same scenario, the technician arrives with a new module, swaps the good with the bad, and the user is off and running in less than ten minutes. In addition to serviceability, PCI Express provides the interconnect capability to perform upgrades without powering down the system.

Although the modules are still under definition and expected to be finalized in 2003, the proposals currently being discussed highlight the benefits of easy to use modules. See Figure 4.4. The PC on the left is based on today's capabilities. In order to install an upgrade, the user must open the box and navigate through the cables and connectors. The PC on the right has the ability to install either in the front or back of the system. PC add-in cards are expected to continue to be supported within the box for standard OEM configurations, but PCI Express provides a revolutionary and easier method to install upgrades versus internal slots. The small module also enables OEMs to provide expansion capability on extremely small form-factor PCs where the PCI Express connectors will minimize the usage of valuable space.

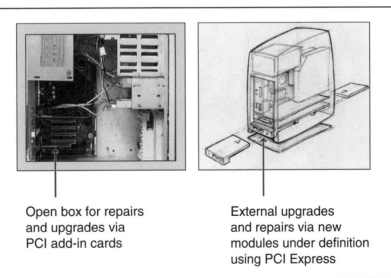

Open box for repairs
and upgrades via
PCI add-in cards

External upgrades
and repairs via new
modules under definition
using PCI Express

Figure 4.4   Ease of Use Module Example

Evolutionary Applications

The following sections within this chapter review both evolutionary and revolutionary applications for PCI Express. To some extent or another, all the following applications are expected to leverage one or more of the five main benefits—high performance, I/O simplification, layered architecture, next generation multimedia, and ease of use.

PCI Express provides a new architecture for the next decade. Over the years, the processor and memory system have scaled in frequency and bandwidth, continually improving the overall system performance. Additionally, platform I/O requirements continue to demand increasing bandwidth, bringing about the creation of several high-speed busses in addition to the general purpose PCI bus within the typical mobile or desktop PC, as shown in Figure 4.5.

Over the next few years, I/O bandwidth requirements will likely continue to outpace the existing PCI capabilities. This section reviews applications benefiting immediately from the bandwidth, scalability, and reliability improvements highlighting where PCI Express is a natural solution due to evolving requirements. The actual applications covered include PC graphics, gigabit Ethernet, high-speed chip interconnects, and general purpose I/O.

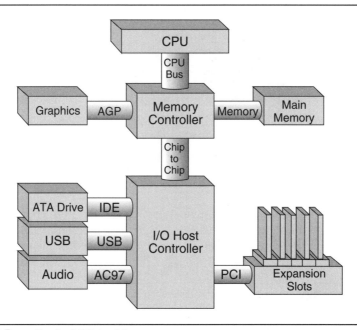

Figure 4.5   Typical PC Architecture

PCI Express for Computing Graphics Applications

The graphics interface on the platform today is AGP (Accelerated Graphics Port) which is moving towards a 16-lane PCI Express implementation. Recall from Chapter 3 that PCI Express has the inherent capability to scale in the number of lanes as well as future scaling capability in frequency. Both of these aspects are critical to providing the bandwidth, performance, and headroom required for next generation graphics. The initial PCI Express-based graphics application will use 16 PCI Express lanes of differential pairs running a total theoretical bandwidth of 4.0 gigabytes per second in each direction. The PCI Express graphics interconnect resides between the core chipset and the graphics controller responsible for driving the monitor display. Reviewing the history of the graphics interconnect is a useful method to highlight the benefits of PCI Express for future graphics applications.

Graphics Evolution

Initial graphics devices were based on the ISA (Industry Standard Architecture) system bus in the early 1980s with a text-only display. The ISA bus provided a 8/16-bit data bus operating at 8.33 megahertz for a total maximum bandwidth of approximately 16 megabytes per second. Although the actual bandwidth of the ISA bus was less due to the inability to transfer data at the peak rate via pipelining, 16 megabytes will be used as a simple comparison. As the CPU and main memory continued to improve in performance, the graphics interconnect also scaled to match system performance and improve the overall end user experience. The early 1990s saw the introduction of the PCI architecture providing a 32-bit bus operating at 33 megahertz for a peak bandwidth of approximately 132 megabytes per second as well as the evolution to two-dimensional rendering of objects improving the user's visual experience. Although the PCI interface added support for a 64-bit interface and 66 megahertz clock, the graphics' interface evolved to AGP implementations. In 1997 to the early years of the following decade, the AGP interface evolved from the 1x mode eventually to the 8x mode. Today the AGP 8x mode operates on a 32-bit bus with a 66 megahertz common clock that is divided eight times in a given clock period to control the data transfer for a total bandwidth of approximately 2,100 megabytes per second. Additional enhancements such as three-dimensional rendering also evolved to improve the overall experience as well as drive the demand for continued bandwidth improvements. See Figure 4.6 for the bandwidth evolution of the graphics interconnect. The graphics interconnect has continued to double in bandwidth every few years to take full advantage of increased computing capability between main memory, the CPU, and the graphics controller. The PC graphics capability will likely have evolved from a text-only, black-and-white display in the 1980s to the high quality, real-time digital virtual reality of Disney's *Toy Story*[†] running on your PC with PCI Express by 2004.

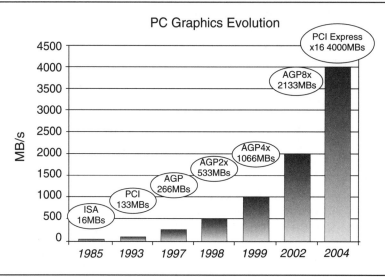

Figure 4.6 Graphics Interconnect Evolution

Immediate Benefits of PCI Express

PCI Express is the next natural evolution as the cost-effective, high-bandwidth, scalable, and isochronous graphics interface. AGP8x represents the end of the line for cost-effective parallel-bus implementations, as the signal lines need to be tightly controlled due to skew and timing dependencies. Pushing the frequency further in a parallel bus architecture pushes motherboard vendors to cost-prohibitive and exotic manufacturing processes. Unlike a parallel bus implementation with external clocks, PCI Express utilizes an embedded clock and encoding scheme to remove platform-clocking limitations experienced on AGP (Refer to Chapter 8 for additional information on the PCI Express Physical Layer). PCI Express also provides a cost-effective solution by improving the bandwidth per pin. Increased bandwidth per pin reduces the overall system cost by reducing the pin count on connectors.

The inherent scalability incorporated into the PCI Express architecture at the Physical Layer provides additional benefits for future implementations. Although the initial solution will provide approximately 4 gigabytes per second per direction of data across the connector utilizing a 2.5 gigabit per second signaling rate, PCI Express technology scales to a 10 gigabit per second signaling rate providing a bandwidth roadmap to 16 gigabytes per second per direction for the same connector. Additional benefits with the PCI Express software model, such as the ability to guarantee bandwidth and resources for real-time applications, provide evolutionary capabilities for future graphics controllers. Future graphics devices should be able to leverage the next generation multimedia aspects and isochrony, ensuring that video streams are delivered to the user free of interruptions.

Applicability to Various Market Segments

The primary market segments most likely to use the PCI Express-based graphics devices are the desktop PC, mobile PC, and workstation markets. The segments are expected to take advantage of the processing capability and bandwidth the PCI Express connection provides. The current challenge facing the mobile PC market is optimizing the design to maximize the Active State Power Management capabilities within PCI Express to consume less power than AGP8x implementations.

For the server market, platform stability is much more critical than screaming graphics performance. For this market segment, graphics products will likely evolve to offer a lower cost and stable solution in a x4 or x8 PCI Express configuration. The PCI Express base card specification allows for the ability to populate a x16 connector with x1, x4, x8, or x16 cards.

PCI Express for Gigabit Ethernet

Gigabit Ethernet is another application that is expected to take full advantage of the immediate increase in bandwidth and performance. Gigabit Ethernet is a local-area-networking standard published by the Institute of Electrical and Electronics Engineers (IEEE) that transfers data at gigabit (1,000 megabits per second) speeds. Gigabit Ethernet will be a single PCI Express lane configuration in most instances. Gigabit Ethernet can transfer up to a theoretical maximum of 125 megabytes per second, which is well matched to the theoretical bandwidth of a single PCI Express lane of 250 megabytes per second. Ethernet is only 25 years old, but has gained tremendous acceptance as the world's dominant data networking standard. A brief review on the evolution to Gigabit Ethernet will highlight the immediate benefits of a PCI Express connection as well the benefits of scalability moving forward.

Ethernet Evolution

Ethernet has continually demonstrated resilience and flexibility in evolving to meet increasing networking demands. Ethernet first hit the market in the early 1980s. As the PC market grew, so did the requirement for computers and users to share data. By 1990, a 10-megabit per second networking technology across standard UTP (unshielded twisted pair) wiring was approved as the IEEE 10BASE-T standard and the next year Ethernet sales nearly doubled (Riley, *Switched Fast Gigabit Ethernet,* pp 15). Networking requirements quickly demanded the evolution to Fast Ethernet and the IEEE 100Base-T standard capable of 100 megabits per second, published in 1994. Fast Ethernet enjoyed a rapid adoption as network interface card suppliers offered both Fast Ethernet (100 megabit per second standard) and Ethernet (10 megabit per second standard) capability on the same card, providing backward compatibility. These dual mode cards are commonly referred to as 10/100Mbps-capable. In fact, as of 2003 almost all Fast Ethernet network interface cards (NICs) are 10/100Mbps-capable and represent a commanding 70 percent of the market only 4 years after introduction (IDC, July 2002 bulletin).

Gigabit Ethernet and specifically the IEEE 1000Base-T standard, capable of 1000 megabits per second across UTP cabling, is the next natural networking technology evolution driven by unprecedented Internet growth and increasing data transfer requirements within the corporate environment. The 1000Base-T standard was published in 1998 and the first major physical layer transceiver (PHY) interoperability testing followed in 1999.

Gigabit Ethernet will most likely experience the same adoption success as Fast Ethernet due to the inherent backward compatibility, low cost structure, and increasing requirements for faster connection rates. Similar to Fast Ethernet, Gigabit Ethernet has the ability to reuse the existing cable within the building as well as the ability to auto-negotiate to a common speed. *Auto-negotiaton* allows each link to advertise the highest possible connection rate. Most network connections support the lower speed capabilities. For example, a Gigabit Ethernet (10/100/1000 megabits per second) switch connection in the wiring closet will be able to operate with a slower Fast Ethernet (10/100 megabits per second) desktop connection at the lowest common denominator of 100 megabits per second. Backward compatibility expedites adoption through removing the requirement for new cable installations or the requirement to replace all of the existing network equipment.

The remaining factor driving Gigabit Ethernet success is the evolving need for additional bandwidth as users are downloading an increasing number of MPEG files, video streaming, webcasts, and so on. According to IDC, in 2000 there were 394 million users accessing the internet. By 2005, the number will almost triple to 941 million users. More important than the number of users is the tremendous growth in bandwidth or downloads per day due to the increasing speed of internet connections. According to IDC, in 2000 users downloaded 24.4 thousand terabits (one terabit is 1,000,000,000 bits) of data. By 2005, this number is expected to grow to 2.3 million terabits of data. To put this in perspective, 2.3 million terabits is over 140 times more than all of the written content in all of the United States academic libraries.

Immediate Benefits

Gigabit Ethernet requires a high performance host interface. As such, PCI Express is well suited as a Gigabit Ethernet host connection. PCI Express provides an immediate boost in performance due to the dedicated bandwidth per link, a direct increase in the usable bandwidth, and the ability to perform concurrent cycles. PCI Express can provide a dedicated link with 100 percent of the bandwidth on each port independent of the system configuration, unlike today's PCI shared bus. An immediate performance gain is realized with PCI Express due to the increase in available bandwidth. PCI provides a total bandwidth of 132 megabytes per second whereas PCI Express operates on a 2.5 gigabits per second encoded link providing 250 megabytes per second per direction. PCI Express additionally supports concurrent data transmissions for a maximum concurrent data transfer of 500 megabytes per second. Devices are able to transmit 250 megabytes per second of data during a write operation while simultaneously receiving 250 megabytes per second of read data due to separate differential pairs. PCI on the other hand is only capable of performing either a read or write operation at any given time. PCI Express is the next obvious connection to deliver Gigabit Ethernet speeds.

Applicability to Various Market Segments

Ethernet is currently the ubiquitous data networking standard throughout the world. Unlike some of the other applications, Gigabit Ethernet spans all of the market segments impacted by PCI Express. Gigabit Ethernet will be the network connection of choice for corporate mobile and desktop computers for sharing files, sending e-mails, and browsing the Internet. Servers as well as communications equipment are expected to implement PCI Express based Gigabit Ethernet connections. The prevalence of Gigabit Ethernet within the enterprise network is shown in Figure 4.7.

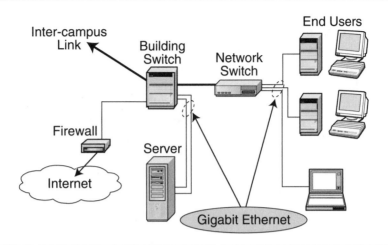

Figure 4.7   Gigabit Ethernet Connections within the Network

Desktop and mobile PCs will likely implement a x1 PCI Express configuration for the Gigabit Ethernet connection into the network. The network switch and building switch could use PCI Express in either the data path or the control plane (refer to the Communications Applications and Advanced Switching section at the end of this chapter). The server connection supplies the data into the network and will also be a PCI Express-based Gigabit Ethernet connection.

PCI Express as a High-Speed Chip-to-chip Interconnect

The chip-to-chip interconnect is a broad category of interconnect technologies enabling multiple devices to communicate with each other and covers a wide range of applications from communications devices and industrial controllers to PCs and servers. To highlight the usage and benefits, this section explores the history of the Intel desktop PC chip-to-chip link implemented over time.

Interconnect History

In 1998, Intel announced the 400 megahertz Pentium® II processor to operate along with the Intel® 440BX chipset. The 440BX used the standard PCI bus to interconnect the memory and processor controller to the PIIX4E I/O controller, as shown in Figure 4.8. Prior to the evolution of bandwidth-intensive I/O devices, the PCI bus provided sufficient bandwidth and performance at 132 megabytes per second as the chip-to-chip interconnect. Adding up the major bandwidth components of the I/O subsystem even under extreme loading conditions was still supported with the bandwidth capability of PCI.

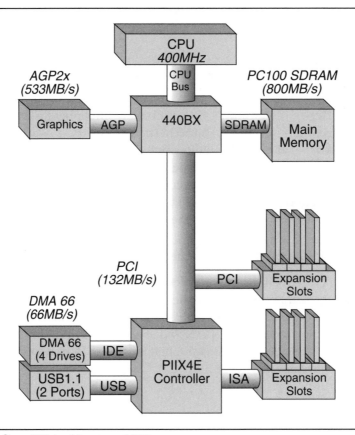

Figure 4.8   PC Architecture 1998

In the few years that followed, several platform I/O technologies evolved placing demand on the chip-to-chip interconnect. Specifically, hard drives were improved from the DMA33 standard to ATA100 increasing the hard drive capability from 33 megabytes per second to 100 megabytes per second. The rapid adoption of Fast Ethernet created integration opportunities for chipset suppliers and increased the network traffic from 10 megabits per second to 100 megabits per second. The removal of ISA slots and the proliferation of faster PCI expansions slots also fueled the demand for a faster I/O interconnects. The introduction of the Intel® 810 chipset in 1999 switched from using the PCI bus as a chip-to-chip interconnect to a proprietary Hub Interface improving the connection performance between the I/O devices to main memory and the CPU to address the evolving requirements. By 2000, the Intel® 815 graphics interface speed doubled from 533 megabytes per second to 1 gigabyte per second, the memory bus evolved from 800 megabytes per second to 1 gigabyte per second, and the CPU frequency more than doubled from 400 megahertz to 1.13 gigahertz, as shown in Figure 4.9.

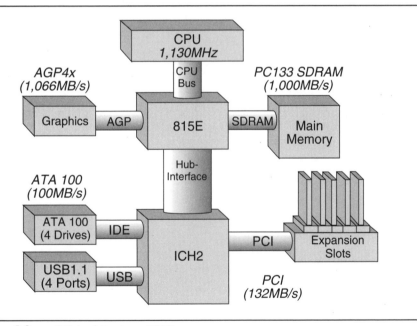

Figure 4.9   PC Architecture 2000

History repeated itself as the platform continued to evolve from 2000 to 2002. Memory bandwidth improved from 1 gigabyte per second to 2.1 gigabytes per second, the graphics interconnect bandwidth doubled once again from 1 gigabyte per second to 2.1 gigabytes per second, and CPU frequency scaled from 1.13 gigahertz to 3.0 gigahertz. Several I/O technologies continued to evolve as well. In 2002, the Universal Serial Bus (USB) evolved from USB 1.1 to USB 2.0, effectively increasing the bandwidth by a factor of 40. The USB 1.1 protocol was originally developed to provide an easy-to-use, low cost, PC peripheral port expansion capability. The USB 1.1 specification was ratified in 1998 and specified up to a maximum of 12 megabits per second or 1.5 megabytes per second bandwidth per host controller. Adding ports to a single controller diminished the total available bandwidth, but was a cost effective method to add additional ports and connectivity. Several applications adopted the USB 1.1 standard due to its availability on virtually all PC platforms and its ease of use with video cameras; and connections to PDAs, printers, and broadband modems. As more applications were developed, the requirement to increase performance materialized. Prior to the release of the Hi-Speed USB 2.0, the USB bandwidth was significantly lower than the other I/O counterparts such as LAN adapters and hard drives. In 2000, the *Hi-Speed USB Specification, Revision 2.0* was published with wide acceptance and in 2002 Intel announced the 845G chipset supporting Hi-Speed USB for a total bandwidth of 60 megabytes per second, as shown in Figure 4.10. Additional platform evolutions increasing the total I/O bandwidth included increasing the number of hard drives. Four years after the introduction of the 440BX AGP chipset, I/O bandwidth demand grew from 132 megabytes per second to more than 1 gigabyte per second.

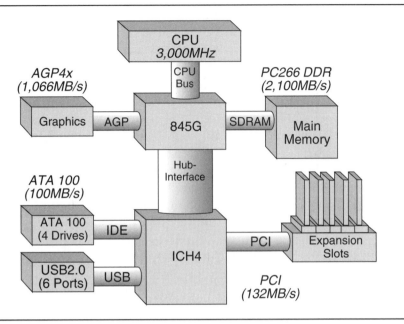

Figure 4.10   PC Architecture 2002

Immediate Benefits

The immediate benefits of PCI Express as a high-speed chipset interconnect are the bandwidth improvements, scalability, and isochrony. I/O evolution will likely continue and several technological changes are underway. The Serial ATA specification was published in 2001 paving the road for new disk transfer rates. The first generation of Serial ATA interconnects will be able to support up to 150 megabytes per second, a 50 percent increase over the existing ATA100 connections. Serial ATA has a plan for reaching 600 megabytes per second by the third generation. In addition, Gigabit Ethernet adoption will eventually drive the requirement for additional bandwidth between the host controller and the I/O controller.

History has demonstrated that bandwidth and performance continue to rise as systems increase the computing power. The inherent scalability in both the numbers of PCI Express lanes as well as the ability to scale the individual frequency of the PCI Express link provides a robust plan for the next decade. For example, if a high-speed interconnect within a chipset requires 1 gigabyte per second per direction of data initially, the system manufacturer could implement a x4 PCI Express link. With changes to the Physical Layer only, the system would be able to scale up to 4 gigabytes per second per direction with a modification to the signaling rate, but leaving the software and existing connectors intact. Due to the benefits, high-speed chip-to-chip interconnects will likely implement PCI Express or proprietary solutions leveraging the PCI Express technology by 2004.

The other immediate benefit evolves from new capabilities within PCI Express. Specifically, isochrony provides revolutionary capabilities for multimedia. Isochrony is discussed later in this chapter and in Chapter 9.

Applicable to Various Market Segments

PCI Express as a high-speed interconnect applies to far more than desktop PCs. Communications equipment are expected to deploy PCI Express links to take advantage of the existing software configuration capability and the scalable nature of PCI Express lanes.

Servers are in a unique position to benefit from several aspects of PCI Express. Servers have a few key distinct requirements, which include increased performance, high connectivity, improved scalability, and improved Reliability, Availability, and Serviceability (RAS). To improve RAS, PCI Express implements a few key features, such as the ability to ensure a robust connection. The Data Link Layer (refer to Chapter 7) ensures that data transfer is not corrupted as well as initiates hardware retries in the event errors are detected.

PCI Express provides an immediate increase in bandwidth while reducing *latency*—the time it takes to receive data after a request by removing the number of bridges between PCI, PCI-X, and proprietary interfaces. PCI Express, unlike current implementations, removes burdensome bridging devices due to its low pin count and dedicated point-to-point link. Bridging solutions and devices evolved due to IO fan-out requirements and layout restrictions associated with PCI/PCI-X. The short bus segment, or the inability to route PCI-X over large distances because of the parallel bus, requires devices to be close to the bus controller chip. In large PCs and servers with multiple slots, the proximity required to support PCI-X is not feasible. I/O fan-out requirements led to bridging devices and proprietary interfaces. The low pin count and dedicated point-to-point link enables greater I/O connectivity and fan-out in a given silicon and package technology while removing the cost and complexity of additional bridging solutions. See Figure 4.11 for a comparison of a server architecture today versus the future.

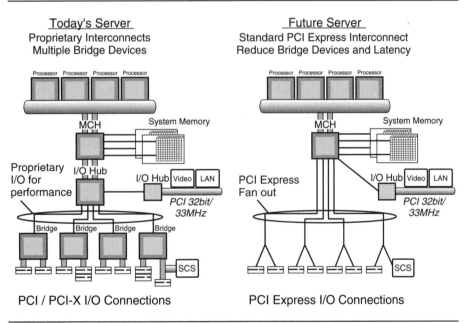

Figure 4.11 Server Architecture Evolution with PCI Express

Given the evolution of multiple I/O technologies, such as disk drives connecting to Serial ATA, networking connections to Gigabit Ethernet, PC peripherals using USB 2.0, chipset designers must revisit their architecture and consider new interconnects. By 2004, proprietary and open architectures are expected to be built around the PCI Express technology.

Revolutionary Applications

Where the previous section covered the applications that will take advantage of the benefits within PCI Express enabling a natural evolution, this section reviews revolutionary applications that PCI Express enables: specifically, isochrony that guarantees glitchless media, future modules that improve ease of use, and communications applications with advanced switching.

Multimedia and Isochronous Applications

Although 1394 and USB2.0 are not necessarily new to the PC platform, there are some specific applications highlighting the revolutionary features of PCI Express—namely isochrony. This section explores 1394 as an example to highlight the impact of PCI Express.

The IEEE 1394 standard was originally "FireWire" from Apple Computer, but was adopted in 1995 as the IEEE 1394-1995 standard, thus the name change from "FireWire" to 1394. The 1394 connection enables a simple, low cost, high bandwidth connection to peripherals such as TVs, printers, cameras, and camcorders for speeds up to 400 megabits per second. The 1394a-2000 protocol ratified in 2000 is a backward-compatible supplement clarifying the 1394-1995 specification to enhance interoperability. The next evolution is to 1394b, which adds new electrical signaling capability to scale from 800 megabits per second to 3,200 megabits per second per direction. 1394b also addresses some protocol enhancements to improve the efficiency of the bus. The 1394 technology has enjoyed a wide acceptance and is found on a wide number of cameras, camcorders, and audio devices. One key aspect of 1394 is the ability to support isochronous traffic or deadline and time-sensitive data.

The easiest way to describe the application and benefit is to walk through an example. Consider trying to record a video clip off a digital camcorder and sending the movie to friends and family via e-mail on the home PC. Easy task, right?

As you start downloading the data from the camera via a 1394 connection to create a simple MPEG file, you decide to check your e-mail and favorite stock price. When you come back to review the MPEG, you notice several dropped frames and an excessive number of glitches in the movie clip. What happened?

This scenario is actually more common than most people think. Essentially, some data types require dedicated bandwidth and a mechanism to guarantee delivery of time-critical data in a deterministic manner. The video stream data needs to be updated on a regular basis between the camera and the application to ensure the time dependencies are met to prevent the loss of video frames. PCI Express-based isochrony solves this problem by providing an interconnect that can deliver time-sensitive data in a deterministic method. In addition to providing the interconnect solution, PCI Express provides a standardized software register set and programming interface easing the burden on the software developer.

In addition to the isochronous support, PCI Express is an excellent choice for 1394b due to the boost in bandwidth and the dedicated connection. Bandwidth for 1394b starts at 800 megabits per second, or 100 megabytes per second. Implementing a PCI (132 megabytes per second) as the interconnect for 1394b quickly becomes the bottleneck throttling performance.

PCI Express Module Applications

The PCI-SIG and the PCMCIA (Personal Computer Memory Card International Association) industry groups are actively defining plug-in modules that will take advantage of the hot plug and hot swap capability within PCI Express. The module developers realized that splitting the effort into multiple industry groups would be more effective than attempting to develop a "one size fits all" approach. The PCI-SIG is currently working on a module for server applications. The PCI-SIG server module objectives are to define a module with two form factors: base and full. The base module form factor is targeted at integrated adapter solutions while the full form factor is targeted at complex adapter solutions requiring the larger volume. The issues currently being worked on include establishing a thermal and power budget based on server needs as well as PCB sizing for cost-effect server IO applications. The current proposals for the full and base modules support x4, x8, and x16 PCI Express configurations for various I/O requirements. The current proposal for the base module measures 75 millimeters × 20 millimeters × 150 millimeters (height ×

width × length) and the full module measures 150 millimeters × 20 millimeters × 150 millimeters (height × width × length). The specification is still being developed and subject to change.

The relevance to server applications is the hot swap capability to add a new I/O function without impacting the system. The technician will be able to insert a new I/O module and the system should dynamically reconfigure automatically, simplifying repairs and upgrades.

The PCMCIA is working on defining a client module (code-named NEWCARD) for mobile and desktop applications because of divergent power and space requirements between the server and client PC (mobile and desktop) market segments. While a server may have sufficient power capability for a 40-watt card and sufficient space, the mobile PC's battery life would be quickly exhausted if the same module were used. The key objective for the PCMCIA is to define a module that will be used by both the desktop PCs and mobile PCs. To achieve this goal, cost must be minimized for the desktop market while space and power must be minimized for the mobile market. Luckily, these two competing objectives are within a reasonable range to resolve for I/O modules. The modules currently under development within the PCMCIA group include a single-wide and a double-wide module. The single-wide module is a small and thin add-in card measuring 33.7 millimeters × 60 millimeters × 5 millimeters (width × length × thickness) and the double-wide module consumes the space of two single-wide modules measuring 68 millimeters × 60 millimeters × 5 millimeters (width × length × thickness). The specification is still under definition—refer to the PCMCIA website (www.pcmcia.org) for the latest information. The 5-millimeter height is critical to enable small and thin notebooks. To accommodate I/O connections such as the RJ45 for LAN, an extended module is under consideration where the I/O connector larger than 5 millimeters will reside outside the desktop or mobile cavity.

The current PC Card is defined by the PCMCIA industry association. PC Card slots on mobile PCs are stacked on top of each other with each of the two slots measuring more than 5 millimeters. The current implementation limits the ability to continue to shrink mobile PCs beyond a certain thickness without sacrificing I/O capability. The smaller modules, in conjunction with a side-by-side configuration, are expected to enable mobile PCs to continue to shrink. The advent of the double-wide module enables a wide variety of applications that might be precluded due to the tight physical space and eases the cost burden for desktop PCs.

In addition, current PC Card implementations require a CardBus controller to translate the PCI interface to the CardBus interface implemented on the PC Card slot. The CardBus controller translates the data from PCI and manages the power states of the PC Card. The introduction of PCI Express provides a cost reduction through the removal of the CardBus controller as PCI Express natively supports hot plug and the advanced power management capabilities. In an effort to ease the industry transition from PC Card, the PCMCIA working group voted in support for USB 2.0 in addition to PCI Express as the electrical interface due to the broad availability of USB 2.0 building blocks. In the long term, PCI Express will displace CardBus as the electrical interface and the newly defined module will displace the current PC Cards defined within the PCMCIA.

Some of the initial applications to embrace the module are flash media, microdrives, wireless LAN, and broadband modems (Cable and DSL routers) because of ease of use. For example, consider the user who orders DSL from the local service provider. Currently, a technician is dispatched to install the unit and must disassemble the PC to install a network connection to an external router via a PCI slot add-in card. The module creates a compelling business scenario for service providers. The service provider could simply ship the module to the user with instructions to connect the phone line to the module and then insert the module into the slot. The user does not need to disassemble or reboot the system. When the card is installed, the operating system detects the presence of a new device and loads the necessary drivers. Additionally, because of the native hot-plug and hot-swap capability within PCI Express, desktop and notebook systems will no longer be burdened with the CardBus controller and the additional system cost associated with the current PC Card.

Communications Applications and Advanced Switching

Communications equipment from embedded applications to chassis-based switching systems requiring high-bandwidth are expected to also adopt PCI Express as a high-speed interconnect. There are two main types of usages within communications equipment for PCI Express, control plane processing and data plane processing. Control plane refers to the control and configuration of the system. Although not originally envisaged by the specification, PCI is used as the interface to configure and control processors and cards within a large number of systems today. Chassis-based building switches typically have various cards that can be inserted and used. Chassis-based switches offer future field-upgradeability. Most switching systems offer the ability to only populate half of the chassis initially and add cards with additional ports or faster speed connections as demand or the number of users increase. PCI Express could be used as a control plane interconnect to configure and monitor the different types of cards installed within the system. The enumeration and established configuration protocol within PCI Express lends itself to a low pin count, high bandwidth and proven methodology to configure cards and services.

The data plane refers to the actual path that the data flows. In the data plane, the advanced switching extension under development within the Arapahoe Work Group, will likely define mechanisms to encapsulate and send PCI Express data packets across peer-to-peer links through the switch fabric. The Arapahoe Work Group consists of promoter companies such as Intel and Microsoft, along with several key developer companies who led the early development of the high-speed interconnect that evolved to the PCI Express specification within the PCI-SIG. The *PCI Express Base Specification* provides the foundation for Advanced Switching extensions, but the AS details are not covered in the *PCI Express Base Specification Revision 1.0*. The following paragraph describes the AS features and benefits. Readers are encouraged to refer to the AS-specific addendums for additional information.

The PCI Express core architecture provides a solid foundation for meeting new interconnects needs. The Advanced Switching (AS) architecture overlays cleanly on this core and establishes an efficient, scalable, and extensible switch fabric through the use of a specific AS header inserted in front of the PCI Express data packet at the Transaction Layer. AS switches only examine the contents of the header that provide routing information (where to send the packet), traffic class ID (quality of service information), congestion avoidance (for preventing traffic jams), packet size, and protocol encapsulation. By separating the routing information, switch designs are simpler and cost-effective. Additionally, adding an external header to the packet enables the switch fabric to encapsulate any number of existing protocols. Features and benefits of Advanced Switching include:

- **Globally flat addressable fabric using path-based routing.** Advanced Switching goes beyond the strict, hierarchical addressing of PCI by employing path-based routing to flatten out the network, increase flexibility and speed the packet delivery process. Instead of using end-point addresses, switches are able to forward packets simply by knowing the correct path at a given point in the network. A 64-bit Advanced Switching route header is added as an extension to the core transaction layer packet.

- **Peer-to-peer transfer between virtually any two devices, anywhere.** Communication can be chip-to-chip, card-to-card, blade-to-blade, or between backplane extensions. All that is required is that both ends of the communication are Advanced Switching capable. They do not have to be using the same operating system.

- **Message passing, both memory and queue based.** Message passing reduces the possibility of inter-node interference. For example, when two boards on a backplane communicate, the packet can simply follow the unique Path ID without providing any visibility into the receiving board.

- **Generalized Upper Layer Protocol (ULP) support.** A set of AS features enables the PCI Express fabric to encapsulate/tunnel arbitrary packets. To illustrate, a group of line cards using different protocols (for example: Ethernet, IP, and SONET) would be able to move data inside the system independent of the ULP.

- **Multicast and Broadcast.** Built-in replication capability enables AS switches to handle multicast and broadcast messages.

- **High availability.** Advanced Switching supports redundant links, switches, fabric managers, control planes and/or data planes, with rapid fail over between them. Additionally, AS adds congestion management capabilities through flow control, deadlock/starvation avoidance, mitigation of Head of Line blocking and additional QoS.

■ **Core and AS in the same fabric.** Core and Advanced Switching components can be designed to co-exist and interoperate in the same fabric. An AS/core bridge provides packet translation at the edge of the fabric where a core device is attached.

■ **Scaleable and extendable.** Support of almost any protocol (past, present, or future) in a way that does not burden AS switches with unnecessary complexity or additional cost. The switches are agnostic to everything in an encapsulated packet with the exception of routing associated information.

The Physical Layer attributes make PCI Express attractive for high-volume backplane switching systems. The inherent scalability provides long term chassis design lifecycles where future system speed upgrades are possible without redefining all of the connectors. Additionally, the advanced encoding scheme allows for high-speed backplane applications with a low pin count. PCI Express with Advanced Switching extensions provides a compelling switch fabric due to the low cost, the ability to leverage the existing industry standard PCI infrastructure, and the ability to address the requirements of converging computing and communications systems.

Chapter 5

PCI Express Architecture Overview

*Always design a thing by considering it in its next larger
context—a chair in a room, a room in a house, a house in
an environment, an environment in a city plan.*

—Eliel Saarinen

This chapter introduces the PCI Express architecture, starting off with
a system level view. This addresses the basics of a point-to-point architecture, the various types of devices and the methods for information
flow through those devices. Next, the chapter drops down one level to
further investigate the transaction types, mainly the types of information
that can be exchanged and the methods for doing so. Lastly, the chapter
drops down one level further to see how a PCI Express device actually
goes about building those transactions. PCI Express uses three transaction build layers, the Transaction Layer, the Data Link Layer and the
Physical Layer. These architectural build layers are touched upon in this
chapter with more details in Chapters 6 through 8.

System Level Overview

Whereas PCI is a parallel, multi-drop interface, PCI Express is a serial,
point-to-point interface. As such, many of the rules and interactions in
PCI are no longer directly applicable to PCI Express. For example, devices no longer need to arbitrate for the right to be the bus driver prior to
sending out a transaction. A PCI Express device is always the driver for its

transmitter pair(s) and is always the target for its receiver pair(s). Since only one device ever resides at the other end of a PCI Express link, only one device can drive each signal and only one device receives that signal.

In Figure 5.1, Device B always drives data out its differential transmitter pair (traces 1 and 2) and always receives data on its differential receiver pair (traces 3 and 4). Device A follows the same rules, but its transmitter and receive pairs are mirrored to Device B. Traces 3 and 4 connect to Device A's transmitter pair (TX), while traces 1 and 2 connect to its receiver pair (RX). This is a very important difference from parallel busses such as PCI; the transmit pair of one device *must* be the receiver pair for the other device. They must be point-to-point, one device to a second device. TX of one is RX of the other and vice versa.

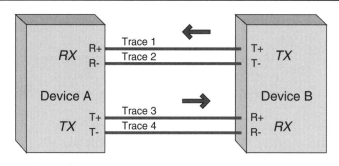

Figure 5.1   Point-to-Point Connection between Two PCI Express Devices

Links and Lanes

The connection between two PCI Express devices is referred to as a *link*. A link consists of a number of lanes, much the same way that a highway consists of a number of driving lanes. With PCI Express, a *lane* is the term used for a single set of differential transmit and receive pairs. A lane contains four signals, a differential pair for unidirectional transmission in both directions (referred to as dual unidirectional). The link shown in Figure 5.1 is a single lane wide. The link shown in Figure 5.2 is 4 lanes wide.

At the device, the collection of transmitter and receiver pairs that are associated with a link is referred to as a *port*. Like links, a device's port can be made up of multiple lanes. A quick aside on terminology: a PCI Express device and its associated port(s) refer to signals as either transmit (TX) or receive (RX) signals. However, when one refers to a link, the signals that make up each lane cannot truly be called "transmitter" or "receiver". No given connection is just a transmitter or a receiver because it is considered both simultaneously. The transmit signal for Device B is the receive signal for Device A.

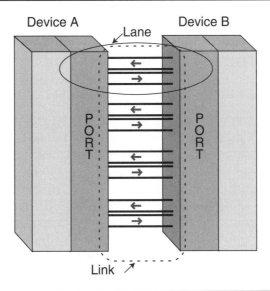

Figure 5.2   Links, Lanes, and Ports

The signaling scheme for PCI Express is tremendously simple. Each lane is just a unidirectional transmit pair and receive pair. There are no separate address and data signals, no control signals like the FRAME#, IRDY# or PME# signals used in PCI, not even a sideband clock sent along with the data. Because of this simplicity and modularity, the architecture can more easily scale into the future, provide additional bandwidth and simplify the adoption of new usage models. However, it also requires the adoption of signaling techniques vastly different from traditional PCI.

Embedded Clocking

PCI Express utilizes 8-bit/10-bit encoding to embed the clock within the data stream being transmitted. At initialization, the two devices determine the fastest signaling rate supported by both devices. The current specification only identifies a single signaling rate, 2.5 gigabits per second (per lane per direction), so that negotiation is pretty simple. Since the transfer rate is determined ahead of time, the only other function of the clock would be for sampling purposes at the receiver. That is where 8-bit/10-bit encoding with an embedded clock comes into play. By transmitting each byte of data as 10 encoded bits, you can control the number of transitions associated with each transmission character—simplifying the sampling procedures on the receiver side. Chapter 8, "Physical Layer Architecture" contains more information on this topic.

Multiple Lanes

You might now be asking yourself, "If the transfer rate is fixed ahead of time at 2.5 gigabits per second per lane per direction, how can this interface scale to meet the needs of high-bandwidth interfaces?" After all, 2.5 gigabits per second per direction is only 250 megabytes per second of actual data that can flow each way (recall that with 8-bit/10-bit encoding, each byte of data is transferred as 10 bits, so you need to divide 2.5 gigabits per second by 10 to get theoretical data transfer rates). A data transfer rate of 250 megabytes per second per direction might be better than traditional PCI, but it certainly is not in the same league as higher bandwidth interfaces like AGP (AGP4x runs at 1 gigabyte per second and AGP8x runs at 2 gigabytes per second total bandwidth). When you add to this the fact that a parallel bus, like PCI or AGP, is substantially more efficient (at the same frequency) than a serial interface like PCI Express, the bandwidth of this new interface seems to be at a disadvantage to some existing platform technologies. Well, that is where PCI Express' scalability comes into play.

Much like lanes can be added to a highway to increase the total traffic throughput, multiple lanes can be used within a PCI Express link to increase the available bandwidth. In order to make its capabilities clear, a link is named for the number of lanes it has. For example, the link shown in Figure 5.2 is called a x4 (read as: "by four") link since it consists of a four lanes. A link with only a single lane, as in Figure 5.1, is called a x1 link. As previously noted, the maximum bandwidth of a x1 is 250 megabytes per second in each direction. Because PCI Express is dual unidirectional, this offers a maximum theoretical bandwidth of 500 megabytes per second between the two devices (250 megabytes per second in both directions). The x4 link shown in Figure 5.2 has a maximum bandwidth of 4 × 250 megabytes per second = 1 gigabyte per second in each direction. Going up to a x16 link provides 16 × 250 megabytes per second = 4 gigabytes per second in each direction. This means that PCI Express can be adjusted to meet a variety of applications with a variety of bandwidth needs. When you consider that the specification will one day support additional transfer rates, such as 5 or even 10 gigabits per second per lane per direction, the scalability and flexibility of the interface begins to come into focus.

Device Types

The *PCI Express Base Specification* identifies several types of PCI Express elements: a *root complex*, a *PCI Express to PCI bridge*, an *endpoint* and a *switch*. These device elements emulate the PCI configuration model, but apply it more closely to the variety of potential point-to-point PCI Express topologies. Figure 5.3 demonstrates how these elements play together within a PCI Express world.

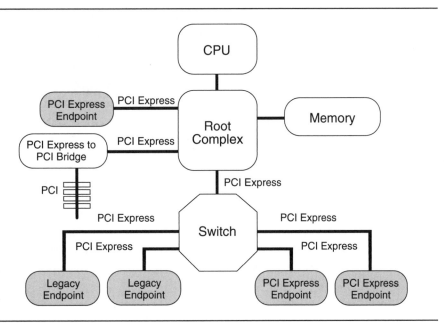

Figure 5.3   PCI Express Topology

■ The root complex is the head or root of the connection of the I/O system to the CPU and memory. For example, in today's PC chipset system architecture, the (G)MCH (Graphics & Memory Controller Hub) or a combination of the (G)MCH and ICH (I/O Controller Hub) could be considered the root complex. Each interface off of the root complex defines a separate hierarchy domain. Supporting transactions across hierarchy domains is not a required capability of root complexes, but may be implemented if desired (for example, to allow direct communications between a PCI Express graphics device connected to the MCH and a USB video camera located off of a PCI Express switch connected to the ICH).

■ An endpoint is a device that can request/complete PCI Express transactions for itself (for example, a graphics device) or on behalf of a non-PCI Express device (translating from a USB interface, for instance). There are two types of endpoints—legacy and PCI Express, and they are differentiated by the types of transactions they support.

■ Switches are used to fan out a PCI Express hierarchy. From a PCI configuration standpoint, they are considered a collection of "virtual" PCI-to-PCI bridges whose sole purpose is to act as the traffic director between multiple links. They are responsible for properly forwarding transactions to the appropriate link. Unlike a root complex, they must always manage peer-to-peer transactions between downstream devices (downstream meaning the side further away from the root complex).

■ A PCI Express to PCI bridge has one PCI Express port and one or multiple PCI/PCI-X bus interfaces. This type of element allows PCI Express to coexist on a platform with existing PCI technologies. This device must fully support all PCI and/or PCI-X transactions on its PCI interface(s). It must also follow a variety of rules (discussed in later chapters) for properly transforming those PCI/PCI-X transactions into PCI Express transactions.

PCI Express Transactions

Transactions form the basis for the transportation of information between PCI Express devices. PCI Express uses a split-transaction protocol. This means that there are two portions to the transaction, the request and the completion. The transaction initiator, referred to as the *requester*, sends out the request packet. It makes its way towards the intended target of the request, referred to as the *completer.* For requests that require completions, the completer later sends back a completion packet (or packets) to the requester. A completion is not necessarily required for each request.

Even though PCI Express links are point-to-point, this does not always mean that one of the devices on the link is the requester and the other the completer. For example, say that the root complex in Figure 5.3 wants to communicate with a PCI Express endpoint that is downstream of the switch. The root complex is the requester and the endpoint is the completer. Even though the switch receives the transaction from the root complex, it is not considered a completer of that transaction. Even though the endpoint receives the transaction from the switch, it does not consider the switch to be the requester of that transaction. The requester identifies itself within the request packet it sends out, and this informs the completer (and/or switch) where it should return the completion packets (if needed).

Transaction Types

The PCI Express architecture defines four transaction types: memory, I/O, configuration, and message. This is similar to the traditional PCI transactions, with the notable difference being the addition of a message transaction type.

Memory Transactions

Transactions targeting the memory space transfer data to or from a memory-mapped location. There are several types of memory transactions: Memory Read Request, Memory Read Completion, and Memory Write Request. Memory transactions use one of two different address formats, either 32-bit addressing (short address) or 64-bit addressing (long address).

I/O Transactions

Transactions targeting the I/O space transfer data to or from an I/O-mapped location. PCI Express supports this address space for compatibility with existing devices that utilize this space. There are several types of I/O transactions: I/O Read Request, I/O Read Completion, I/O Write Request, and I/O Write Completion. I/O transactions use only 32-bit addressing (short address format).

Configuration Transactions

Transactions targeting the configuration space are used for device configuration and setup. These transactions access the configuration registers of PCI Express devices. Compared to traditional PCI, PCI Express allows for many more configuration registers. For each function of each device, PCI Express defines a configuration register block four times the size of PCI. There are several types of configuration transactions: Configuration Read Request, Configuration Read Completion, Configuration Write Request, and Configuration Write Completion.

Message Transactions

PCI Express adds a new transaction type to communicate a variety of miscellaneous messages between PCI Express devices. Referred to simply as messages, these transactions are used for functions like interrupt signaling, error signaling or power management. This new transaction type is necessary since these functions are no longer available via sideband signals such as PME#, SERR#, and so on.

Build Layers

The specification defines three abstract layers that "build" a PCI Express transaction, as shown in Figure 5.4. The first layer, logically enough, is referred to as the *Transaction Layer*. The main responsibility of this layer is to begin the process of turning requests or completion data from the device core into a PCI Express transaction. The *Data Link Layer* is the second architectural build layer. The main responsibility of this layer is to ensure that the transactions going back and forth across the link are received properly. The third architectural build layer is called the *Physical Layer*. This layer is responsible for the actual transmitting and receiving of the transaction across the PCI Express link.

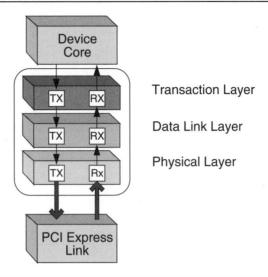

Figure 5.4   The Three Architectural Build Layers

Since each PCI Express link is dual uni-directional, each of these architectural layers has transmit as well as receive functions associated with it. Outgoing PCI Express transactions may proceed from the transmit side of the Transaction Layer to the transmit side of the Data Link Layer to the transmit side of the Physical Layer. Incoming transactions may proceed from the receive side of the Physical Layer to the receive side of the Data Link Layer and then on to the receive side of the Transaction Layer.

Packet Formation

In a traditional parallel interface like AGP, sideband signals (such as C/BE[3:0]# and SBA[7:0]) transmit the information for command type, address location, length, and so on. As discussed previously, no such sideband signals exist in PCI Express. Therefore, the packets that are being sent back and forth must incorporate this sort of information.

The three architectural build layers accomplish this by "building up" the packets into a full scale PCI Express transaction. This buildup is shown in Figure 5.5.

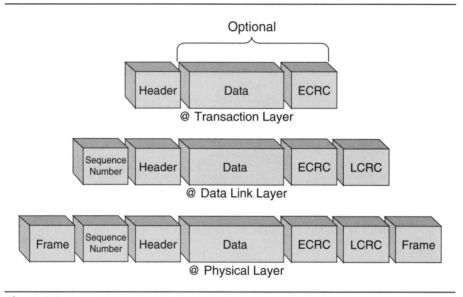

Figure 5.5   Transaction Buildup for a TLP through Architectural Layers

Each layer has specific functions and contributes to a portion of the pyramid in Figure 5.5. As a transaction flows through the transmitting PCI Express device, each layer adds on its specific information. The Transaction Layer generates a header and adds the data payload (if required) and an optional ECRC (end-to-end CRC). The Data Link Layer adds the sequence number and LCRC (link CRC). The Physical Layer frames it for proper transmission to the other device. When it gets to the receiver side of the link mate, the complete reversal of this build occurs. The Physical Layer decodes the framing characters and passes along the rest of the information (sequence number, header, data, ECRC, and LCRC) to its Data Link Layer. The Data Link Layer checks out the sequence number and LCRC, and then passes the header, data, and ECRC on to the Transaction Layer. The Transaction Layer decodes the ECRC (if applicable) and header, and then passes the appropriate information on to its device core.

Note

> The *PCI Express Base Specification* defines three types of CRCs: an ECRC, an LCRC, and a CRC. Each of these CRC types provides a method for PCI Express devices to verify the contents of received packets. The transmitting device performs a calculation on the bit values of the outgoing packet and appends the result of that calculation to the packet. The appropriate receiver then performs the same calculation on the incoming packet and compares the result to the attached value. If one or more bit errors occurred during the transmission of that packet, the two calculated values do not match and the receiver knows that the packet is unreliable.
>
> The differences between the three CRC types consist of the sizes (32 bits long versus 16 bits long), and the PCI Express layer that is responsible for generating and checking the values. Additional details on ECRCs are contained in Chapter 6, "Transaction Layer Architecture" and additional details on LCRCs and CRCs are contained in Chapter 7, "Data Link Layer Architecture."

The Big Picture

Before getting into all the architectural details of how this happens, the following section takes a step back to look at the big picture. From an architectural standpoint, what is it that PCI Express is actually trying to do? The answer is quite simple. It is trying to get data from one PCI Express device to another as quickly and reliably as possible. Great, but what does that mean in a real computer system? The simplified block diagram in Figure 5.6 shows how PCI Express could help get a computer up and running.

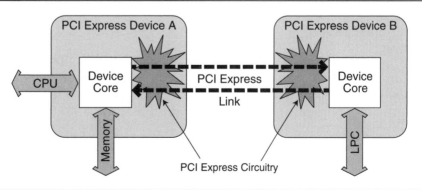

Figure 5.6   PCI Express in the Pathway between the CPU and System Firmware

The following hypothetical example details how PCI Express may be used to help boot up a standard computer. Once the system has powered up, the CPU sends out a memory read request for the first BIOS instruction. This request comes to Device A across the processor's system bus. Device A's core decodes this transaction and realizes that the requested address is not its responsibility and this transaction needs to be forwarded out to Device B. This is where PCI Express comes into play.

Device A's core passes this memory read request to its PCI Express block. This block is then responsible for turning the request into a legitimate PCI Express request transaction and sending it out across the PCI Express link. On the other side of the link, Device B's PCI Express block is responsible for receiving and decoding the request transaction, verifying its integrity, and passing it along to the Device B core.

Now the Device B core has just received a memory read request, so it sends that request out its LPC (low pin count) bus to read that address location from the system's flash/BIOS device that is attached to it. Once the Device B core receives the requested data back, it passes the data along to its PCI Express block.

Device B's PCI Express block is then responsible for turning this data into a legitimate PCI Express completion transaction and sending it back up the PCI Express link. On the other side of the link, Device A's PCI Express block is responsible for receiving and decoding the transaction, verifying its integrity, and passing it along to the Device A core. The Device A core now has the appropriate information and forwards it along to the CPU. The computer is now ready to start executing instructions.

With this big picture in mind, the following sections start to examine how each of the PCI Express architectural layers contributes to accomplishing this task.

Transaction Layer

As mentioned earlier, the Transaction Layer is the uppermost PCI Express architectural layer and starts the process of turning request or data packets from the device core into PCI Express transactions. This layer receives request (such as "read from BIOS location FFF0h") or completion packet ("here is the result of that read") from the device core. It is then responsible for turning that request/data into a Transaction Layer Packet (TLP). A TLP is simply a packet that is sent from the Transaction Layer of one device to the Transaction Layer of the other device. The TLP uses a header to identify the type of transaction that it is (for example, I/O versus memory, read versus write, request versus completion, and so on).

Please note that the Transaction Layer has direct interaction only with its device core and its Data Link Layer, as shown in Figure 5.7. It relies on its device core to provide valid requests and completion data, and on its Data Link Layer to communicate with its Physical Layer to get that information to and from the Transaction Layer on the other side of the link.

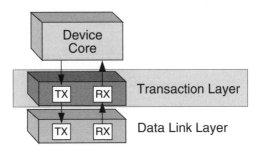

Figure 5.7   Transaction Layer

How might this layer behave in the previous "Big Picture" startup example? The Device A core issues a memory read request with associated length and address to its PCI Express block. The Transaction Layer's transmit functions turn that information into a TLP by building a memory read request header. Once the TLP is created, it is passed along to the transmit side of the Data Link layer. Some time later, Device A's Transaction Layer receives the completion packet for that request from the receive side of its Data Link Layer. The Transaction Layer's receive side then decodes the header associated with that packet and passes the data along to its device core.

The Transaction Layer also has several other functions, such as flow control and power management. Chapter 6, "Transaction Layer Architecture" contains additional details on the Transaction Layer and TLPs. Chapter 9, "Flow Control" contains additional details on the flow control mechanisms for those TLPs, and Chapter 11, "Power Management" contains additional details on the various power management functions.

Data Link Layer

The Data Link Layer is the middle PCI Express architectural layer and interacts with both the Physical Layer and the Transaction Layer, as shown in Figure 5.8. The main responsibility of this layer is error correction and detection. Basically, it makes sure that all data being sent back and forth across the link is wholesome. It is responsible for making sure that each packet makes it across the link, and makes it across intact.

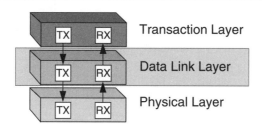

Figure 5.8   Data Link Layer

This layer receives TLPs from the transmit side of the Transaction Layer and continues the process of building that into a PCI Express transaction. It does this by adding a sequence number to the front of the packet and an LCRC error checker to the end. The sequence number serves the purpose of making sure that each packet makes it across the link. For example, if the last sequence number that Device A successfully received was #6, it expects the next packet to have a sequence number of 7. If it instead sees #8, it knows that packet #7 got lost somewhere and notifies Device B of the error. The LCRC serves to make sure that each packet makes it across intact. As mentioned previously, if the LCRC does not check out at the receiver side, the device knows that there was a bit error sometime during the transmission of this packet. This scenario also generates an error condition. Once the transmit side of the Data Link Layer applies the sequence number and LCRC to the TLP, it submits them to the Physical Layer.

The receiver side of the Data Link Layer accepts incoming packets from the Physical Layer and checks the sequence number and LCRC to make sure the packet is correct. If it is correct, it then passes it up to the receiver side of the Transaction Layer. If an error occurs (either wrong sequence number or bad data), it does not pass the packet on to the Transaction Layer until the issue has been resolved. In this way, the Data Link Layer acts a lot like the security guard of the link. It makes sure that only the packets that are "supposed to be there" are allowed through.

The Data Link Layer is also responsible for several link management functions. To do this, it generates and consumes Data Link Layer Packets (DLLPs).Unlike TLPs, these packets are created at the Data Link Layer. These packets are used for link management functions such as error notification, power management, link-specific flow control and so on.

How might this layer behave in the previous "Big Picture" startup example? The Transaction Layer in Device A creates a memory read request TLP and passes it along to the Data Link Layer. This layer adds the appropriate sequence number and generates an LCRC to append to the end of the packet. Once these two functions are performed, the Data Link Layer passes this new, larger packet along to the Physical Layer. Some time later, Device A's Data Link Layer receives the completion packet for that request from the receive side of its Physical Layer. The Data Link Layer then checks the sequence number and LCRC to make sure the received read completion packet is correct.

What happens if the received packet at Device A was incorrect (assume the LCRC did not check out)? The Data Link Layer in Device A then creates a DLLP that states that there was an error and that Device B should resend the packet. Device A's Data Link Layer passes that DLLP on to its Physical Layer, which sends it over to Device B. The Data Link Layer in Device B receives that DLLP from its Physical Layer and decodes the packet. It sees that there was an error on the read completion packet and resubmits that packet to its Physical Layer. Please note that the Data Link Layer of Device B does this on its own; it does *not* send the DLLP on to its Transaction Layer. The Data Link Layer, not the Transaction Layer, of Device B is responsible for the retry attempt.

Eventually, Device A receives that resent packet and it proceeds from the receive side of the Physical Layer to the receive side of the Data Link Layer. If the sequence number and LCRC check out this time around, it then passes that packet along to the Transaction Layer. The Transaction Layer in Device A has no idea that a retry was needed for this packet; it is totally dependent on its Data Link Layer to make sure the packet is correct.

Additional details on this layer's functions, sequence numbers, LCRCs and DLLPs are explained in Chapter 7, "Data Link Layer Architecture."

Physical Layer

Finally, the lowest PCI Express architectural layer is the Physical Layer. This layer is responsible for actually sending and receiving all the data to be sent across the PCI Express link. The Physical Layer interacts with its Data Link Layer and the physical PCI Express link (wires, cables, optical fiber, and so on), as shown in Figure 5.9. This layer contains all the circuitry for the interface operation: input and output buffers, parallel-to-serial and serial-to-parallel converters, PLL(s) and impedance matching circuitry. It also contains some logic functions needed for interface initialization and maintenance.

On the transmit side of things, the Physical Layer takes information from the Data Link Layer and converts it into the proper serial format. The packet goes through an optional data scrambling procedure, 8-bit/10-bit conversion, and parallel-to-serial conversion. The Physical Layer also adds framing characters to indicate the beginning and ending of a packet. It is then sent out across the link using the appropriate transfer rate (for example, 2.5 gigahertz) as well as link width (for example, using four lanes if the link is a x4).

On the receive side, the Physical Layer takes the incoming serial stream from the link and turns it back into a chunk of data to be passed along to its Data Link Layer. This procedure is basically the reverse of what would occur on the transmit side. It samples the data, removes the framing characters, descrambles the remaining data characters and then converts the 8-bit/10-bit data stream back into a parallel data format.

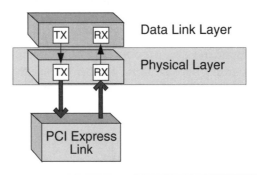

Figure 5.9   Physical Layer

How might this layer behave in the previous "Big Picture" startup example? Once power up occurs, the Physical Layers on both Device A and Device B are responsible for initializing the link to get it up and running and ready for transactions. This initialization process includes determining how many lanes should be used for the link and at what speed the interface should operate. To make this example simple, both devices support a x1 link and operate at the initial 2.5 gigabits per second rate. Sometime after the link is properly initialized, that memory read request starts to work its way through Device A. Eventually it makes its way down to Device A's Physical Layer, complete with a sequence number, memory read request header, and LCRC. The Physical Layer takes that packet of data and transforms it into a serial data stream after it applies 8-bit/10-bit encoding and data scrambling to each character. The Physical Layer knows the link consists of a single lane running at 2.5 gigahertz, so it sends that data stream over its transmit pairs at that speed. In doing this, it needs to meet certain electrical and timing rules that are discussed in Chapter 8, "Physical Layer Architecture." The Physical Layer on Device B sees this data stream appear on its differential receiver input buffers and samples it accordingly. It then decodes the stream, builds it back into a data packet and passes it along to its Data Link Layer.

Please note that the Physical Layers of both devices completely insulate the rest of the layers and devices from the physical details for the transmission of the data. How that data is transmitted across the link is completely a function of the Physical Layer. In a traditional computer system, the two devices would be located on the same FR4 motherboard and connected via copper traces. There is nothing in the *PCI Express Base Specification*, however, that would require this sort of implementation. If designed properly, the two devices could implement their PCI Express transmit/receive circuitry as optical circuits that are connected via a 6-foot-long optical fiber cable. The rest of the layers would not know the difference. This provides PCI Express an enormous amount of flexibility in the ways it can be implemented. As speed or transmission media changes from system to system, those modifications can be localized to one architectural layer.

Additional details on this layer's functions, 8-bit/10-bit encoding, electrical requirements and timing requirements are explained in Chapter 8, "Physical Layer Architecture."

Chapter 6

Transaction Layer Architecture

The following are the universally fundamental laws of ... communication: 1) one must have something to communicate; 2) one must have someone to whom to communicate it; 3) one must really communicate it, not merely express it for oneself alone.

—Friedrich von Schlegel

This chapter goes into the details of the uppermost PCI Express architectural layer: the Transaction Layer. This layer creates and consumes the request and completion packets that are the backbone of data transfer across PCI Express. The chapter discusses the specifics for Transaction Layer Packet (TLP) generation, how the header is used to identify the transaction, and how the Transaction Layer handles incoming TLPs. Though TLP flow control is a function of the Transaction Layer, that topic is discussed in Chapter 9, "Flow Control" and is not discussed in this chapter.

Transaction Layer Overview

This layer's primary responsibility is to create PCI Express request and completion transactions. It has both transmit functions for outgoing transactions, and receive functions for incoming transactions. On the transmit side, the Transaction Layer receives request data (such as "read from BIOS location FFF0h") or completion data ("here is the result of that read") from the device core, and then turns that information into an outgoing PCI Express transaction. On the receive side, the Transaction Layer accepts incoming PCI Express transactions from its Data Link Layer, as shown in Figure 6.1. This layer assumes all incoming information is correct, because it relies on its Data Link Layer to ensure that incoming information is error-free and received in the proper sequence.

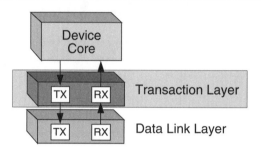

Figure 6.1   Transaction Layer

The Transaction Layer uses TLPs to communicate request and completion data with other PCI Express devices. TLPs may address several address spaces and have a variety of purposes, for example: read versus write, request versus completion, and memory versus configuration. Each TLP has a header associated with it to identify the type of transaction. The Transaction Layer of the originating device generates the TLP and the Transaction Layer of the destination device consumes the TLP. The Transaction Layer also has several other responsibilities, such as managing TLP flow control (discussed in Chapter 9, "Flow Control") and controlling some aspects of power management.

Transaction Layer Packets

The Transaction Layer Packet (TLP) is the means through which request and completion information is communicated between PCI Express devices. A TLP consists of a header, an optional data payload, and an optional TLP digest. The Transaction Layer generates outgoing TLPs based on the information it receives from its device core. The Transaction Layer then passes the TLP on to its Data Link Layer for further processing. The Transaction Layer also accepts incoming TLPs from its Data Link Layer. The Transaction Layer checks the ECRC (optional) and decodes the header information, and then passes along the appropriate information and data payload (again optional) to its device core. A generic TLP is shown in Figure 6.2.

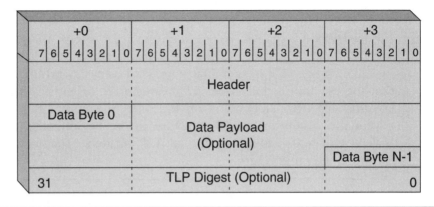

Figure 6.2   Generic TLP Format

The TLP always begins with a header. The header is DWord aligned (a multiple of four bytes; DWord equals four bytes or 32 bits) but varies in length based on the type of transaction. Depending on the type of packet, TLPs may contain a data payload. If present, the data payload is also DWord-aligned for both the first and last DWord of data. DWord Byte Enable fields within the header indicate whether "padding" bytes are appended to either the beginning or ending of the payload to achieve this DWord alignment. Finally, the TLP may consist of a digest at the end of the packet.

Like the data payload, the digest is optional and is not always used. If used, the digest field contains an ECRC (end-to-end CRC) that ensures the contents of the TLP are properly conveyed from the source of the transaction to its ultimate destination. The Data Link Layer ensures that the TLP makes it across a given link properly, but does not necessarily guarantee that the TLP makes it to its destination intact. For example, if the TLP is routed through an intermediate device (such as a switch), it is possible that during the handling of the TLP, the switch introduces an error within the TLP. An ECRC may be appended to the TLP to ensure that this sort of error does not go undetected. The ECRC should not be confused with the LCRC or the CRC. The ECRC is a 32-bit value that is generated at the Transaction Layer of the originating device and checked at the Transaction Layer of the destination device. It is not necessarily checked on a link-by-link basis in the manner that LCRCs and CRCs are (Chapter 7 contains a more detailed description of LCRCs and CRCs). Additional details on ECRCs are contained later in this chapter.

TLP Headers

All TLPs consist of a header that contains the basic identifying information for the transaction. The TLP header may be either three or four DWords in length, depending on the type of transaction. This section covers the details of the TLP header fields, beginning with the first DWord (bytes 0 through 3) for all TLP headers. The format for this DWord is shown in Figure 6.3.

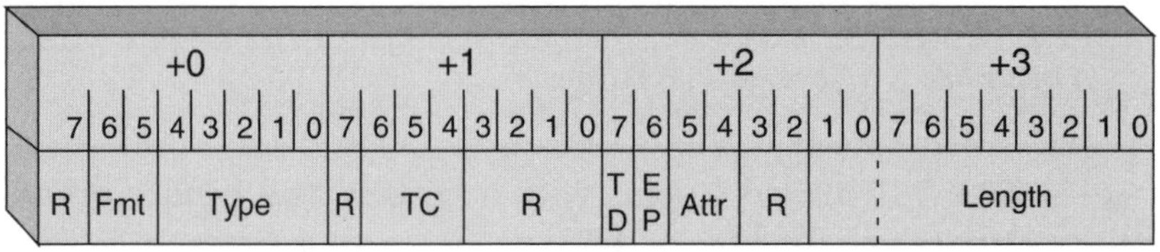

Figure 6.3   Format of First DWord for All TLP Headers

TLP fields marked with an R indicate a reserved bit or field. Reserved bits are filled with 0's during TLP formation, and are ignored by receivers. The Format (Fmt) field indicates the format of the TLP itself. Table 6.1 shows the associated values for that field.

Table 6.1   Fmt[1:0] Field Values

Fmt [1:0] Encoding	TLP Format
00b	3 DWord header, no data payload
01	4 DWord header, no data payload
10	3 DWord header, with data payload
11	4 DWord header, with data payload

As can be seen in Table 6.1, the Format field indicates the length of the TLP header, but does not directly identify the type of transaction. This is determined by the combination of the Format and Type fields, as shown in Table 6.2.

Table 6.2   Type[4:0] Field Values

Fmt [1:0] Encoding	Type [4:0] Encoding	TLP Type	Description
00	0 0000	MRd	Memory Read Request
01			Fmt = 00b indicates a 32 bit address; Fmt = 01b indicates a 64 bit address
00	0 0001	MrdLk	Memory Read Request—Locked
01			Fmt = 00b indicates a 32 bit address; Fmt = 01b indicates a 64 bit address
10	0 0000	MWr	Memory Write Request
11			Fmt = 10b indicates a 32 bit address; Fmt = 11b indicates a 64 bit address
00	0 0010	IORd	I/O Read Request
10	0 0010	IOWr	I/O Write Request
00	0 0100	CfgRd0	Configuration Read Type 0
10	0 0100	CfgWr0	Configuration Write Type 0
00	0 0101	CfgRd1	Configuration Read Type 1
10	0 0101	CfgWr1	Configuration Write Type 1
01	1 0$r_2 r_1 r_0$	Msg	Message Request (with no data payload)
11	1 0$r_2 r_1 r_0$	MsgD	Message Request (with data payload)
00	0 1010	Cpl	Completion (with no data payload)
10	0 1010	CplD	Completion (with data payload)
00	0 1011	CplLk	Completion for Locked Memory Read (with no data payload)—used only in error case
10	0 1011	CplDLk	Completion for Locked Memory Read (with data payload)—otherwise like CplD
			All other encodings are reserved

r[2:0] indicate the routing scheme that a message uses. The messages section of this chapter contains a full explanation of these bits.

Additional details on each of these types of transactions are provided later in this chapter. As can be seen from Table 6.2, the most significant bit in the Fmt field differentiates between reads (Fmt[1]=0) and writes (Fmt[1]=1) for memory, I/O and configuration requests. For completion and message transactions, that same bit differentiates packets that contain a data payload from those that do not. For memory transactions, the least significant format bit (Fmt[0]) differentiates 32-bit address formats from 64-bit address formats.

The TC field (bits 6:4 of byte 1) indicates the traffic class of the packet. This 3-bit field allows for differentiation of transactions into eight distinct traffic classes. Devices use this information, in conjunction with virtual channels, to provide differentiated servicing policies. The default traffic class is a value of 000b indicating a traffic class of TC0. This classification is used for general purpose I/O traffic and is serviced using a best effort policy. Values between 001b and 111b in this field indicate traffic classes between TC1 and TC7. These traffic classes may have differentiated service policies based on the implementation of the devices within the system. Chapter 9, "Flow Control" has a full description of virtual channels, traffic classes and differentiated servicing policies.

The TD bit (bit 7 of byte 2) indicates whether a TLP digest is provided at the end of the TLP. As previously discussed, the TLP digest field may contain an ECRC (end-to-end CRC) to ensure the integrity of the TLP as it travels through the PCI Express system. A value of 1b in this location indicates that a TLP digest is attached, while a value of 0b indicates that no TLP digest is present. Additional details on ECRCs are contained later in the chapter.

The EP bit (bit 6 of byte 2) indicates whether a TLP is poisoned. A poisoned TLP is a known bad TLP that is forwarded along. This may be used for the controlled propagation of an error through the system.

The Attr field (bits [5:4] of byte 2) contains attributes information for the TLP. This field provides additional information that allow for traffic handling optimization. The first bit (bit 5 of byte 2) identifies if PCI-X relaxed ordering applies to the TLP. A value of 0b at that bit indicates default, PCI strongly ordered model. A value of 1b indicates that PCI-X relaxed ordering model applies. This information is used when determining transaction ordering. The level of support for this attribute is dependent upon the target applications of the individual PCI Express devices. Please refer to the *PCI-X 2.0 Specification* for additional details on relaxed ordering. The second bit of this field (bit 4 of byte 2) indicates whether "snooping" (cache coherency) is required for the transaction. A value of 0b in this field indicates that hardware enforced cache coherency is expected, while a value of 1b indicates that cache coherency is not expected.

The Length field (bits[1:0] of byte 2 and all of byte 1) indicates the length of the data payload in DWords. The length in this field only identifies the length of the data payload and not of the entire TLP. A value of 00 0000 0001b in this location indicates a data payload that is one DWord long. A value of 00 0000 0010b indicates a two DWord value, and so on up to a maximum of 1024 DWords (which rolls over and is represented by 00 0000 0000b). As mentioned previously, if a data payload is present, it must be aligned on a DWord boundary on both the first and last DWord. The overall size of the TLP can be determined from this field, along with the Fmt (indicating whether the TLP header is three or four DWords) and TD (indicating whether a single DWord digest is attached at the end) fields.

Memory Request Headers

Memory requests are used for normal memory reads, reads to locked memory, or for memory writes. Memory requests are also differentiated by the addressing format, as PCI Express supports both 32-bit and 64-bit memory addressing. All memory requests have the common DWord shown in Figure 6.3 as the first DWord of the header. The second DWord for all memory requests contains the same information: the Requester ID, the Tag, and the Byte Enable fields. If a memory request uses 64-bit addressing, it then places that 64 bit address into the third and fourth DWords, making the entire 64-bit memory address header a four DW header. This can be seen in Figure 6.4. As a result, the associated Format field for a 64-bit memory request is either 01b if a read or 11b if a write. If a memory request uses 32-bit addressing, it then places that 32 bit address into the third DWord—making the entire 32-bit memory address header a three DW header. This can be seen in Figure 6.5. As a result, the associated Format field for a 32-bit memory request is either 00b if a read or 10b if a write.

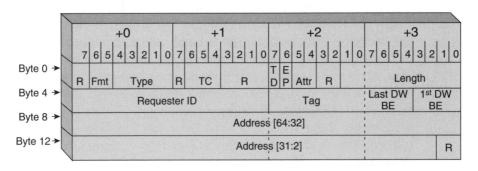

Figure 6.4 64-bit Address Memory Request Header

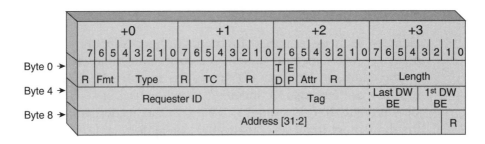

Figure 6.5 32-bit Address Memory Request Header

The address mapping for TLP headers is outlined in Table 6.3. Please note that address bits [31:2] are not in the same location for 64-bit address formats as they are for 32-bit addressing formats. If addressing a location below 4 gigabytes, requesters must use the 32-bit address format.

Table 6.3 Address Field Mapping

Address Bits	32 Bit Addressing	64 Bit Addressing
63:56	Not Applicable	Bits 7:0 of Byte 8
55:48	Not Applicable	Bits 7:0 of Byte 9
47:40	Not Applicable	Bits 7:0 of Byte 10
39:32	Not Applicable	Bits 7:0 of Byte 11
31:24	Bits 7:0 of Byte 8	Bits 7:0 of Byte 12
23:16	Bits 7:0 of Byte 9	Bits 7:0 of Byte 13
15:8	Bits 7:0 of Byte 10	Bits 7:0 of Byte 14
7:2	Bits 7:2 of Byte 11	Bits 7:2 of Byte 15

The Requester ID field (bytes 4 and 5 in Figure 6.5) contains the logical bus, device and function number of the requester. This is a 16-bit value that is unique for every PCI Express function within a hierarchy. Bus and device numbers within a root complex may be assigned in an implementation specific manner, but all other PCI Express devices (or functions within a multi-function device) must comprehend the bus and device number they are assigned during configuration. PCI Express devices (other than the root complex) cannot make assumptions about their bus or device number. Each device is responsible for capturing the bus and device from any configuration write that targets that device (Type 0). Since this information is necessary to generate any request TLP, a device cannot initiate a request until it receives at least one configuration write containing its assigned bus and device numbers. This model is consistent with the existing PCI/PCI-X model for system initialization and configuration. Figure 6.6 shows the requester ID format.

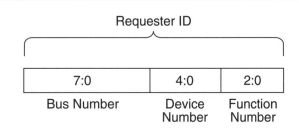

Figure 6.6   Requester ID Format

The Tag field (byte 6 in Figure 6.5) is an 8-bit field that helps to uniquely identify outstanding requests. The requester generates a unique tag value for each of its outstanding requests that requires a completion. Requests that do not require a completion do not have a tag assigned to them (the tag field is undefined and may have any value). If a completion is required, the requester ID and tag value are copied into the completion header. This allows the system to route that completion packet back to the original requester. The returned tag value identifies which request the completion packet is responding to. These two values form a global identification (referred to as a *Transaction ID*) that uniquely identifies each request with an accompanying completion. Requests from different devices (or functions within a device) have different requester IDs, and multiple requests (that require a completion) from a single device function have differing tag values.

The Byte Enable fields contain the byte enables for the first and last DWord referenced by a request TLP. This allows the system to complete data transactions that are not DWord aligned. The First DW BE field (bits [3:0] of byte 7 in Figure 6.5) contains the byte enables for the first (or only) DWord, while the Last DW BE field (bits [7:4] of byte 7 in Figure 6.5) contains the byte enables for the last DWord of a request. Each bit within the Byte Enable fields identifies whether its associated byte is valid. A value of 0b for any Byte Enable bit indicates that the completer device must not write or, if non-prefetchable, read the corresponding byte of data. A value of 1b for any Byte Enable bit indicates that the completer device should write or read the corresponding byte of data. Table 6.4 details the mapping between byte enable bits and their corresponding data bytes.

Table 6.4   Byte Enables and Corresponding Data Bytes

Byte Enable	Header Location	Corresponding Data Byte
1st DW BE[0]	Bit 0 of byte 7	Byte 0
1st DW BE[1]	Bit 1 of byte 7	Byte 1
1st DW BE[2]	Bit 2 of byte 7	Byte 2
1st DW BE[3]	Bit 3 of byte 7	Byte 3
Last DW BE[0]	Bit 4 of byte 7	Byte N-4
Last DW BE[1]	Bit 5 of byte 7	Byte N-3
Last DW BE[2]	Bit 6 of byte 7	Byte N-2
Last DW BE[3]	Bit 7 of byte 7	Byte N-1

If the request indicates a length greater than a single DWord, neither the First DW BE field nor the Last DW BE field can be 0000b. Both must specify at least a single valid byte within their respective DWord. For example, if a device wanted to write six bytes to memory, it needs to send a data payload of two DWords, but only six of the accompanying eight bytes of data would be legitimately intended for that write. In order to make sure the completer knows which bytes are to be written, the requester could indicate a First DW BE field of 1111b and a Last DW BE field of 1100b. This indicates that the four bytes of the first DWord and the first two bytes of the second (and last) DWord are the six bytes intended to be written. The completer knows that the final two bytes of the accompanying data payload are not to be written.

If the request indicates a data length of a single DWord, the Last DW BE field must equal 0000b. If the request is for a single DWord, the First DW BE field can also be 0000b. If a write request of a single DWord is accompanied by a First DW BE field of 0000b, that request should have no effect at the completer and is not considered a malformed (improperly built) packet. A memory read request of one DWord with no bytes enabled is referred to as a "zero length read". These reads may be used by devices as a type of flush request, allowing a device to ensure that previously issued posted writes have been completed. If a read request of a single DWord is accompanied by a First DW BE field of 0000b, the corresponding completion for that request should have and indicate a data payload length of one DWord. The contents of that data payload are unspecified, however, and may be any value.

I/O Request Headers

I/O requests are used for reads or writes to I/O locations. Unlike memory requests, which can use either 32-bit or 64-bit addressing, all I/O requests use just the 32-bit address format. All I/O requests have the common DWord shown in Figure 6.3 as the first DWord of the header. The second DWord for all I/O requests utilizes the same format as the second DWord of memory requests, with a Requester ID, Tag and Byte Enables in the exact same locations. Since all I/O requests are 32-bit addressed, I/O request headers end up looking remarkably similar to 32-bit addressed memory request headers. The differentiation between the two comes mainly from the different Format and Type values placed in the first DWord. Figure 6.7 shows the format for an I/O request header.

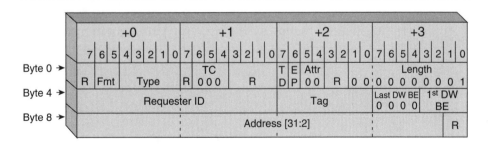

Figure 6.7   I/O Request Header

As mentioned, the format for I/O request headers is quite similar to that of the 32-bit memory request header (seen in Figure 6.5). However, a 32-bit addressed memory request header has a value of 0 0000b (or 0 0001b for reads to locked memory) in the Type field, whereas I/O requests use a value of 0 0010b in the Type field. As with memory requests, the Fmt field identifies whether an I/O request is a read request (Fmt = 00b, indicating no data payload) or a write request (Fmt = 10b, indicating a data payload is attached). Since all I/O requests use 32-bit addressing, all I/O request headers are three DWords in length.

Along with using different values for the Type field, I/O requests handle some of the common fields in slightly different ways than memory requests. For example, the TC field (Traffic Class) must always be 000b for I/O requests. Additionally, the Attr (Attributes) field must have a value of 00b, and the Last DW BE (Last DWord Byte Enable) field must have a value of 0000b. For I/O requests, the Length field must always have a value of 00 0000 0001b.

Configuration Request Headers

Configuration requests are used for reads or writes to configuration registers of PCI Express devices. Unlike memory or I/O requests, configuration requests are routed based on destination ID, and not address. All configuration requests have the common DWord shown in Figure 6.3 as the first DWord of the header. The second DWord for all configuration requests uses the same format as the second Dword of memory and I/O requests, with a Requester ID, Tag and Byte Enables in the exact same locations. However, since configuration requests are routed based on Destination ID and not address, the third and final DWord for configuration request headers is markedly different than those used for memory or I/O requests. Figure 6.8 shows the format for a configuration request header.

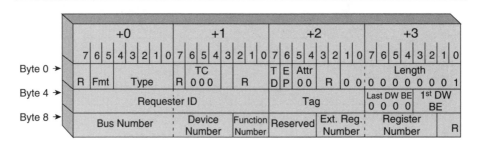

Figure 6.8   Configuration Request Header

A configuration request header has a value of 0 0100b (for Type 0 configuration transactions) or 0 0101b (for Type 1 configuration transactions) in the Type field. For a brief refresher on Type 0 versus Type 1 configuration transactions, refer to Chapter 10, "PCI Express Software Overview." As with memory and I/O requests, the Fmt field identifies whether a configuration request is a read request (Fmt = 00b, indicating no data payload) or a write request (Fmt = 10b, indicating a data payload is attached). All configuration request headers are three DWords in length (which is why bit 0 of the Fmt field is always 0).

Configuration requests handle some of the common fields in a manner quite similar to I/O requests. For example, as with I/O requests, the TC field (Traffic Class) must always be 000b for configuration requests. Likewise, the Attr (Attributes) field must have a value of 00b, the Last DW BE (Last DWord Byte Enable) field must have a value of 0000b, and the Length field must always have a value of 00 0000 0001b.

Unlike I/O request headers, however, configuration requests do not use a 32-bit address field as the third DWord. Configuration destinations are differentiated based on their bus, device, and function numbers, so these packets are routed based on that ID and not by address. As can be seen in Figure 6.8, the destination bus, device, and function number have the identical format as those used to identify the requester. In addition to those fields, Register Number (bits [7:2] of byte 11) and Extended Register Number (bits [3:0] of byte 10) fields are located in the third DWord.

Message Headers

Recall that since PCI Express has no sideband signals (such as INTA#, PME#, and so on), all special events must be transmitted as packets (called messages) across the PCI Express link. Messages are used for INTx interrupt signaling, power management, error signaling, locked transaction support, slot power limit support, hot plug signaling, and for other vendor defined messaging.

All messages have the common DWord shown in Figure 6.3 as the first DWord of the header. The second DWord for all messages uses the Transaction ID (Requester ID + Tag) in the same location as memory, I/O and configuration requests. It then adds a Message Code field to specify the type of message. Figure 6.9 shows the format for a message header.

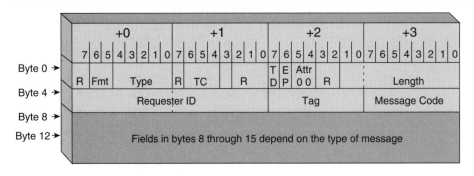

Figure 6.9   Message Header

Most messages use the Msg encoding for the Type field. Exceptions to this include the Slot Power Limit message, which uses the MsgD format, and vendor defined messages, which may use either the Msg or MsgD encoding. Recall from Table 6.2 that the Msg encoding is 01b for Format and 1 $0r_2r_1r_0$ for Type, where r[2:0] indicates message routing. The MsgD encoding is similar, but with 11b in the Fmt field indicating that a data payload is attached. In addition to the address-based routing used by memory and I/O requests, and the ID-based routing employed by configuration requests, messages may use several other routing schemes. The r[2:0] sub-field indicates the type of routing scheme that a particular message employs. Table 6.5 outlines the various routing options.

Table 6.5   Message Routing Options

r[2:0]	Description
000	Routed to root complex
001	Routed by address
010	Routed by ID
011	Broadcast from root complex
100	Local—terminate at receiver
101	Gathered and routed to root complex
110-111	Reserved—terminate at receiver

Interrupt Messages

PCI Express supports interrupts in two different formats: INTx emulation and Message Signaled Interrupt (MSI). MSI interrupt support (as defined in the *PCI Local Bus Specification, Revision 2.3*) is required for all PCI Express devices. In this model, which is the preferred interrupt mechanism for PCI Express, devices deliver interrupts through memory write transactions. As such, MSI interrupts take on the format of memory write requests and not messages. For legacy support, however, devices can emulate the INTx interrupt model through the use of messages. This model virtualizes PCI physical interrupt signals via in-band message packets. This is necessary to maintain backward compatibility with existing devices and software models without requiring the additional cost and complexity of sideband pins. A PCI Express to PCI (or PCI-X) bridge, for instance, must translate the INTx signals the bridge sees on the downstream interface into proper INTx messages on its PCI Express interface.

There are eight distinct INTx messages. As shown in Table 6.6, these messages simulate the assertion or de-assertion of the four INTx signals.

Table 6.6   INTx Messages

Code[7:0]	Name/Description
0010 0000	Assert INTA
0010 0001	Assert INTB
0010 0010	Assert INTC
0010 0011	Assert INTD
0010 0100	De-assert INTA
0010 0101	De-assert INTB
0010 0110	De-assert INTC
0010 0111	De-assert INTD

The Assert/De-assert INTx messages constitute four "virtual interrupt wires." An assert message represents the active transition of that virtual wire, and a de-assert message represents the inactive transition.

For all INTx messages, the routing field r[2:0] is 100b, indicating that the message is terminated locally. However, this does not mean that the interrupt message "disappears" at the local device. If necessary, the interrupt message may be forwarded on to an appropriate downstream port. This means that the Requester ID associated with the INTx message corresponds to the transmitter of that message for that link, and not necessarily the originator of the interrupt. INTx messages do not include a data payload, and they treat the Length field as reserved. INTx messages must use the default traffic class, TC0 (this is different than MSI interrupts, which are not restricted to the default traffic class).

Power Management Messages

These messages are used to support power management operations. There are four distinct power management TLP messages, as shown in Table 6.7.

Table 6.7   Power Management Messages

Code[7:0]	Routing r[2:0]	Name/Description
0001 0100	100	PM_Active_State_Nak
0001 1000	000	PM_PME
0001 1001	011	PME_Turn_Off
0001 1011	101	PME_TO_Ack

Power management messages do not contain a data payload and they treat the Length field as reserved. Power management messages must use the default traffic class, TC0. Additional details on these messages and PCI Express power management (including DLLP packets used for power management) are found in Chapter 11.

Error Signaling Messages

Error signaling messages indicate errors associated with particular transactions, as well as generic error conditions (for example, link training failures). Error messages are initiated by the component that detects the error. There are three distinct error signaling messages, as shown in Table 6.8.

Table 6.8   Error Messages

Code[7:0]	Name/Description
0011 0000	ERR_COR—Correctable error
0011 0001	ERR_NONFATAL—Uncorrectable but nonfatal error
0011 0011	ERR_FATAL—Uncorrectable and fatal error

Correctable errors are error conditions where the PCI Express protocol (and specifically hardware) can recover without any loss of information. An example of this type of error is an LCRC error that is detected by the Data Link Layer and corrected through normal retry means. An uncorrectable error is one that impacts the functionality of the interface and may be classified as either fatal or nonfatal. A fatal error is uncorrectable and renders that particular link unreliable. A reset of the link may be required to return to normal, reliable operation. Platform handling of fatal errors is implementation specific. Nonfatal errors are uncorrectable and render a particular transaction unreliable, but do not impact the link as a whole. Additional details on error signaling and handling is located in Chapter 10, "PCI Express Software Overview."

For all error signaling messages, the routing field r[2:0] is 000b, indicating that the message should be routed to the root complex. The Requester ID associated with an error message is that of the initiator of that error. Error signaling messages do not include a data payload and treat the Length field as reserved. Error signaling messages must use the default traffic class, TC0.

Locked Transaction Messages

Locked transaction sequences are generated by the CPU as one or more reads followed by a number of writes to the same location. When a locked transition sequence is established (indicated through TLPs that use MRdLk and CplDLk type), all other traffic is blocked from using the path between the root complex and the locked legacy endpoint or bridge. In addition to the TLPs that indicate a locked sequence, there is a single defined locked transaction message. The Unlock message defined here is used to indicate the end of a locked sequence. It is sent from the root complex down the locked transaction path to the completer and may be broadcast to all endpoints and bridges. The unlock DLLP follows the format outlined in Table 6.9.

Table 6.9   Locked Transaction Message

Code[7:0]	Routing r[2:0]	Name/Description
0000 0000	011	Unlock

The Unlock message does not include a data payload and treats the Length field as reserved. Unlock messages must use the default traffic class, TC0. As evidenced by the r[2:0] value, the root complex initiates and broadcasts this message.

Slot Power Limit Messages

PCI Express provides a mechanism for a system to control the maximum amount of power provided to a PCI Express slot or module. The message identified here is used to provide a mechanism for the upstream device (for example, root complex) to modify the power limits of its downstream devices. A card or module must not consume more power than it was allocated by the Set Slot Power Limit message. The format for this message is shown in Table 6.10.

Table 6.10   Slot Power Limit Message

Code[7:0]	Routing r[2:0]	Name/Description
010010000	100	Set Slot Power Limit

The Set Slot Power Limit message contains a one DWord data payload with the relevant power information. This data payload is a copy of the slot capabilities register of the upstream device and is written into the device capabilities register of the downstream device. Slot Power messages must use the default traffic class, TC0. As evidenced by the r[2:0] value, this message is only intended to be sent from an upstream device (root complex or switch) to its link mate.

Hot Plug Messages

The PCI Express architecture is defined to natively support both hot plug and hot removal of devices. There are seven distinct Hot Plug messages. As shown in Table 6.11, these messages simulate the various states of the power indicator, attention button, and attention indicator.

Table 6.11   Hot Plug Messages

Code[7:0]	Name/Description
0100 0101	Power Indicator On
0100 0111	Power Indicator Blink
0100 0100	Power Indicator Off
0100 1000	Attention Button Pressed
0100 0001	Attention Indicator On
0100 0011	Attention Indicator Blink
0100 0000	Attention Indicator Off

Hot plug messages do not contain a data payload and treat the Length field as reserved. Hot plug messages must use the default traffic class, TC0. Additional details on PCI Express hot plug support are found in Chapter 10.

Completion Packet/Header

Some, but not all, of the requests outlined so far in this chapter may require a completion packet. Completion packets always contain a completion header and, depending on the type of completion, may contain a number of DWords of data as well. Since completion packets are really only differentiated based on the completion header, this section focuses on that header format.

Completion headers are three DWords in length and have the common DWord shown in Figure 6.3 as the first DWord of the header. The second DWord for completion headers make use of some unique fields: a Completer ID, Completion Status, Byte Count Modified (BCM) and Byte Count. The third and final DWord contains the Requester ID and Tag values, along with a Lower Address field. Figure 6.10 shows the format for a completion header.

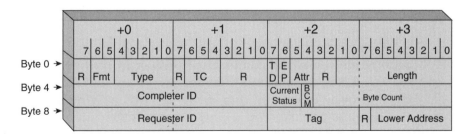

Figure 6.10   Completion Header

Completion packets are routed by ID, and more specifically, the Requester ID that was supplied with the original request. The Completer ID field (bytes 4 and 5) is a 16-bit value that is unique for every PCI Express function within the hierarchy. It follows the exact same format as the Requester ID, except that it contains the component information for the completer instead of the requester. The Completer ID format is shown in Figure 6.11.

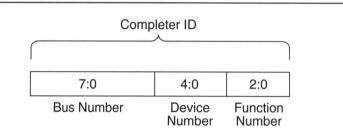

Figure 6.11   Completer ID

The Completion Status field (bits [7:5] of byte 6) indicates if the request has been completed successfully. There are four defined completion status responses, as shown in Table 6.12. The TLP Handling section later in this chapter contains the details for when each of these completion options is used.

Table 6.12   Completion Status

Completion Status[2:0] Value	Status
000b	Successful Completion (SC)
001b	Unsupported Request (UR)
010b	Configuration Request Retry Status (CRS)
100b	Completer Abort (CA)
All others	Reserved

A single memory read request may result in multiple completion packets. Individual read completion packets may provide a portion of the requested data, as long as all completions for a given request, when combined, provide exactly the amount of data originally requested. The *PCI Express Base Specification* defines several fields within the completion packet header to deal with this scenario. The Byte Count field (bits [3:0] of byte 6 and all of byte 7) indicates the remaining number or bytes required to complete a memory read request. It is represented as a binary number with 0000 0000 0001b indicating 1 byte, 1111 1111 1111b indicating 4095 bytes and 0000 0000 0000b indicating 4096 bytes. Since a single memory read request can be returned with multiple completion packets, this field is used to indicate how many bytes (including the existing completion packet) are still to be returned. If a memory read request is completed with multiple completion packets, the Byte Count field for each successive completion packet is the value indicated by the previous packet, minus the number of bytes returned with that packet. This field is used to help the requester determine if any of the read completion packets are missing. For all other types of completions (non-memory read), the Byte Count is set to four.

The BCM field (bit 4 of byte 6) may be used by PCI-X completers to indicate that the Byte Count field has been modified and is not being used in its normal manner. For PCI-X burst reads, the initial completion transaction may use the Byte Count field to indicate the size of just that first transaction, and not the entire burst read. In this case, that PCI-X completer sets the BCM field to a 1 for that first transaction, indicating that the Byte Count field is not being used in its normal manner. Subsequent completion transactions for that read do not have the BCM bit set (set to 0), and the Byte Count fields in those packets indicate the remaining byte count in the normal manner.

The Requester ID and Tag fields make up bytes 8–10 of the completion header. This information is provided in the original request packet and, along with the Attr and TC fields, must have the same values as the originating request. The completion packet is routed back to the requester based on the Requester ID and the requester then uses the tag value to identify which request is being completed. The Lower Address field (bits [6:0] of byte 11) indicates the byte address for the first *enabled* byte of data returned with a memory read completion. Again, since memory read requests may be completed with multiple completion packets, this field helps ensure that all read data makes it back to the requester intact and in order. For any completion other than a memory read, the Lower Address field must be all 0s.

TLP Data Payload

As shown in Figure 6.2, if a packet uses a data payload, it is appended to the end of the TLP header. Whether or not a TLP contains a data payload depends on the type of packet. If present, the data payload is DWord-aligned for both the first and last DWord of data. DWord byte enables within the header indicate if "padding" bytes are appended to either the beginning or ending of the payload to achieve this DWord alignment.

The Length field (bits[1:0] of byte 2 and all of byte 1 in the header) indicates the length of the data payload in DWords. This length value only identifies the length of the data payload and not of the entire TLP. The header and TLP digest lengths are not directly accounted for in this field (though they are implied by the values of other header fields). A value of 00 0000 0001b in this location indicates a data payload that is one DWord long. A value of 00 0000 0010b indicates a two DWord value, and so on up to a maximum of 1024 DWords. The data payload for a TLP must not exceed the maximum allowable payload size, as defined in the device's control register (and more specifically, the Max_Payload_Size field of that register). TLPs that use a data payload must have the value in the Length field match the actual amount of data contained in the payload. Receivers must check to verify this rule and, if violated, consider that TLP to be malformed and report the appropriate error. Additionally, requests must not specify an address and length combination that crosses a 4 kilobyte boundary.

When a data payload is included in a TLP, the first byte of data corresponds to the lowest byte address (that is to say, closest to zero) and subsequent bytes of data are in increasing byte address sequence. For example, a 16 byte memory write to location 100h would place the data in the payload as shown in Figure 6.12.

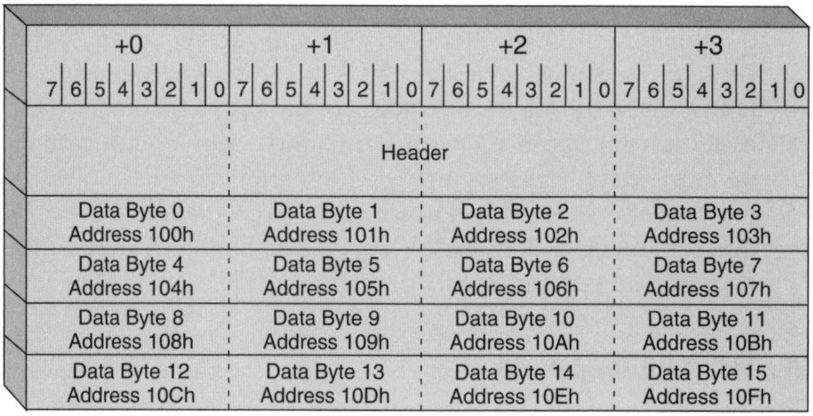

Figure 6.12   Example Data Payload

TLP Digest

The Data Link Layer provides the basic TLP data reliability mechanism within PCI Express via the use of a 32-bit LCRC. This LCRC code can detect errors in TLPs on a link-by-link basis and allows for a retransmit mechanism for error recovery. This LCRC, however, is based upon the TLP the Data Link is provided by its Transaction Layer. If an error is induced within the TLP prior to being provided to the Data Link Layer (for example, by a switch processing the TLP), the resultant LCRC has no ability to detect that the TLP itself was in error.

To ensure end-to-end data integrity, the TLP may contain a digest that has an end-to-end CRC. This optional field protects the contents of the TLP through the entire system and can be used in systems that require high data reliability. The Transaction Layer of the originating device generates the 32-bit ECRC. It incorporates the entire TLP header and, if present, the data payload. The exact details for the ECRC algorithm are contained in the *PCI Express Base Specification*. Once calculated, that ECRC value is placed in the digest field at the end of the TLP (refer to Figure 6.2). If the ECRC is present and support is enabled, the destination device applies the same ECRC calculation and compares the value to what is received in the TLP digest.

The TD bit (bit 7 of byte 2 in the header) indicates whether a TLP digest is provided at the end of the TLP. A value of 1b in this location indicates that a TLP digest is attached, while a value of 0b indicates that no TLP digest is present. Now what happens if, during the handling of the TLP, a switch induces an error on the TD bit? It could accidentally switch it from a 1 to a 0, which would negate the use of the ECRC and could lead to other undetected errors. The *PCI Express Base Specification* does not really have a way to avoid this potential issue, other than to highlight that it is the utmost of importance that switches maintain the integrity of the TD bit.

The capability to generate and check ECRCs is reported to software (by an Advanced Error Capabilities and Control register), which also controls whether the capability is enabled. If a device is enabled to generate and/or check ECRCs, it must do so for all TLPs.

TLP Handling

This section details how the Transaction Layer handles incoming TLPs, once they have been verified by the Data Link Layer. A TLP that makes it through the Data Link Layer has been verified to have traversed the link properly, but that does not necessarily mean that the TLP is correct. A TLP may make it across the link intact, but may have been improperly formed by its originator. As such, the receiver side of the Transaction Layer performs some checks on the TLP to make sure it has followed the rules described in this chapter. If the incoming TLP does not check out properly, it is considered a malformed packet, is discarded (without updating receiver flow control information) and generates an error condition. If the TLP is legitimate, the Transaction Layer updates its flow control tracking and continues to process the packet. This is seen in the flowchart in Figure 6.13.

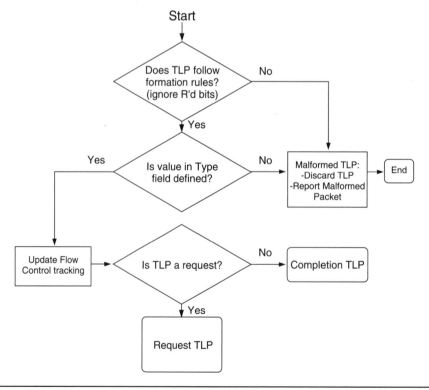

Figure 6.13   Flowchart for TLP Handling

Request Handling

If the TLP is a request packet, the Transaction Layer first checks to make sure that the request type is supported. If it is not supported, it generates a non-fatal error and notifies the root complex. If that unsupported request requires a completion, the Transaction Layer generates a completion packet with completion status of UR (unsupported request). The Transaction Layer then checks to see if the TLP should be handled as a message request or a "normal" request. This is shown in Figure 6.14.

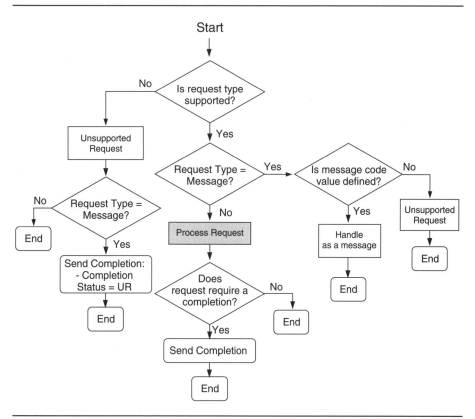

Figure 6.14 Flowchart for Request Handling

The shaded Process Request box indicates that there are optional implementation methods that may be employed by a PCI Express device. For example, if a device wanted to restrict the supported characteristics of requests (for performance optimizations), it is permitted to issue a Completer Abort if it receives a request that violates its restricted model.

Another implementation-specific option may arise with configuration requests. Some devices may require a lengthy self-initialization sequence before they are able to properly handle configuration requests. Rather than force all configuration requests to wait for the maximum allowable self-initialization time, PCI Express allows for devices to respond to a configuration request with a Configuration Request Retry Status (CRS) completion packet. If a device receives a configuration request prior to coming out of its self-initialization, it can respond with a CRS completion packet to effectively stall the configuration request.

Data Return for Read Requests

As discussed previously, a single memory read request may result in multiple completion packets. Individual read completion packets may provide a portion of the requested data, as long as, when combined, all completions for a given request provide exactly the amount of data originally requested. If a memory read request results in multiple completion packets, those packets must follow the rules for the BCM, Byte Count and Lower Address fields that are discussed earlier in the chapter. However, while a single request may correlate to multiple completion packets, a single completion cannot correlate to multiple request packets. The PCI Express does not allow a device to "collapse" the response to multiple requests into a single completion.

Completion Handling

If a device receives a completion that does not correspond to any outstanding request, that completion is referred to as an *unexpected completion*. Receipt of an unexpected completion causes the completion to be discarded and results in an error condition (nonfatal). The receipt of unsuccessful completion packets generates an error condition that is dependent on the completion status. The details for how successful completions are handled and impact flow control logic are contained in Chapter 9, "Flow Control."

Chapter **7**

Data Link Layer Architecture

An error the breadth of a single hair can lead one a thousand miles astray.

—Chinese Proverb

This chapter describes the details of the middle PCI Express architectural layer, the Data Link Layer. The Data Link Layer's main responsibility is error detection and correction as well as link management support. The chapter discusses the sequence number and LCRC (Link CRC), and how they are added to the Transaction Layer Packet (TLP) to ensure data integrity. It then describes the functions specific to the Data Link Layer, particularly the creation and consumption of Data Link Layer Packets (DLLPs).

Data Link Layer Overview

The Data Link Layer serves as the "gatekeeper" for each individual link within a PCI Express system. It ensures that the data being sent back and forth across the link is correct and received in the same order it was sent. The Data Link Layer makes sure that each packet makes it across the link, and makes it across intact.

This layer takes TLPs from the transmit side of the Transaction Layer and continues the process of building them into a PCI Express transaction. The Data Link Layer adds a sequence number to the front of the packet and an LCRC error checker to the tail. Once the transmit side of

123

the Data Link Layer has applied these to the TLP, the Data Link Layer forwards it on to the Physical Layer. Like the Transaction Layer, the Data Link Layer has unique duties for both outgoing packets and incoming packets. For incoming TLPs, the Data Link Layer accepts the packets from the Physical Layer and checks the sequence number and LCRC to make sure the TLP is correct. If it is correct, the Data Link Layer removes the sequence number and LCRC, then passes the TLP up to the receiver side of the Transaction Layer. If an error is detected (either wrong sequence number or LCRC does not match), the Data Link Layer does not pass the "bad" packet on to the Transaction Layer. Instead, the Data Link Layer communicates with its link mate to try and resolve the issue through a retry attempt. The Data Link Layer only passes a TLP through to the Transaction Layer if the packet's sequence number and LCRC values check out. It is important to note this because this "gate-keeping" allows the Transaction Layer to assume that everything it receives from the link is correct. As seen in Figure 7.1, the Data Link Layer forwards outgoing transactions from the Transaction Layer to the Physical Layer, and incoming transactions from the Physical Layer to the Transaction Layer.

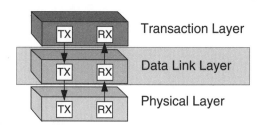

Figure 7.1   Data Link Layer

In order to accomplish several link management functions, the Data Link Layer generates and processes Data Link Layer Packets (DLLPs). The Data Link Layer uses these packets for error notification, power management, flow control, and so on.

Building on the TLP

The TLP transmission path through the Data Link Layer prepares the packet for reliable transmission across the link. The Data Link Layer adds the sequence number and LCRC code before passing it along to its Physical Layer. It does not process or modify the contents of the TLP—the Data Link Layer simply appends information to the beginning and end of the packet, as seen in Figure 7.2.

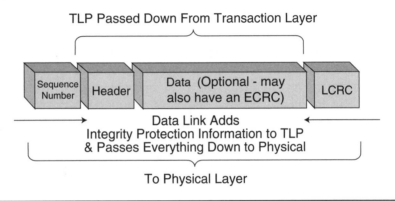

Figure 7.2   Impact of Data Link Layer on TLPs

Sequence Number

The Data Link Layer assigns a 12-bit sequence number to each TLP as it is passed from the transmit side of its Transaction Layer. The Data Link Layer applies the sequence number, along with a 4-bit reserved field to the front of the TLP. Refer to Figure 7.3 for the sequence number format. To accomplish this, the transmit side of this layer needs to implement two simple counters, one indicating what the next transmit sequence number should be, and one indicating the most recently acknowledged sequence number. When a sequence number is applied to an outgoing TLP, the Data Link Layer refers to its next sequence counter for the appropriate value. Once that sequence number is applied, the Data Link Layer increments its next sequence counter by one.

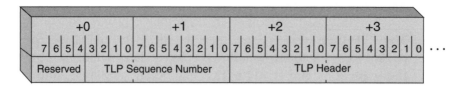

Figure 7.3   Sequence Number Appended to the Front of the TLP

On the receiver side, the Data Link Layer receives incoming TLPs from the Physical Layer, then checks the sequence number and LCRC. If they check out properly, the TLP is passed on to the Transaction Layer. If the sequence number (or LCRC) is incorrect, the Data Link Layer requests a retry. To accomplish this, the receive side of this layer needs to implement a counter for the next receiver sequence number, which indicates the next expected sequence number. If the sequence number of the received TLP matches that counter (and the LCRC checks), the Data Link Layer then removes the sequence number, associated reserved bits, and the LCRC. Once the layer removes that data, it forwards the incoming TLP on to the receive side of the Transaction Layer. When this occurs, the Data Link Layer increments its next receiver sequence counter.

If the sequence number does not match the value stored in the receiver's next sequence counter, that Data Link Layer discards that TLP. The Data Link Layer checks to see if the TLP is a duplicate. If it is, it schedules an acknowledgement (Ack) DLLP to be sent out for that packet. If the TLP is not a duplicate, it schedules a negative acknowledgement (Nak) DLLP to report a missing TLP. The "Retries" section of this chapter explains this procedure in more detail.

The Data Link Layer does not differentiate among types of TLP when assigning the sequence number. Transactions destined to I/O space do not have a different set of sequence numbers than memory transactions. Nor are sequence numbers dependent on the ultimate completer of the transaction. The Data Link Layer of the transmitting device is the sole determinant of the sequence number assigned to a TLP.

The sequence number is used on a link-by-link basis. If a TLP passes through a PCI Express device (such as a switch), it has different sequence numbers associated with it on the various links it traverses. The TLP header contains all the global identifying information. The sequence number only has meaning for a single transmitter and receiver. For example, if a PCI Express switch receives a request TLP from its upstream link, it processes that packet through its upstream receiver logic. That packet has a sequence number associated with it that the upstream Data Link Layer verifies. Once verified and acknowledged on the upstream side, that sequence number no longer means anything. After the request TLP is passed through the Transaction Layer of the upstream port, it is sent along to the appropriate downstream port. There, the TX side of the downstream Data Link Layer appends its own sequence number as the request TLP is sent out the downstream port. The Data Link Layer of the endpoint verifies and acknowledges this sequence number. If the TLP requires a completion packet, the sequence numbers for the completion TLP is also completely independent. The sequence number for the completion TLP on the downstream link has no relationship to the request TLP's sequence number or the upstream link's sequence number (once it is forwarded). Refer to Figure 7.4 for additional clarification: sequence numbers A, B, C, and D are completely independent of one another.

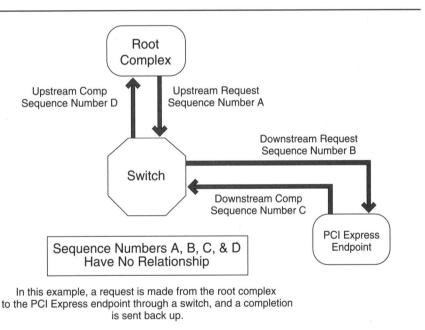

In this example, a request is made from the root complex to the PCI Express endpoint through a switch, and a completion is sent back up.

Figure 7.4   Sequence Numbers in a PCI Express Topology

LCRC

The Data Link Layer protects the contents of the TLP by using a 32-bit LCRC value. The Data Link Layer calculates the LCRC value based on the TLP received from the Transaction Layer *and* the sequence number it has just applied. The LCRC calculation utilizes each bit in the packet, including the reserved bits (such as bits 7:4 of byte 0). The exact details for the LCRC algorithm are contained in the *PCI Express Base Specification*.

On the receiver side, the first step that the Data Link Layer takes is to check the LCRC value. It does this by applying the same LCRC algorithm to the received TLP (not including the attached 32-bit LCRC). If a single or multiple-bit error occurs during transmission, the calculated LCRC value should not match the received LCRC value. If the calculated LCRC value does not equal the received value, the TLP is discarded and a Nak DLLP is scheduled for transmission. If the calculated value equals the received value, the Data Link Layer then proceeds to check the sequence number.

Like sequence numbers, the LCRC protects the contents of a TLP on a link-by-link basis. If a TLP travels across several links (for example, passes through a switch on its way to the root complex), an LCRC value is generated and checked for each link. In this way, it is different than the ECRC value that may be generated for a TLP. The ECRC serves to protect the TLP contents from one end of the PCI Express topology to the other end (refer to Chapter 6), while the LCRC only ensures TLP reliability for a give link. The 32-bit LCRC value for TLPs is also differentiated from the 16-bit CRC value that is used for DLLP packets and discussed later in this chapter.

Retries

The transmitter cannot assume that a transaction has been properly received until it gets a proper acknowledgement back from the receiver. If the receiver sends back a Nak (for something like a bad sequence number or LCRC), or fails to send back an Ack in an appropriate amount of time, the transmitter needs to retry all unacknowledged TLPs. To accomplish this, the transmitter implements a Data Link Layer retry buffer.

All copies of transmitted TLPs must be stored in the Data Link Layer retry buffer. Once the transmitter receives an appropriate acknowledgement back, it purges the appropriate TLPs from its retry buffer. It also updates its acknowledged sequence number counter.

Note   A quick note on retry terminology: the *PCI Express Base Specification* often flips back and forth between the terms *retry* and *replay*. For example, the buffer that is used during retry attempts is called a retry buffer, but the timeout counter associated with that buffer is called a replay timer. To avoid as much confusion as possible, this chapter sticks to the term retry as much as possible and only uses replay when referring to a function that uses that term expressly within the specification.

TLPs may be retried for two reasons. First, it is retried if the receiver sends back a Nak DLLP indicating some sort of transmission error. The second reason for a retry deals with a replay timer, which helps ensure that forward progress is being made. The transmitter side of the Data Link Layer needs to implement a replay timer that counts the time since the last Ack or Nak DLLP was received. This timer runs anytime there is an outstanding TLP and is reset every time an Ack or Nak DLLP is received. When no TLPs are outstanding, the timer should reset and hold so that it does not unnecessarily cause a time-out. The replay timer limit depends upon the link width and maximum payload size. The larger the maximum payload size and the narrower the link width, the longer the replay timer can run before timing out (since each packet requires more time to transmit). If the replay timer times out, the Data Link Layer reports an error condition.

If either of these events occurs—either a Nak reception or a replay timer expiration—the transmitter's Data Link Layer begins a retry. The Data Link Layer increments a replay number counter. This is a 2-bit counter that keeps track of the number of times the retry buffer has been retransmitted. If the replay counter rolls over from 11b to 00b (that is, this is the fourth retry attempt) the Data Link Layer indicates an error condition that requires the Physical Layer to retrain the link (refer to Chapter 8, "Physical Layer Architecture" for details on retraining). The Data Link Layer resets its replay counter every time it successfully receives an acknowledgement, so the retrain procedure only occurs if a retry attempt continuously fails. In other words, four unsuccessful attempts at a single retry create this error. Four unsuccessful retry attempts across numerous packets with numerous intermediate acknowledgements do not.

If the replay counter does not roll over, then the Data Link Layer proceeds with a normal retry attempt. It blocks acceptance of any new outgoing TLPs from its Transaction Layer and completes the transmission of any TLPs currently in transmission. The Data Link Layer then retransmits all unacknowledged TLPs. It begins with the oldest unacknowledged TLP and retransmits in the same order as the original transmission. Once all unacknowledged TLPs have been retransmitted, the Data Link Layer resumes normal operation and once again accepts outgoing TLPs from its Transaction Layer.

During the retry attempt, the Data Link Layer still needs to accept incoming TLPs and DLLPs. If the layer receives an Ack or Nak DLLP during the retry attempt it must be properly processed. If this occurs, the transmitter may fully complete the retry attempt or may skip the retransmission of any newly acknowledged TLPs. However, once the Data Link Layer starts to retransmit a TLP it must complete the transmission of that TLP. For example, imagine the transmitter has sequence numbers #5–8 sitting unacknowledged in its retry buffer and initiates a retry attempt due to a timeout of the replay timer. The transmitter starts to retransmit all four TLPs, beginning with sequence number #5. If, during the retransmission of TLP #5, the transmitter receives an Ack associated with sequence number #7, it must complete the retransmission of TLP #5. Depending on the implementation, the transmitter either continues with the retransmission of TLPs #6, #7, and #8, or skips the newly acknowledged TLPs (that is, up through #7) and continues retransmitting the remaining unacknowledged TLPs—in this example, #8.

If the transmitter receives multiple Acks during a retry, it can "collapse" them into only the most recent. If in the previous example the transmitter had seen separate individual Acks for #5, #6, and then #7, it could discard the individual Acks for #5 and #6 and only process the Ack for #7. Acknowledging #7 implies that all previous outstanding sequence numbers (#5 and #6) are also acknowledged. Likewise, if, during retry, the transmitter receives a Nak followed by an Ack with a later sequence number, the Ack supercedes the Nak and that Nak is ignored.

Data Link Layer Packets (DLLPs)

DLLPs support link operations and are strictly associated with that given link. DLLPs always originate at the Data Link Layer and are differentiated from TLPs when passed between the Data Link Layer and Physical Layer. Additionally, TLPs have an originator and destination that are not necessarily link mates, while a DLLP is always intended for the device on the other side of the link. DLLPs have four major functions (types):

- Ack DLLP: TLP sequence number acknowledgement. These indicate a successful receipt of some number of TLPs.

- Nak DLLP: TLP sequence number negative acknowledgement. These indicate an error condition (for example, a sequence number or LCRC issue, but do not differentiate between the two). Includes the last successfully received sequence number, and initiates a Data Link Layer retry attempt.

- FC DLLPs: Flow control. The three types of flow control DLLPs are InitFC1, InitFC2 and Update FC. The InitFC1 and InitFC2 DLLPs are sent during the flow control initialization for each virtual channel. Update FC packets are then sent during normal link operation to indicate how much buffer space is available for incoming TLPs. Additional details on the use of these packets is in Chapter 9, "Flow Control."

- PM DLLPs: Power management. The four types of power management DLLPs are PM_Enter_L1, PM_Enter_L23, PM_Request_Ack and PM_Active_State_Request_L1. Chapter 11, "Power Management" contains additional details about these power management functions.

DLLPs consist of four bytes of data followed by a 16-bit CRC. Please note that this is not the same as the 32-bit LCRC appended by the Data Link Layer for TLPs. Nor is it the same as the 32-bit ECRC appended (optionally) by the Transaction Layer. The size and creation procedures for the DLLP CRC differ from the LCRC and ECRC procedures for TLPs. The algorithm details for the generation of this 16-bit DLLP specific CRC are found in the *PCI Express Base Specification*. The smaller CRC size (16 bits versus 32 bits used for TLPs) is due to the fact that DLLPs are smaller than TLPs. Since less data is being protected, the CRC does not need to have as fine a granularity.

DLLP transmitters must fill any DLLP Reserved fields with 0s, but the DLLP receiver must ignore these (a 1 in a Reserved field cannot cause an error). The first byte of the DLLP specifies the type of DLLP. Table 7.1 details the encodings for this byte.

Table 7.1   DLLP Type Encodings

Encodings	DLLP Type
0000 0000	Ack
0001 0000	Nak
0010 0000	PM_Enter_L1
0010 0001	PM_Enter_L23
0010 0011	PM_Active_State_Request_L1
0010 0100	PM_Request_Ack
0011 0000	Vendor Specific—Not used in normal operation
0100 0$v_2v_1v_0$	InitFC1-P (v[2:0] specifies virtual channel)
0101 0$v_2v_1v_0$	InitFC1-NP
0110 0$v_2v_1v_0$	InitFC1-Cpl
1100 0$v_2v_1v_0$	InitFC2-P
1101 0$v_2v_1v_0$	InitFC2-NP
1110 0$v_2v_1v_0$	InitFC2-Cpl
1000 0$v_2v_1v_0$	UpdateFC-P
10010$v_2v_1v_0$	UpdateFC-NP
1010 0$v_2v_1v_0$	UpdateFC-Cpl
All other encodings	Reserved

Ack and Nak DLLPs

Ack DLLPs acknowledge that a given number of TLPs have successfully been received. Though the Data Link Layer requires acknowledgement for every TLP sent out, it does not require an individual Ack DLLP for each TLP. As mentioned previously, a Data Link Layer that has received multiple TLPs can accumulate acknowledgements and collapse them into a single Ack DLLP. An Ack DLLP indicates that all TLPs up to and including the specified sequence number have been successfully received.

A Nak DLLP indicates a negative acknowledgement of a TLP. This type of packet indicates that a TLP did not successfully make it across the link. The Data Link Layer issues a Nak for several reasons, but does not specify the cause within the Nak itself. Unexpected sequence numbers, bad LCRCs, TLP framing, or other Physical Layer receive errors all result in a Nak DLLP transmission. Though a Nak indicates a negative acknowledgement, it may also imply a positive acknowledgement for previous TLPs. For example, a receiver successfully receives TLPs #5 and #6 but has not acknowledged either with an Ack DLLP yet. The receiver expects TLP #7 as the next TLP, but instead receives TLP #8. This causes the Data Link Layer of the receiver to send out a Nak with the sequence number of 6 (the last successfully received sequence number). This indicates an issue with TLP #7 and initiates a retry attempt at the transmitter. However, it also implies that TLPs #5 and #6 successfully made it through to the receiver. Therefore, the transmitter's Data Link Layer increments its acknowledged sequence counter to 6, removes TLPs #5 and #6 from its retry buffer and begins the retry attempt with TLP #7.

Ack and Nak DLLPs follow the format shown in Figure 7.5.

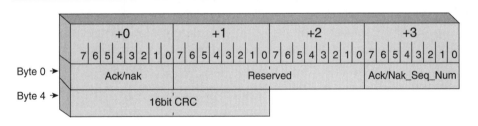

Figure 7.5   Ack/Nak DLLP Format

Ack and Nak Impact on Performance

Ack and Nak policies impact device designs and link bandwidth efficiencies. Designers must account for tradeoffs between large retry buffers or requiring the receiver at the other end of the link to issue a large number of Ack and Nak DLLPs. If Device A implements a small retry buffer, it forces its link mate, Device B, to issue a large number of Acks or risk stalling the flow of data. If Device B constantly needs to send Ack DLLPs out, it reduces the amount of bandwidth available for transmitting "real" data from B to A. Implementing large retry buffers avoids this bandwidth issue, but larger buffers require more transistors and that could lead to a more costly piece of silicon.

Since a device's ability to clear its buffers is dependent on receiving timely Ack DLLPs from its link mate, it is important to ensure that all devices transmit Acks in a timely manner. To help ensure that Acks are being sent out appropriately, the Data Link Layer implements an AckNak latency timer. The timer ensures that TLPs do not linger around in an unacknowledged state, taking up space in the transmitter's retry buffer. This timer is dependent on the maximum payload size as well as the link width. Additionally, the specified Ack latency values ensure that the link does not stall due to too many outstanding sequence numbers. This latency timer is used in association with *received* TLPs and helps ensure that the receiver of a TLP acknowledges it in an appropriate amount of time. It should not be confused with the replay timer, which tracks the amount of time since a *transmitted* TLP has been acknowledged.

If a device has received TLPs but not yet acknowledged them and its AckNak latency timer times out, it requires the device to send out an Ack or Nak DLLP. Ack DLLPs may be transmitted more frequently than required, though constant Ack DLLPs may impact link efficiency. The *PCI Express Base Specification* outlines a recommended priority list for situations when multiple DLLPs or TLPs await transmission. It also recommends that devices implement some sort of fairness mechanism to ensure that no type of traffic completely blocks transmission of another type of traffic. The recommended priority is as follows:

1. Highest Priority: Complete any transmission (TLP or DLLP) currently in progress

2. Nak DLLP

3. Ack DLLP due to either:

   ■ Receipt of a duplicate TLP or

   ■ Ack latency timer expiration

4. FC DLLP required for operation (see Chapter 9, "Flow Control")

5. Retry buffer retransmission

6. TLP directly from Transaction Layer

7. FC DLLP other than those required in priority #4

8. Lowest Priority: All other DLLPs

Flow Control DLLPs

Flow Control Data Link Layer Packets (FC DLLPs) contain information relevant to the flow control logic in the Transaction Layer. Unlike Ack and Nak DLLPs, incoming FC DLLPs are passed on to the receiver's Transaction Layer. Flow control mechanisms identify three separate types: P (Posted), NP (Non-Posted) and Cpl (Completion). A mapping of flow control types (P, NP, and Cpl) to PCI Express transaction types (memory request, I/O completion, and so on) is located in Chapter 9, "Flow Control."

The Data Link Layer triggers the transmission of FC DLLPs when initializing flow control for a virtual channel. After initialization, the Transaction Layer can trigger (not create; the Data Link Layer must create all DLLPs) an FC DLLP. At the receiver, the Data Link Layer checks the integrity of the FC DLLP by checking its CRC value. If correct, the DLLP continues on to the Transaction Layer. If the CRC check fails, the Data Link Layer discards the DLLP.

FC DLLPs follow the format shown Figure 7.6. The first four bits indicate whether it is an InitFC1, InitFC2, or Update FC packet, along with the associated FC type: P, NP, or Cpl (refer to Table 7.1). The VC ID field contains the virtual channel number that is being referenced (recall that separate virtual channels have separate flow control resources). The HdrFC field contains the credit value for the headers of the indicated type (P, NP, or Cpl). The DataFC field contains the credit value for payload data for the indicated type. Chapter 9 contains additional details on flow control procedures, including the use of FC DLLPs for initialization and updates.

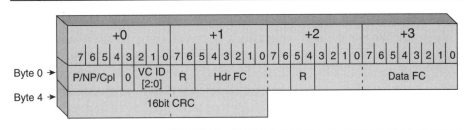

Figure 7.6   Flow Control DLLP Format

Power Management DLLPs

Power management DLLPs contain information relevant to the power management logic. The power management functions are not necessarily contained within any one architectural layer, but instead impact all of them. Power management is explored in more detail in Chapter 11.

The power management logic triggers the transmission of power management DLLPs. At the receiver, the Data Link Layer checks the integrity of the PM DLLP by checking its CRC value. If correct, the DLLP continues on to the power management logic. If the CRC check fails, the Data Link Layer discards the DLLP.

Power management DLLPs follow the format shown in Figure 7.7. The three bits represented with *xxx* indicate whether the DLLP is an Enter_L1, Enter_L23, Active_State_Request_L1, or Request_Ack power management DLLP as shown in Table 7.1.

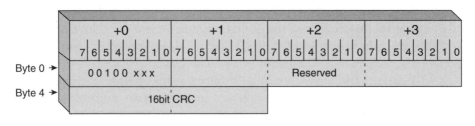

Figure 7.7   Power Management DLLP Format

Processing a DLLP

The Physical Layer passes the received DLLP up to its Data Link Layer. If the Physical Layer indicates a receiver error, it (and not the Data Link Layer) reports the error condition. In this situation, the Data Link Layer discards that DLLP. If the Physical Layer does not indicate a receiver error, the Data Link Layer calculates the CRC for the incoming DLLP. The Data Link Layer then checks to see if the calculated value matches the CRC attached to that DLLP. If the CRCs check out, the DLLP is processed. In the event that the CRCs do not match, the DLLP is discarded and an error is reported. This flow can be seen in Figure 7.8. Please note that neither device expects to retry a DLLP. As such, DLLPs are not placed into the retry buffer.

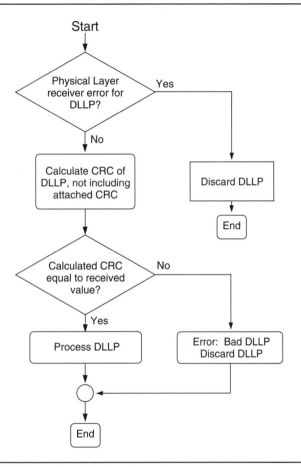

Figure 7.8   DLLP Processing Flowchart

A DLLP that uses an unsupported DLLP type encoding is discarded without further action and is not considered an error. Nonzero values in reserved fields should be ignored by the receiver. Incoming FC DLLPs continue on to the Transaction Layer. Incoming power management DLLPs continue on to the component's power management control logic. Acks and Naks stay within the Data Link Layer for processing.

If the DLLP is an Ack or Nak, the Data Link Layer first looks at the Ack_Nak sequence number contained within the DLLP. If the sequence number does not correspond to an unacknowledged TLP (or the most recently acknowledged TLP), the DLLP is discarded. In the event that an Ack DLLP has this issue, a Data Link Layer protocol error is reported.

If the sequence number refers to an appropriate unacknowledged TLP, the Data Link Layer purges that, and any older TLPs, from the retry buffer. From the earlier example, if the retry buffer contains TLPs # 5-8 and an Ack #7 DLLP comes in, TLPs #5, #6, and #7 should be purged from the buffer. The Data Link Layer also updates its acknowledged sequence counter with the value from the DLLP. Finally, if the DLLP indicates an acknowledgement of a previously unacknowledged TLP, the replay timer and replay number counter get reset. Recall that the replay timer tracks the time since the last acknowledgement came in, and the replay number counter tracks how many times the current retry has been attempted. If the DLLP is a Nak, the Data Link Layer initiates a retry attempt of its entire retry buffer.

Data Link Layer Control

The Data Link Layer tracks the state of the link and communicates this status with both the Transaction and the Physical Layer. The Data Link Layer keeps track of the link status via a state machine with the following parameters:

■ States:

  – DL_Inactive: Physical Layer reporting that link is nonoperational or nothing is connected

  – DL_Init: Physical Layer reports that link is operational, initialize flow control for the default virtual channel

  – DL_Active: normal operation mode

■ Status Outputs:

  – DL_Down: Data Link Layer is not communicating with the component on the other side of the link

  – DL_Up: Data Link Layer is communicating with the component on the other side of the link

Figure 7.9 shows the relationships between the various states.

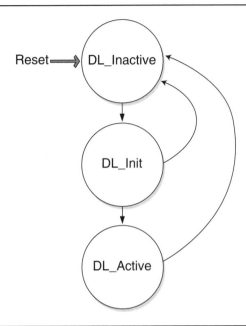

Figure 7.9   Data Link Layer State Machine

The DL_Inactive state is the initial state following a reset event. Upon entry into this state, all Data Link Layer state information resets to default values. Additionally, the Data Link Layer purges any entries in the retry buffer. While in this state, the Data Link Layer reports DL_Down to the Transaction Layer. This causes the Transaction Layer to discard any outstanding transactions and cease any attempts to transmit TLPs. Just as well, because while in this state, the Data Link Layer does not accept any TLPs from either the Transaction or the Physical Layer. The Data Link Layer also does not generate or accept any DLLPs while in the Inactive state. The state machine proceeds to the Init state if two conditions are met: the Transaction Layer indicates the link is not disabled by software, and the Physical Layer reports that the link is up (Physical LinkUp = 1).

The DL_Init state takes care of flow control initialization for the default virtual channel. While in this state, the Data Link Layer initializes the default virtual channel according to the methods outlined in Chapter 9. The DL status output changes during this state. It reports out DL_Down while in FC_Init1 and switches over to DL_Up when in gets to FC_Init2. The state machine proceeds to the Active state if FC initialization completes successfully and the Physical Layer continues to report that the Physical Link is up. If the Physical Layer does not continue to indicate the link is up (Physical LinkUp = 0), the state machine returns to the DL_Inactive state.

The DL_Active state is the normal operating state. The Data Link Layer accepts and processes incoming and outgoing TLPs, and generates and accepts DLLPs as described in this chapter. While in this state, the Data Link Layer reports DL_Up. If the Physical Layer does not continue to indicate the link is up (Physical LinkUp = 0), the state machine returns to the DL_Inactive state.

Chapter 8

Physical Layer Architecture

Things should be made as simple as possible, but not any simpler.

—Albert Einstein

This chapter looks more closely at the Physical Layer architecture of PCI Express. To start, the logical and electrical divisions of the Physical Layer are investigated along with the functions that each performs. This takes into account several mechanisms such as scrambling, encoding, the preparation of data for transmission across the PCI Express link, and the signaling method used to transmit data. A large portion of this chapter focuses on the training and configuration of the PCI Express link by detailing the primary Physical Layer link training states. Finally, this chapter investigates the link responses to surprise insertion and removal of devices as well as the link's power management capabilities.

Physical Layer Organization

The Physical Layer of PCI Express is the engine that will power next generation busses to frequencies that exceed the transmission capabilities (10 gigahertz) of copper wire. The objective of this section is not to explore what mediums will be used once the bandwidth limits of copper wire have been reached; however, to satisfy curiosity it can be noted that optical wires are a likely solution.

The Physical Layer contains all the necessary digital and analog circuits required to configure and maintain a link. Additionally, the Physical Layer may contain a phase locked loop (PLL) to provide the necessary clocking to drive the serial shift registers of the transmitter output stages. Given the understanding that PCI Express may support data rates greater than 2.5 gigabits per second, the data rate detect mechanisms have been predefined to minimize the changes required to support future generations of PCI Express. Additionally, the layers of PCI Express are organized to provide isolation of the circuits and logic that need to be modified and/or tuned in order to support next generation speeds. As an example, the Physical Layer is a separate entity from the Data Link and Transaction Layers, as illustrated in Figure 8.1. Next generation frequency changes will only require changing the Physical Layer. This eases the transition of upgrading the technology by allowing maximum reuse of the upper layers.

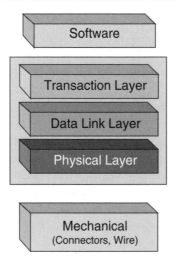

Figure 8.1 Physical Layer Positioning

There are two key sub-blocks that make up the Physical Layer architecture: a logical sub-block and an electrical sub-block. Both sub-blocks have dedicated transmit and receive paths that allow dual unidirectional communication between two PCI Express devices. These sub-blocks ensure that data gets to and from its destination quickly and in good order, as shown in Figure 8.2.

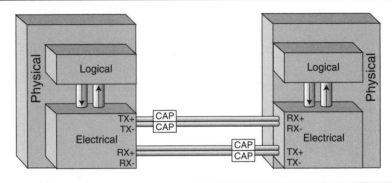

Figure 8.2   Physical Architecture Sub-Blocks between Two PCI Express Devices

Logical Sub-Block

The logical sub-block is the key decision maker for the Physical Layer. As mentioned above, the logical sub-block has separate transmit and receive paths, referred to hereafter as the *transmit unit* and *receive unit*. Both units are capable of operating independently of one another.

The primary function of the transmit unit is to prepare packets received from the upper layers for transmission across the link. This process involves three primary stages: data scrambling, 8-bit/10-bit encoding, and packet framing. The receive unit functions similarly to the transmit unit, but in reverse. The receive unit takes the deserialized physical packet received from the wire by the electrical sub-block, removes the framing, decodes it, and finally descrambles it. Figure 8.3 gives a description of each of these stages along with a description of the benefits received by each stage.

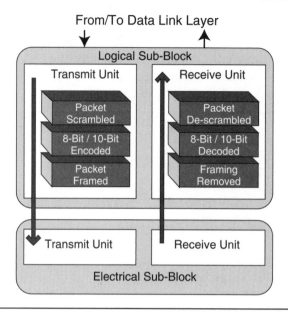

Figure 8.3   Logical Sub-Block Primary Stages

Data Scrambling

PCI Express employs a technique called data scrambling to reduce the possibility of electrical resonance on the link. Electrical resonance can cause unwanted effects such as excessive radiation, data corruption and in some cases circuit damage, due to electrical overstresses caused by large concentrations of voltage. Since electrical resonance is somewhat difficult to predict, the simplest solution is usually to prevent conditions that can cause electrical resonance. Most electrical resonance conditions are caused by repeated data patterns at some constant frequency. To avoid repeated data patterns the *PCI Express Base Specification* defines a scrambling/descrambling algorithm that is implemented using a linear feedback shift register. PCI Express accomplishes scrambling or descrambling by performing a serial XOR operation to the data with the seed output of a Linear Feedback Shift Register (LFSR) that is synchronized between PCI Express devices. Scrambling is enabled by default; however, it can be disabled for diagnostic purposes.

8-Bit/10-Bit Encoding

The primary purpose of 8-bit/10-bit encoding is to embed a clock signal into the data stream. By embedding a clock into the data, this encoding scheme renders external clock signals unnecessary. An investigation of parallel bus technologies, like conventional PCI, has shown that as clock frequencies increase, the length matching requirements become increasingly more stringent. The dependency of a group of signals to a single clock source acts to severely reduce setup and hold margins in a particular data transaction. Take for example two data lines named Data Line 1 and Data Line 2 that are both referenced to a high-speed clock signal called Data Clock. At a transmitting source both Data Line 1 and Data Line 2 have signals placed on the bus at the same instance in reference to Data Clock. However, due to a slight mismatch in interconnect length between Data Line 1, Data Line 2, and Data Clock, they all reach the receiving device at slightly different times. Since the receiving device samples the data based on the reception of the Data Clock, the overall margin may be reduced significantly or the wrong data may be clocked into the receiving device if the mismatch is bad enough. As bus frequencies increase, the amount of allowable mismatch decreases or essentially becomes zero. For an illustration of this concept see Figure 8.4.

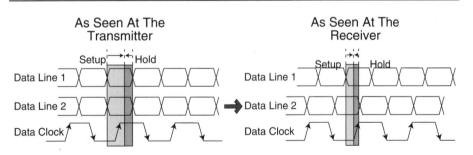

Figure 8.4   Parallel Bus Data/Clock Length Mismatch Example

Because PCI Express embeds a clock into the data, setup and hold times are not compromised due to length mismatch between individual PCI Express lanes within a link.

The concept of 8-bit/10-bit encoding is not something new that is unique to PCI Express. This data encoding concept was actually patented by IBM and used in Fibre Channel to increase data transfer lengths and rates. Since then it has also been adopted and used in Serial ATA, Infini-Band, and Gigabit Ethernet because of the benefits that it provides. The 8-bit/10-bit encoding process involves converting a byte (8 bits) of data into an encoded 10-bit data symbol.

Encoded data byte and special symbols are generally described by code and are referred to throughout this book by the given code for a particular byte or symbol. For instance the data byte value 25h is referred to as D5.1 where D stands for data and 5.1 is related to the hexadecimal representation of bits making up the data byte value 25h. A byte value represented by bits HGFEDCBA is broken into two separate bit streams, mainly HGF and EDCBA. In the case of data byte value 25h (00100101), this equates to 001 and 00101. The code D5.1 is formed by taking the decimal equivalent of bits EDCBA, which is 5, followed by a period and then the decimal equivalent of bits HGF, which is 1. Special symbols are coded according to the same process except that the prefix K is used instead of the prefix D. Note also that there are only twelve special symbols as opposed to the 256 possible data characters. Table 8.1 describes these special symbols.

Table 8.1   PCI Express Special Symbols

Special Symbol Code	Special Symbol Name	Special Symbol Value	Bits HGFEDCBA	Description
K28.0	Skip	1C	000 11100	Used for compensating for different bit rates for two communicating ports
K28.1	Fast Training Sequence	3C	001 11100	Used within an ordered set to exit from L0s to L0 (power states)
K28.2	Start DLLP	5C	010 11100	Marks the start of a Data Link Layer Packet
K28.3	Idle	7C	011 11100	Symbol used in the electrical idle ordered set
K28.4		9C	100 11100	Reserved
K28.5	Comma	BC	101 11100	Used for lane and link initialization and management
K28.6		DC	110 11100	Reserved
K28.7		FC	111 11100	Reserved
K23.7	Pad	F7	111 10111	Used in framing and link width and lane ordering negotiations
K27.7	Start TLP	FB	111 11011	Marks the start of a Transaction Layer Packet
K29.7	End	FD	111 11101	Marks the end of a Transaction Layer Packet or a Data Link Layer Packet
K30.7	End Bad	FE	111 11110	Marks the end of a nullified Transaction Layer Packet.

Note: Reserved symbols have not been given a name

The process of 8-bit/10-bit encoding adds twenty-five percent more overhead to the system through the addition of two extra bits. However, many side benefits make this additional overhead tolerable. All of these benefits, as they relate to PCI Express, are described briefly here.

Benefit 1: Embedded Clocking. The process of 8-bit/10-bit encoding actually embeds a clock signal into the data stream. This is accomplished by forcing a minimum number of bit-level transitions within a particular symbol. Bit-level clock synchronization is achieved at the receive side with every bit-level transition. From this perspective it is desirable to have as many bit transitions as possible to ensure the best possible synchronization between devices. To illustrate this concept, consider the data byte value 00h. It is conceivable that without 8-bit/10-bit encoding, eight bits could be sent without giving the receiving device a chance to synchronize. Consequently, this could result in data corruption if the receiving device sampled a bit at the wrong time.

By definition, 8-bit/10-bit encoding allows at most five bits of the same polarity to be transmitted before a bit-level transition must occur. Recall that a byte value represented by bits HGFEDCBA is broken into two separate bit streams, mainly a 3-bit stream HGF and a 5-bit stream EDCBA. Each of these bit streams has a control variable appended to it to form a 4-bit stream and a 6-bit respectively. Concatenating the 4-bit stream and the 6-bit stream together forms a 10-bit symbol. As a result, bits HGF become JHGF, where J is a control variable. Bits EDCBA become IEDCBA where I is a control variable. Figure 8.5 shows 8-bit/10-bit encoded byte value 00h.

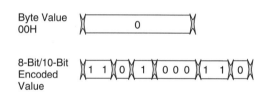

Figure 8.5   8-Bit/10-Bit Encoding Example

From another perspective, namely platform real estate, there are other benefits to getting rid of the length-matching requirement between data and clock signals. In many instances board designers have to weave or "snake" traces across the platform in order to meet the length-matching requirement between the clock and data signals. This weaving of traces is required to ensure correct operation, but comes at a high cost to system designers in both extra design time and platform real estate as shown in Figure 8.6. At frequencies in which PCI Express operates (2.5 gigahertz and beyond) this length matching would become so stringent that it would be nearly impossible to route. Since each PCI Express lane has a clock embedded into the data, the lanes can be routed to their destination with relaxed guidelines for length matching the individual lane lengths within the link. The *PCI Express Base Specification* defines the maximum skew between lanes that form the link to be 20 nanoseconds. As a result, the amount of allowable lane-to-lane skew for PCI Express is governed by the flight time characteristics of the platform.

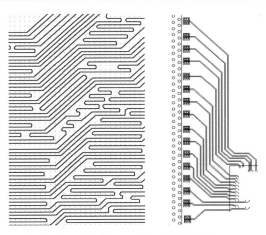

Left side shows a cut-out of a routing example in which the traces are "snaked" to length-match them to the clock in order to guarantee data is sampled with the clock.

Right side shows a PCI Express routing solution, which does not require length matching to a clock signal thereby freeing up board space and simplifying the routing.

Figure 8.6   Embedded Clocking Simplifies Routing

Benefit 2: Error Detection. A secondary benefit of 8-bit/10-bit encoding is to provide a mechanism for error detection through the concept of *running disparity*. Running disparity is essentially trying to keep the difference between the number of transmitted 1s and 0s as close to zero as possible. This allows the receiving device to determine the health of the received symbol by registering the effect that the symbol had on disparity.

Benefit 3: DC Balance. DC balancing is accomplished through running disparity. It is called out separately here to discuss the benefits received from maintaining the balance of 1s and 0s from an electrical perspective instead of an error-checking mechanism. Maintaining a proportionate number of 1s and 0s allows an individual data line to have an average DC voltage of approximately half of the logical threshold. This reduces the possibility of having inter-symbol interference, which is the inability to switch from one logic level to the next because of system capacitive charging. Inter-symbol interference is discussed in more detail within the electrical sub-block section.

Packet Framing

In order to let the receiving device know where one packet starts and ends, there are identifying 10-bit special symbols that are added and appended to a previously 8-bit/10-bit encoded data packet. The particular special symbols that are added to the data packet are dependent upon where the packet originated. In the case where the packet originated from the Transaction Layer the special symbol Start TLP (encoding K27.7) would be added to the front of the data packet. In the case the packet originated from the Data Link layer the special symbol Start DLLP (encoding K28.2) would be added to the beginning of the data packet. To end either a TLP or DLLP the special symbol END (encoding K29.7) is appended, as shown in Figure 8.7.

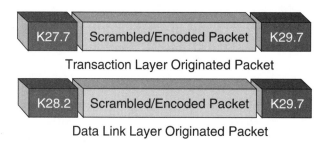

Figure 8.7 Packet Framing Example

Electrical Sub-Block

As the logical sub-block of the Physical Layer fulfils the role as the key decision maker, the electrical sub-block functions as the delivery mechanism for the physical link. The electrical sub-block contains transmit and receive buffers that transform the data into/from electrical signals. The electrical sub-block may also contain the phase locked loop circuitry, which drives the serial shift registers of the transmitter output stages. The following paragraphs describe exactly how the signaling of PCI Express works and why, and what a phase locked loop (PLL) actually does. The concepts of AC coupling and de-emphasis are also discussed briefly.

Serial/Parallel Conversion

The transmit buffer in the electrical sub-block takes the encoded/packetized data from the logical sub-block and converts it into serial format. Once the data has been serialized it is then routed to an associated lane for transmission across the link. On the receive side the receivers deserialize the data and feed it back to the logical sub-block for further processing.

Clock Extraction

In addition to the parallel-to-serial conversion described above, the receive buffer in the electrical sub-block is responsible for recovering the link clock that has been embedded in the data. With every incoming bit transition, the receive side PLL circuits are resynchronized to maintain bit and symbol (10 bits) lock.

Lane-to-Lane De-Skew

The receive buffer in the electrical sub-block de-skews data from the various lanes of the link prior to assembling the serial data into a parallel data packet. This is necessary to compensate for up to the allowable 20 nanoseconds of lane-to-lane skew. Depending on the flight time characteristics of a given transmission medium this could correlate to several inches of variance between the individual lanes that make up the link. The actual amount of skew the receive buffer must compensate for is discovered during the training process for the link.

Differential Signaling

PCI Express signaling differs considerably from the signaling technology used in conventional PCI. Conventional PCI uses a parallel bus, which sends a signal across the wire at given amplitude referenced to the system ground. In order for that signal to be received properly, it must reach its destination at a given time in reference to some external clock signal. In addition to this the signal must arrive at the destination with a given amplitude in order to register at the receiver. For relatively slow signals this type of signaling has worked quite well. However, as signals are transmitted at very high frequencies over distances of 12 inches or more, the low pass filter effects of the common four-layer FR4 PC platform cause the electrical signals to become highly attenuated. In many cases the attenuation is so great that a parallel bus receiver cannot detect the signal as valid. Electrically there are two options to overcome this signal attenuation. One option is to shorten the length of the transmission path in order to reduce signal attenuation. In some cases this is possible. However, in most cases it makes design extremely difficult, if not impossible. The other option is to use a different type of signaling technique that can help overcome the effects of attenuation.

PCI Express transmit and receive buffers are designed to convert the logical data symbols into a differential signal. *Differential signaling,* as its name might give away, is based on a relative difference between two different signals referred to as a differential pair. A differential pair is usually signified by a positively notated signal and a negatively notated signal. Logical bits are represented by the relative swing of the differential pair. To illustrate how logical bits are represented electrically on a differential pair, take the following example, as illustrated in Figure 8.8. A differential pair has a given voltage swing around 1 volt, which means the positively notated signal swings to +1 volt when representing a logical 1 and to a –1 volt when representing a logical 0. The negatively notated signal likewise swings to –1 volt when representing a logical 1 and to a +1 volt when representing a logical 0. The peak-to-peak difference between the differential pair is 2 volts in the case either logical bit is represented. The logical bit is determined by the direction in which the signals swing.

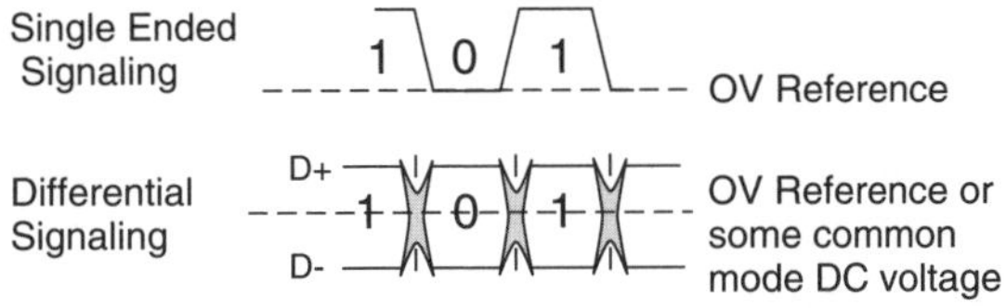

Figure 8.8   Signaling Comparison

There are several advantages that differential signaling offers over conventional single-ended signaling used commonly for parallel bus applications. A comparison of a differential pair to a single-ended signal illustrates these advantages. Assume that a single-ended bus signal swings from 0 volts to +1 volt to represent logical bits electrically. Also consider the differential pair mentioned above, which swings the positively notated signal and the negatively notated signal to +/-1 volt. The single-ended buffer output swings the signal line to 1 volt, consequently sending the electrical equivalence of the logical bit 1 down the bus. As the signal travels it becomes attenuated before it reaches the receive buffers on the other side. For now, assume that the receive buffers have been designed sensitive enough to detect the signal after it has been attenuated to some extent. Next suppose that the line is held at 0 volts to transmit the logical bit 0 down the bus. At the transmit side the buffer holds the line at 0 volts. However, at some point along the bus some noise couples onto the line and propagates down to the receiving device. To counteract signal attenuation, the receive buffers have been designed to be very sensitive to detect bus transitions. Unfortunately, the noise that has coupled onto the bus is large enough in magnitude to register a logical 1 transition at the receive side even though the transmit buffers were holding the bus low. The end result is data corruption. This is the big problem with single-ended signaling. The challenge is to have receive buffers with sensitivity suitable to register electrical transitions yet somewhat immune to noise.

Now take the case of the differential buffers sending the same bits down the bus as was done in the single-ended case. To send a logical 1 bit down the bus, the positively notated line swings to +1 volt and the negatively notated bit swings to −1 volt. As the signal travels it becomes attenuated before it reaches the receive buffers on the other side. If the signal were to be attenuated by 50 percent the relative difference between the positively notated line and the negatively notated line would still be 1 volt. The receive buffers need not be nearly as sensitive in design as the single-ended case. Now consider the case that the logical bit 0 is transferred down the bus. For the differential bus the positively and negatively notated lines swing to the opposite voltage signifying a switch in bit polarity. Also consider that the same noise source that coupled onto the single-ended line couples onto the differential pair. Since the differential receiver measures the relative difference between the differential pair, any noise that gets coupled equally onto each signal of the pair is inconsequential. Differential signaling allows designers to deal with platform level signal attenuation and noise coupling by providing a better method to transfer energy between devices and eliminating common mode elements that interfere with signal quality.

Phase Locked Loop (PLL) Circuit

A clock derived from a PLL circuit may provide the internal clocking to drive the serial shift registers of the transmitter output stages of the PCI Express device. Each PCI Express device is given a 100 megahertz differential clock signal. This clock can be fed into a PLL circuit, which multiplies it by 25 to achieve the 2.5 gigahertz PCI Express frequency.

AC Coupling

PCI Express requires AC coupling on the transmit side of the differential pair to eliminate the DC common mode element. These capacitors can be included on the motherboard or integrated into the PCI Express device itself for soldered down devices. Likewise, PCI Express add in devices are required to place these capacitors on the add-in card itself or integrate them into the add-in card device silicon. By removing the DC common mode element, the buffer design process for PCI Express becomes much simpler. Each PCI Express device can have a unique DC common mode voltage element, which is used during the detection process. The link AC coupling removes the common mode element from view of the receiving device. The range of AC capacitance that is allowed by the *PCI Express Base Specification* is 75 to 200 nanofarads.

De-Emphasis

PCI Express utilizes a concept referred to as *de-emphasis* to reduce the effects of inter-symbol interference. In order to best explain how de-emphasis works it is important to understand what inter-symbol interference is. As frequencies increase, bit times decrease. As bit times decrease the capacitive effects of the platform become much more apparent.

Inter-symbol interference comes into play when bits change rapidly on a bus after being held constant for some time prior. Take under consideration a differential bus that transmits five logical 1s in a row. This is the maximum number of same-bit transmissions allowable under 8-bit/10-bit encoding. Suppose that following the five logical 1s was a logical 0 followed by another logical 1. The transmission of the first five logical 1s charges the system capacitance formed by the layering process of the PCB stackup (Plate Capacitor). When the system follows the five logical 1s with a logical 0 and then another logical 1 the system cannot discharge quick enough to register the logical 0 before the next logical 1. The effect is inter-symbol interference, as shown in Figure 8.9.

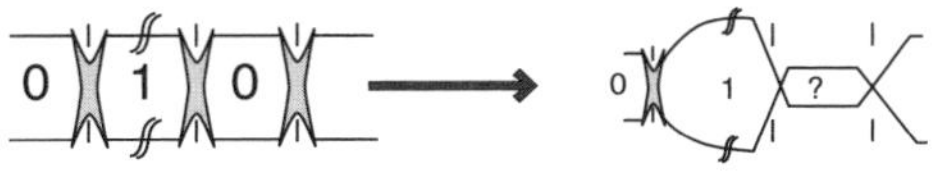

Figure 8.9   Inter-Symbol Interference

In order to minimize the effect of inter-symbol interference, subsequent bits of the same polarity that are output in succession are de-emphasized. When discussing PCI Express this translates into a 3½ decibels reduction in power of each subsequent same polarity bits as shown in Figure 8.10. This does not mean that each and every bit continues to be reduced in power; it only refers to the first subsequent bit. Further bits would continue at the same "de-emphasized" strength. It may not be immediately apparent just how this technique actually helps to reduce the effects of inter-symbol interference, but this will soon become clear.

As seen at Transmit side

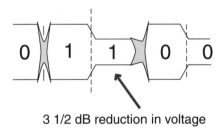

3 1/2 dB reduction in voltage

Figure 8.10   De-emphasis Example

Instead of thinking of each subsequent same polarity bit as being reduced by 3½ decibels, think of the first initial bit as being pre-emphasized. As discussed above, the difficulty with inter-symbol interference is the inability to overcome the capacitive discharging of the system quick enough to reach the electrical thresholds to register a logical event. By pre-emphasizing the first bit transition, or as the PCI Express specification defines it, by de-emphasizing subsequent same polarity bit transmissions, the first initial bit transition is given extra drive strength. Through this mechanism, bit transitions occurring after multiple same polarity transmissions are given enough strength to overcompensate for the capacitive effects of the system. See Table 8.2 for the DC characteristics of de-emphasis.

Table 8.2   PCI Express De-Emphasis Electricals

Initial Bit Transition Peak-to-Peak Voltage	Subsequent Bit Transmission Peak-to-Peak Voltage
800 mV minimum	505 mV minimum

Link and Lane Training

Recall from Chapter 3 that a lane is a set of differential transmit and receive pairs and that a link is a collection of lanes forming a dual unidirectional communication between two PCI Express devices. The link and lane training process is a coordinated effort between the logical and the electrical sub-blocks. These sub-blocks work together to configure individual lanes into a functioning link. Training the link requires an understanding of the link data rate, lane ordering and link width, lane-to-lane skew, and lane polarity. There are seven link training states, the detect, polling, configuration, disable, recovery, hot reset, and loopback states, as shown in Figure 8.11. The following discussion focuses on the details associated with the detect, polling, and configuration link training states, which are considered the primary states used during the training process. The other training states are touched upon briefly.

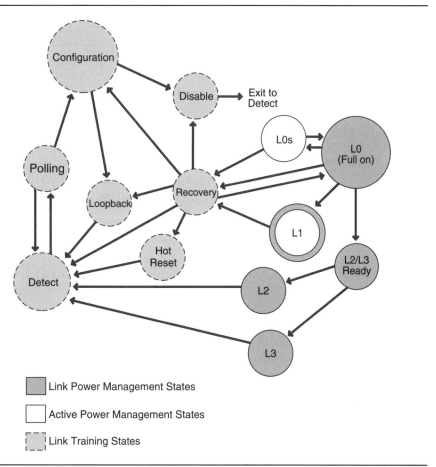

Figure 8.11 Physical Layer Link Training States

Electrical Idle

Before describing the link configuration states it seems appropriate to define electrical idle since it will be referred to throughout the remainder of this chapter. The electrical idle state is a steady state condition where the Transmit pairs TX+ and TX- are held at a constant value. The *PCI Express Base Specification* defines constant as meaning that the differential pair lines have no more than 20 millivolts of difference between the pair after factoring out any DC common element. The minimum time that a transmitter must remain in electrical idle is 20 nanoseconds, however, the transmitter must attempt to detect a receiving device within 100 milliseconds. Electrical idle is primarily used in power saving mode and common mode voltage initialization.

Detect State

The first state that the PCI Express link enters into is the detect state upon cold reset (power-up), warm reset, and if the configuration protocol fails to establish a configured link. It is also a transitioned into if the other link states do not succeed. The detect state is also entered into upon a hot reset condition, a surprise removal of a device, or an exit from the link disabled state. The detect state determines whether or not there is a device connected on the other side of the link. The detection process takes place in the progression through two sub-states called quiet and active as shown in Figure 8.12.

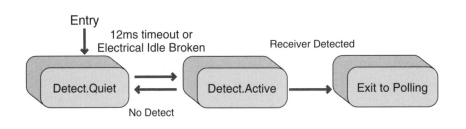

Figure 8.12   Detect Sub-State Machine

Quiet Sub-State. During the quiet sub-state, three primary tasks are completed. First the transmitter in both the upstream and downstream device enters the electrical idle state while driving its DC common mode voltage. The relationship between an upstream and downstream device is shown in Figure 8.13.

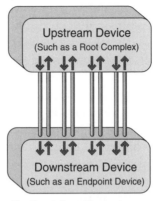

The *PCI Express Base Specification* defines the upstream and downstream device relationship as following: The downstream device on a link is the device farther from the root complex. The upstream device on a link is the device closer to the root complex.

Figure 8.13   Downstream Device/Upstream Device Relationship

Next both devices select the data rate, which is always 2.5 gigabits per second during link training regardless of frequency advances of the technology. This assures frequency backward compatibility in the future. Finally, both devices clear the status of the LinkUp indicator to inform the system that a link connection is not currently established (refer to Chapter 7 on Data Link Layer Control). A register in the Data Link Layer monitors the LinkUp status to ensure that data packets are not generated in the event that the link is not established and active.

The upstream or downstream device will progress to the active sub-state after a 12 millisecond timeout or if electrical idle has been broken on any of the device's lanes.

Active Sub-State. Primary detection is completed during the active sub-state. Detection is done on a per-lane basis by analyzing the loading effect the other device's receiver has on the transmitted operating DC common mode voltage. If no device is connected to the other end of the lane, the rate of change of the applied DC common mode voltage of the transmitting device is much faster than if a terminated device receiver were setting out on the lane. If a device is detected the next state is the polling state. If no device can be detected the sub-state machine returns to the quiet sub-state and wait for 12 milliseconds or for electrical idle to be broken before checking again for the presence of a device.

The previous example assumes a simplistic case where two equal port width devices (two x4 devices for example) are connected together. If, for example, a x4 upstream device is connected to a x2 downstream device, two of the lanes of the upstream device detect a device and the remaining two unconnected lanes do not detect a device. In this case the upstream device waits 12 milliseconds and tries the detection again. Assuming the x2 downstream device is still connected, the upstream device again detects that two of the lanes do not have a device connected to them. If the upstream device is capable of forming a separate x2 link (now becomes two x2 port devices) the unconnected lanes become associated with another link training state machine. If the device does not have this capability, the unconnected lanes return to the Electrical Idle state. This example also applies if the situation is reversed with a x4 downstream device and a x2 upstream device.

Polling State

The polling state is the first state where training instructions called training ordered sets are sent out on all the individual PCI Express lanes to initialize the link. PCI Express currently defines two training ordered sets called TS1 and TS2. There are not many differences between the two sets except for the indicator used to distinguish which training ordered set it actually is. Some sub-states use TS1 training ordered sets and others use TS2 training ordered sets. The use of a particular training ordered set helps the PCI Express device determine the current state and sub-state. Both training ordered sets are used during the polling process to establish bit and symbol alignment and to exchange Physical Layer parameters. During the polling state TS1 and TS2 ordered sets are used.

Training ordered sets are nothing more than a group of 16 8-bit/10-bit encoded special characters and data. Training ordered sets are never scrambled. These training instructions are used to establish the link data rate, establish clock synchronization down to the bit level, configure link and lane numbering, and check lane polarity, force resets, disable a link, enter test modes, and enable data scrambling. Table 8.3 shows the training ordered set that is sent out during the polling state.

Table 8.3   TS1 Ordered Sets Used during the Polling State

Symbol Number	Allowed Values	Encoded Values	Description
0		K28.5	COMMA code group for symbol alignment
1	0 - 255	D0.0 – D31.7, K23.7	Link Number within device
2	0 - 31	D0.0 – D31.0, K23.7	Lane Number within Port
3	0 - 255	D0.0 – D31.7	N_FTS. This is the number of fast training ordered sets required by the receiver to obtain reliable bit and symbol lock.
4	2	D2.0	Data Rate Identifier Bit 0 – Reserved, set to 0 Bit 1 = 1, generation 1 (2.5 Gb/s) data rate supported Bit 2:7 – Reserved, set to 0

5	Bit 0 = 0, 1
	Bit 1 = 0, 1
	Bit 2 = 0, 1
	Bit 3 = 0, 1
	Bit 4:7 = 0,
		D0.0, D1.0, D2.0, D4.0, D8.0	Training Control
			
			Bit 0 – Hot Reset
			    Bit 0 = 0, De-assert Reset
			    Bit 0 = 1, Assert Reset
			
			Bit 1 – Disable Link
			    Bit 1 = 0, Enable Link
			    Bit 1 = 1, Disable Link
			
			Bit 2 – Loopback
			    Bit 2 = 0, No Loop back
			    Bit 2 = 1, Enable Loop back
			
			Bit 3 – Disable Scrambling
			    Bit 3 = 0, Enable Scrambling
			    Bit 3 = 1, Disable Scrambling
			
			Bit 4:7, Reserved

6–15		D10.2	TS1 Identifier

Note: The TS2 Training Ordered Set is exactly the same as the TS1 Training Ordered Set with one exception. In the place of symbols 6–15 is the TS2 encoded value D5.2.

Similar in concept to the detect state, the polling state has four defined sub-states that are used in the link training process. The polling sub-states are referred to as active, configuration, speed, and compliance as shown in Figure 8.14. A short description of the transition in and out of these sub-states follows.

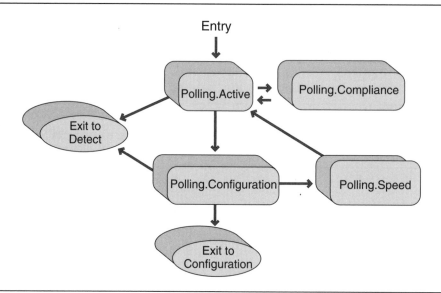

Figure 8.14 Polling State Machine

Active Sub-State. In this sub-state both the upstream and downstream device send out a minimum of 1024 consecutive TS1 training ordered sets. This is done to achieve bit and symbol (10-bit) lock. If eight consecutive TS1 or TS2 training ordered sets or their complements are received, the device has achieved bit and symbol lock and advances to the configuration sub-state (the minimum number of TS1 training ordered sets must still be sent before advancing). A complement is received if the transmit and receive polarities are backwards.

If a 24 millisecond timeout occurs and a device has not progressed to another sub-state, the device advances to either the configuration sub-state, the compliance sub-state or the detect state. The configuration sub-state is entered into if any lane received eight consecutive training ordered sets or their complement and all connected lanes (determined during the detect state) detected an exit from electrical idle at least one time since the device entered the polling state. The compliance sub-state is entered if any single lane has never detected an exit from the electrical idle state since the device entered the polling state. If a device's transmitter has transmitted 1024 TS1 ordered sets and has not successfully received a single training ordered set or its complement with the link and lane numbers set to the special symbol PAD (encoding K23.7), then the device exits the polling active sub-state and re-enters the detect state.

Compliance Sub-State. In the compliance sub-state, the device sends out the compliance pattern defined in the *PCI Express Base Specification* to each lane known to have a device connected. The compliance pattern is composed of a sequence of four symbols (encodings K28.5, D21.5, K28.5, D10.2), which are repeated. This continues until the device detects that electrical idle has been broken on all connected lanes. The compliance sub-state is generally entered into as the result of test equipment being connected to the link instead of a PCI Express component. The compliance sub-state is intended for a compliance lab environment and is not intended for normal operation.

Configuration Sub-State. The configuration sub-state ensures the proper polarization of each receiving lane. If during the active sub-state the device of a training ordered set is received by the downstream port then the receive logic performs a logical inversion on each incoming lane that has received an inverted training ordered set, as shown in Figure 8.15. The ability to perform a logical inversion on incoming signals (due to polarity inversion of the differential pair) gives the designer flexibility in cases where it would otherwise be necessary to bow-tie the signals.

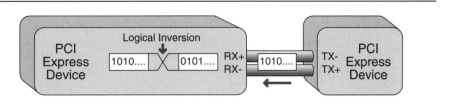

Figure 8.15 Logical Inversion

During the configuration sub-state both the upstream and downstream devices transmit TS2 training ordered sets to each other on each connected lane. After a device receives a single TS2 training ordered set on any lane, the corresponding transmitter associated with that lane will send out sixteen TS2 training ordered sets. These TS2 training ordered sets continue to have the link and lane numbers set to the special symbol PAD to indicate that they have not yet been configured. As soon as eight consecutive TS2 training ordered sets are received on any of the connected lanes with the data rate identifier set 2.5 gigabits per second, the device enters the configuration state. Do not confuse this with the configuration sub-state currently being discussed. If eight consecutive TS2 training ordered sets are received on all of the connected lanes and one of the lanes receives a data rate identifier greater than 2.5 gigabits per second (indicating the ability to operate at a higher frequency) then the device enters the speed sub-state.

Speed Sub-State. The speed sub-state is only entered if either the downstream or upstream device supports a data rate higher than the initial PCI Express data rate of 2.5 gigabits per second (if symbol 4 of the TS1 or TS2 training ordered sets contains anything other than D2.0). During the speed sub-state, the electrical idle ordered set—the special symbol COM (encoding K28.5) followed by three IDL special symbols (encoding K28.3)—is sent to cause each transmitter on the other device to enter electrical idle. While in electrical idle for at least the minimum 20 nanoseconds but not longer than 2 milliseconds, information in symbol 4 of the training ordered sets is changed to the highest common data rate supported by both ports. Upon selecting the highest common data rate the device enters the active sub-state once again.

Configuration State

The configuration state establishes link width and lane ordering. Prior to this state, bit and symbol lock should have been established, link data rate determined, and polarity corrections made on incoming data if necessary. Within the configuration state there are six sub-states, linkwidth.start, linkwidth.accept, lanenum.accept, lanenum.wait, complete, and idle, as shown in Figure 8.16.

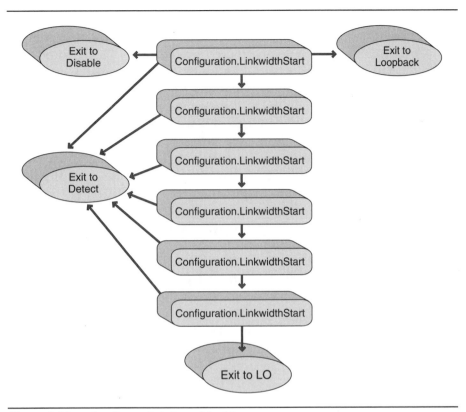

Figure 8.16   Configure Sub-State Machine

Linkwidth.Start Sub-State. During the linkwidth.start sub-state, link width is established. The linkwidth.start sub-state is the first sub-state where the upstream and downstream devices begin to act a bit differently. First, however, the similarities are investigated. If either the upstream or downstream device is directed by a higher layer to disable the link or enter loopback, the device enters either the disabled or loopback state and the corresponding bit is set in the TS1 and TS2 training ordered sets. These training ordered sets are then transmitted to the other device. This will force the device on the other side of the link to enter either the disabled or the loopback state. In the case where the loopback bit is received, the receiving device becomes the loopback slave to the transmitting loopback master (the other device).

When in this sub-state, assuming that the device did not transition to the disabled state or the loopback state, the upstream device begins transmitting TS1 training ordered sets to the downstream device with selected link numbers. If the upstream device is capable of forming multiple links then unique link numbers will be sent out on the lanes capable of forming multiple links. For example, if the upstream device is a x4 port and capable of forming either a x4 link or two x2 links then two of the lanes would transmit the link number N and the other two lanes would transmit the link number N+1. Once the downstream device receives two consecutive TS1 training ordered sets with the link number set, the link number negotiation process begins. The downstream device responds to the upstream device by selecting a single link number (assuming that more than one was received) and transmitting that link number back to the upstream device on all lanes capable of forming a link by means of symbol 2 of the TS1 training ordered set as shown in Figure 8.17. Any lanes that are connected and incapable of forming a link continue to respond with the special symbol PAD (encoding K23.7) in place of the link number. This informs the upstream device that those lanes are not capable of forming a link. At this point the downstream device advances to the linkwidth.accept sub-state. The upstream device advances to the linkwidth.accept sub-state upon receiving two consecutive TS1 training ordered sets with the link number set to anything except the special symbol PAD.

If nothing happens within a 24 millisecond timeout window, the device enters back into the detect state. The linkwidth.start sub-state has hooks to support the optional cross-link feature for advanced switching. However, this case is not discussed in this book. For more details reference the *PCI Express Base Specification.*

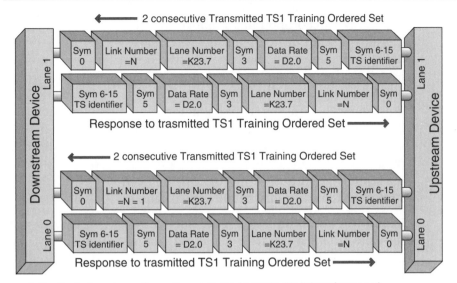

Figure 8.17 Link Training

Linkwidth.Accept Sub-State. After the link number is established, the upstream device changes the lane numbers from PAD to the lane numbers associated with the particular lane in question on the upstream device. The upstream device sends a recommended lane number for each connected lane on the lanes capable of forming a link to the downstream device. This is accomplished by replacing symbol 2 (formally the special symbol PAD) of the TS1 training ordered set with the recommended lane numbering. The upstream device then proceeds to the lanenum.wait sub-state. If a 2 millisecond timeout occurs or a link cannot be configured the upstream device transitions to the detect state.

Upon receiving two consecutive TS1 training ordered sets with the previously agreed upon link number and unique lane numbers now set, the downstream device transmits a response to the upstream device. If the lane numbers recommended by the upstream device are acceptable to the downstream device, the downstream devices echoes back the lane numbers suggested by the upstream device through sending TS1 training ordered sets with the corresponding lane numbers included. If the downstream device prefers to use some other lane numbering it responds with those lane numbers instead. The downstream device then progresses to the lanenum.wait sub-state. Similar to the upstream device, if a 2 millisecond timeout occurs or a link can not be configured the upstream device transitions to the detect state.

Lanenum.Wait Sub-State. The lanenum.wait sub-state is a transition sub-state between the time when the lane numbers of the link are proposed and when they are accepted. In this state the upstream device is waiting for a response from the downstream device regarding the lane numbers it has proposed. The downstream device is waiting for a response from the upstream device regarding the lane numbers it either echoed back during the previous sub-state or the new lane number proposal it countered with.

Both the downstream and upstream devices progress to the lanenum.accept sub-state if any of the lanes receive two consecutive TS1 training ordered sets with a lane number different from when it first entered the lanenum wait sub-state. The downstream device will also transition to the lanenum.accept sub-state if any lane receives two consecutive TS2 training ordered sets. In other words, the upstream device transitions out of this state when it receives the first response from the downstream device regarding the suggested lane numbers. The downstream device transitions out of this state upon confirmation of the previously transmitted lane numbers or an alternative suggestion from the upstream device.

Lanenum.Accept Sub-State. The lanenum.accept sub-state is the seal-the-deal state between the two devices. The upstream device will seal the deal if a link can be formed by all lanes in question with the lane numbers received on all lanes through two consecutive TS1 training ordered sets. The lane numbers can either be the original lane numbers that the upstream device proposed or reversed lane numbers if that ability is supported in the upstream device. Refer to Figure 8.18 for an example of lane reversal. This deal is sealed from the upstream devices perspective by advancing to the configuration.complete sub-state.

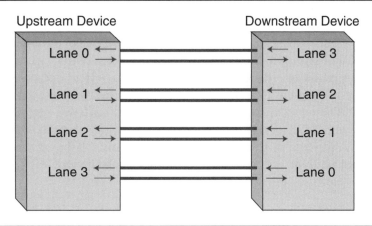

Figure 8.18   Lane Reversal between the Upstream and Downstream Device

If no link can be configured or for some reason two consecutive TS1 training ordered sets are received with the link and lane numbers effectively cleared (set to the special symbol PAD), then the device will transition to the detect state. This applies to both the upstream and downstream device.

Complete Sub-State. During the complete sub-state, the TS2 training ordered sets are transmitted by each device with the previously agreed upon link and lane numbers. Once a device receives a TS2 training ordered set it must then transfer sixteen TS2 training ordered sets. For links greater than a x1 configuration each device's receiver must compensate for the allowable 20 nanoseconds of lane-to-lane skew that the *PCI Express Base Specification* allows between the lanes that form the link. To accomplish this each device is assumed to transmit lane data at the same time. The receiving device determines the amount of lane-to-lane deskew required by noting when data is received on each lane. Since each lane is being sent the same data (TS2 training ordered sets) the determination of the skew parameters becomes relatively simpler. During this state the devices also exchange additional information through the TS2 training ordered sets. One piece of information that is exchanged is whether or not to enable data scrambling. This ability is enabled sending out two consecutive TS2 training ordered sets with the disable scrambling bit cleared. Additionally each device reports the number of Fast Training Sequences—an ordered set composed of the following special symbols: one COM (encoding K28.5) followed by three FTS (encoding K28.1)—needed to re-establish bit and symbol lock when transitioning out of the

L0s Active Power Management State. For more information on Active State Power Management refer to Chapter 11.

During this sub-state, scrambling may be also disabled if desired. This is accomplished by sending out two consecutive TS2 training ordered sets with the disable scrambling bit set. If a device sets the disable scrambling bit it must also cease to scramble future data transmissions.

Once eight consecutive TS2 training ordered sets are received, the device advances to the idle sub-state. Each device must complete the transmission of the 16 required TS2 training ordered sets. If a 2 millisecond timeout occurs on either device each device will respectively enter the detect state.

Idle Sub-State. As soon as the idle sub-state is reached the link is fully configured. At this point bit and symbol lock are established, the link data rate is selected, and link and lane numbering are fixed. In this sub-state both the devices transmit the special symbol IDL (encoding K28.3) (Idle). As soon as each device receives the idle symbol it transmits at least 16 consecutive idle symbols in return. Once a device receives eight consecutive IDL symbols the device transitions to the L0 state, which is the operating state. If the devices receive no idle symbols within 2 milliseconds, a timeout condition occurs and the devices respectively transition to the detect state, as shown in Figure 8.16.

Recovery State

The recovery state is the only state that cannot be entered into through the link training process. Based on this argument, it is logical to dismiss it as a training state. This state is considered a training state because of the things that are accomplished while in this state. The recovery state is entered into as needed by a functioning link or a link that is in transition from an Active State Power Management (ASPM) state (discussed more below and in Chapter 11). In the recovery state, the link and lane numbering are preserved as well as the link operating frequency, which is always 2.5 gigabits per second for first generation PCI Express devices. The recovery state is used to achieve bit and symbol level synchronization as needed, as well as re-establish the number of fast training sequences required to quickly recover from the Active State Power Management states.

Loopback State

The loopback state is a test feature for the lab and debug environment and is not intended to be used during normal link training. A downstream or upstream device may initiate entry into the loopback state if this feature is supported by the Data Link Layer. This ability is an optional feature. However, all devices must be able to enter this state if directed by another device. A device must request this state through sending out TS1 or TS2 training ordered sets with the loopback bit set while in the configuration or recovery states. Refer to Table 8.3. A device that requests the loopback state becomes the loopback master. A loopback master may transmit any pattern of 8-bit/10-bit encoded symbols to the other device, which becomes the loopback slave. The loopback slave must retransmit all received valid 8-bit/10-bit symbols exactly as received. This means that the received symbols are not scrambled and disparity errors are not corrected. This state may be used to test many different parameters such as general device functionality, the integrity of the data paths between the two devices, buffer receive sensitivity, and more. The ability to test beyond a pure functional level may be provided through a proprietary set of extensions that each device manufacturer can add to their PCI Express design.

Hot Reset State

The hot reset state is simply a state used to reset a link without requiring a full system reset. An upstream device may initiate a hot reset as directed by the upper PCI Express layers setting the Secondary Bus Reset bit in the Bridge Control Register of the PCI Express configuration space header. Setting this bit causes an upstream device to send out TS1 training ordered sets with the hot reset bit set. This state is generally used to reset a malfunctioning link. Both the device that receives a hot reset state request and the device that initiated the request must prepare to enter the detect state.

Disabled State

The disabled state is used to transition the lanes to electrical idle. Entry into this state is the result of receiving TS1 training ordered sets with the disable bit asserted or as directed by an upper layer through setting a bit in the Link Control Register. This particular register is part of the PCI Express capability structure, which is illustrated in Chapter 11, Figure 11.8. An upper layer would likely cause a transition into this state as a result of a surprise removal of a device.

Surprise Insertion/Removal

The concept of surprise removal is often equated to hot swapping. For the most part this is accurate since a hot swap is the removal of a device without any software interaction. Unfortunately the concept of no software interaction is pretty broad. In the context of this section, PCI Express buffer architecture and detect mechanisms are addressed.

PCI Express physical architecture is designed with ease of use in mind. To support this concept PCI Express has built in the ability to handle surprise insertion and removal of PCI Express devices. All transmitters and receivers must support surprise insertion/removal without damage to the device. The transmitter and receiver must also be capable of withstanding sustained short circuit to ground of the differential inputs/outputs TX/RX+ and TX/RX–.

A PCI Express device can assume the form of an add-in card, module, or a soldered-down device on a PC platform. In the case of an add-in card or module, PCI Express allows a user to insert or remove a device (an upstream port) while the system is powered.

Surprise Insertion

A link that is missing a downstream device causes the upstream device to remain in the detect state. Every 12 milliseconds the downstream port checks the link to see whether or not downstream device has been connected. As soon as a user inserts a device into the system it is detected and the link training process as previously described begins.

Surprise Removal

If a downstream device is removed from the system during normal operation, the upstream device's receiver(s) detect an electrical idle condition (a loss of activity). Because the electrical idle condition was not preceded by the electrical idle ordered set, the link changes to the detect state.

Power Management Capabilities

PCI Express has several power management states that can either be driven by the request of software or are actively managed by the Physical Layer. This section focuses on the actively managed link power states controlled by the Physical Layer. For additional power management details not covered here, refer to Chapter 11.

The *PCI Express Base Specification* defines two Active State Power Management states to lower the power consumption of the link. The first state is called L0s. According to the *PCI Express Base Specification* this state must be supported. The second Active State Power Management state is the L1 state. Support for this state is optional. Software enables the use of these states. However, the Physical Layer actually handles the autonomous function of managing the power states. By default, PCI Express devices power up with this functionality turned off.

L0s Active Power Management State

When the L0s state is enabled, the Physical Layer transitions the link to this state whenever the link is not in use, as shown in Figure 8.11. This power-saving state is managed on a per-direction basis. In other words, the transmit path from the upstream device could be in the L0s state while the receive path to the upstream device could remain in the fully functional L0 state. Because the link transitions into and out of this state often, the latencies associated with coming in and out of this state must be relatively small (a maximum of several microseconds). During this state the transmitter continues to drive the DC common mode voltage and all devices on chip clocks continue to run (PLL clocks and so on).

To enable the L0s power management state, the transmitter must send the electrical idle ordered set, the special symbol COM (encoding K28.5) followed by three IDL special symbols (encoding K28.3). After sending the electrical idle ordered set, the transmitter has to transition to a valid electrical idle within 20 UI (Unit Intervals). A Unit Interval is defined as a single bit time or the inverse of the frequency. Given the initial PCI Express frequency of 2.5 gigahertz, the transition time equates to approximately 8 nanoseconds.

$$\frac{1}{2.5\exp^9} = 0.4\,ns \Rightarrow 0.4\,ns * 20 = 8\,ns$$

Sample Timing Calculation

As soon as the transmitter enters the L0s state, it must remain in the state for a minimum of 50 UI or 20 nanoseconds. To exit the L0s state the transmitter must begin sending out Fast Training Sequences to the receiver. As mentioned earlier in this chapter, a Fast Training Sequence is an ordered set composed of one COM special symbol (encoding K28.5) and three FTS special symbols (encoding K28.1). Fast Training Sequences are used to resynchronize the bit and symbol times of the link in question. The exit latency from this state depends upon the amount of time it takes the receiving device to acquire bit and symbol synchronization. If the receiver is unable to obtain bit and symbol lock from the Fast Training Sequence the link must enter a recovery.

L1 Active Power Management State

The L1 active power management state allows for additional power savings over the L0s state but at the cost of much higher exit latency. During this state the transmitter continues to drive the DC common mode voltage and all devices on chip clocks are turned off. The details of transitioning into and out of the L1 state are very similar to the L0s state. However, the Data Link Layer and not the Physical Layer controls the active management of this state. Refer to Chapter 11 for more details.

Chapter **9**

Flow Control

My expressway runneth over.

—Victor Ross, spokesman for NY Bureau of Traffic Operations

This chapter goes into the details of the various flow control mechanisms within PCI Express. It begins with a description of the ordering requirements for the various transaction types and then explains key aspects of the credit-based flow control mechanisms. The rest of the chapter then deals with some of the advanced mechanisms that PCI Express uses to manage the traffic within the system, namely virtual channels and traffic classes. Following that, the chapter briefly describes how these mechanisms are used to support isochronous data streams.

Transaction Ordering

The *PCI Express Base Specification* defines several ordering rules to govern which types of transactions are allowed to pass or be passed. Passing occurs when a newer transaction bypasses a previously issued transaction and the device executes the newer transaction first. The ordering rules apply uniformly to all transaction types—memory, I/O, configuration, and messages—but only within a given traffic class. There are no ordering rules between transactions with different traffic classes. It follows that there are no ordering rules between different virtual channels, since a single traffic class cannot be mapped to multiple virtual channels within a given link. Further details on this are located in the section on virtual channels and traffic classes later in this chapter. Please note that the ordering rules for completions are somewhat decoupled from request ordering. Completions use their own ordering rules and do not necessarily follow the same ordering as their associated requests.

Table 9.1 illustrates the various rules for when a transaction must, may, or cannot be allowed to pass a previously issued transaction. An entry of Yes indicates that to avoid deadlock, the subsequent transaction (identified by that row) must be allowed to pass the previous transaction (as identified by that column). An entry of Y/N indicates that there are no specified requirements. The subsequent transaction may pass or be blocked by the previous transaction. An entry of No indicates that the subsequent transaction must not pass the previous transaction.

Table 9.1   Ordering Rules

Row Pass Column? (Row letter or column number in parentheses)		**Posted Request** Memory Write or Message Request (1)	**Non-Posted Request**		**Completion**	
			Read Request (2)	I/O or Config Write Request (3)	Read Completion (4)	I/O or Config Write Completion (5)
Posted Request	Memory Write or Message Request (A)	a) No b) Y/N	Yes	Yes	a) Y/N b) Yes	a) Y/N b) Yes
Non-Posted Request	Read Request (B)	No	Y/N	Y/N	Y/N	Y/N
Non-Posted Request	I/O or Config Write Request (C)	No	Y/N	Y/N	Y/N	Y/N
Completion	Read Completion (D)	a) No b) Y/N	Yes	Yes	a) Y/N b) No	Y/N
Completion	I/O or Config Write Completion (E)	Y/N	Yes	Yes	Y/N	Y/N

A subsequent memory write or message request interacts with previous transactions as follows. As seen in cell A1, there are two potential ordering rules when dealing with two memory write or message requests. If the relaxed ordering bit (bit 5 of byte 2 in the TLP header) contains a value of 0, then the second transaction is not permitted to bypass the previously submitted request (A1a). If that bit is set to a 1, then the subsequent transaction is permitted to bypass the previous transaction (A1b). A memory write or message request must be allowed to pass read requests (A2) as well as I/O or configuration write requests (A3) in order to avoid deadlock. The ordering rules between memory write or message requests and completion packets depend on the type of PCI Express device. Endpoints, switches, and root complexes may allow memory write or message requests to pass or be blocked by completions (A4a and A5a). PCI Express to PCI or PCI-X bridges, on the other hand, must allow memory write or message requests to pass completions in order to avoid deadlock (A4b and A5b). This scenario only occurs for traffic flowing from the upstream (PCI Express) side of the bridge to the downstream (PCI or PCI-X) side of the bridge.

A subsequent non-posted request (any read request or an I/O or configuration write request) interacts with previous transactions in the following way. As seen in cells B1 and C1, these requests are not allowed to pass previously issued memory write or message requests. Non-posted requests may pass or be blocked by all other transaction types (B2, B3, B4, B5, C2, C3, C4, and C5).

A subsequent read completion interacts with previous transactions as follows. As seen in cell D1, there are two potential ordering rules when determining if a read completion can pass a previously issued memory write or message request. If the relaxed ordering bit (bit 5 of byte 2 in the TLP header) contains a value of 0, then the read completion is not permitted to bypass the previously submitted request (D1a). If that bit is set to a 1, then the read completion may bypass the previously enqueued transaction (D1b). A read completion must be allowed to pass read requests (D2) as well as I/O or configuration write requests (D3) in order to avoid deadlock. Read completions from different read requests are treated in a similar fashion to I/O or configuration write completions. In either case (D4a or D5), the subsequent read completion may pass or be blocked by the previous completion transaction. Recall however, that a single completion may be split up amongst several completion packets. In this scenario, a subsequent read completion packet is not allowed to pass a previously enqueued read completion packet for that same request/completion (D4b). This is done in order to ensure that read completions return in the proper order.

A subsequent I/O or configuration write completion interacts with previous transactions as follows. As seen in cell E1, these completions may pass or be blocked by previously issued memory write or message requests. Like read completions, I/O or configuration write completions must be allowed to pass read and I/O or configuration write requests in order to avoid deadlocks (E2 and E3). Finally, as seen in E4 and E5, I/O and configuration write completions may pass or be blocked by previously issued completions.

Flow Control

PCI Express enacts flow control (FC) mechanisms to prevent receiver buffer overflow and to enable compliance with the ordering rules outlined previously. Flow control is done on a per-link basis, managing the traffic between a device and its link mate. Flow control mechanisms do not manage traffic on an end-to-end basis, as shown in Figure 9.1.

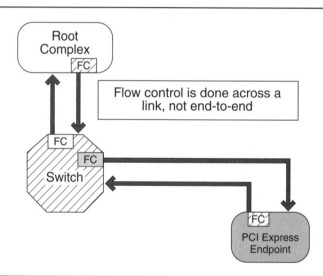

Figure 9.1   Link by Link Flow Control

In the example in Figure 9.1, the root complex issues a request packet destined for the PCI Express endpoint and transmits that packet across the outgoing portion of its link to the switch. The switch then sends that packet across its downstream port to the endpoint. The flow control mechanisms that PCI Express implements, however, are local to each link. The flow control block in the root complex only deals with managing the traffic between the root complex and the switch. The downstream port of the switch and the endpoint then manage the flow control for that packet between the switch and the endpoint. In Figure 9.1, there are no flow control mechanisms in the root complex that track the packet all the way down to the endpoint.

Link mates share flow control information to ensure that no device transmits a packet that its link mate is unable to accept. Each device indicates how many flow control credits it has available for use. If the next packet allocated for transmission exceeds the available credits at the receiver, that packet cannot be transmitted. Within a given link, each virtual channel maintains its own flow control credit pool.

As mentioned in Chapter 7, DLLPs carry flow control details between link mates. These DLLPs may initialize or update the various flow control credit pools used by a link. Though the flow control packets are DLLPs and not TLPs, the actual flow control procedures are a function of the Transaction Layer in cooperation with the Data Link Layer. The Transaction Layer performs flow control accounting for received TLPs and gates outgoing TLPs if they exceed the credits available. The flow control mechanisms are independent of the data integrity mechanisms of the Data Link Layer (that is, the flow control logic does not know if the Data Link Layer was forced to retry a given TLP, and retry cannot be used as a form of flow control).

Flow Control Rules

What is flow control really doing? It helps to ensure that traffic flows through a system in an orderly manner. Just imagine trying to drive down the highway if there were no rules governing how to drive. What would stop somebody else from driving down your side of the road? What would stop somebody in the next lane from pulling directly into your lane? During high traffic times, what if nobody bothered to use their brakes? Cars that tried to occupy the same space at the same time would collide, and cars that had no place to go could be forced to swerve off the road and be lost. Traffic rules help to avoid these sorts of issues on the highway, and flow control rules help avoid these same sorts of issues on a PCI Express link.

First consider a single lane bridge that must service cars in both directions. To get access to the road, a driver must arbitrate for control of the road with other drivers going both the same direction and the opposite direction. This is a good representation of how conventional PCI and PCI-X flow control works. Additionally, once a car gains access to the road, it needs to determine how fast it can go. If there is a lot of traffic already on the road, the driver may need to throttle his or her advancement to keep from colliding with other cars on the road. PCI accomplishes this through signals such as IRDY# and TRDY#.

Now consider that the road is changed into a highway with four lanes in both directions. This highway has a carpool lane that allows carpoolers an easier path to travel during rush hour traffic congestion. There are also fast lanes for swifter moving traffic and slow lanes for big trucks and other slow moving traffic. Drivers can use different lanes in either direction to get to a particular destination. Each driver occupies a lane based upon the type of driver he or she is. Carpoolers take the carpool lane while fast drivers and slow drivers occupy the fast and slow lanes respectively. This highway example represents the PCI Express flow control model. Providing additional lanes of traffic increases the total number of cars or bandwidth that can be supported. This is what is accomplished by adding additional lanes to a PCI Express link. Prioritizing who gets to use the available bandwidth (especially during high traffic times) is what virtual channels and traffic classes add to the picture.

PCI Express does not have the same sideband signals (IRDY#, TRDY#, RBF#, WBF#, and so on) that PCI or AGP have in order to implement this sort of flow control model. Instead, PCI Express uses a flow control credit model. Data Link Layer Packets (DLLPs) are exchanged between link mates indicating how much free space is available for various types of traffic. This information is exchanged at initialization, and then updated throughout the active time of the link. The exchange of this information allows the transmitter to know how much traffic it can allow on to the link, and when the transmitter needs to throttle that traffic to avoid an overflow condition at the receiver.

Flow control differentiates between various types of TLPs and allocates separate credit pools for each type. TLPs are divided up into the following types for flow control purposes: posted request header (PH), posted request data (PD), non-posted request header (NPH), non-posted request data (NPD), completion header (CplH), and completion data (CplD). Posted request credits (Px) apply to message and memory write requests. Non-posted request credits (NPx) apply to IO and configuration write, as well as all read requests. Completion credits (Cplx) apply to the completions associated with a corresponding request.

For the various data credits, the corresponding unit of credit is equal to 16 bytes of data (that is to say that 1 CplD unit equals 16 bytes of completion data). For the various header credits, the corresponding unit of credit is the maximum-size header plus TLP digest. Table 9.2 identifies the credits associated with the various types of traffic.

Table 9.2   TLP Flow Control Credits

TLP	Credits Consumed
Memory, I/O, configuration read request	1 NPH
Memory write request	1 PH + n PD
I/O, configuration write request	1 NPH + 1 NPD (note: size of data written for these TLPs is never more than one aligned DWord)
Message request without data	1 PH
Message request with data	1 PH + n PD
Memory read completion	1 CplH + n CPLD
I/O, configuration read completions	1 CplH + 1 CPLD
I/O, configuration write completions	1 CplH

The n units used for the data credits are calculated by rounding up the data length by 16 bytes. For example, a memory read completion with a data length of 10 DWords (40 bytes) uses 1 CplH unit and 3 ($40/16 = 2.5$, which rounds up to 3) CplD units. Please note that there are no credits and hence no flow control processes for DLLPs. The receiver must process these packets at the rate that they arrive.

Each virtual channel has independent flow control, and thus maintains independent flow control pools (buffers) for PH, PD, NPH, NPD, CplH, and CplD credits. Each device autonomously initializes the flow control for its default virtual channel (VC0). As discussed in Chapter 7, this is done during the DL_Init portion of the Data Link Layer state machine. The initialization procedures for other virtual channels flow control are quite similar to that of VC0, except that VC0 undergoes initialization by default (and before the link is considered active) while other virtual channels undergo initialization after the link is active. Once enabled by software, multiple virtual channels may progress through the various stages of initialization simultaneously. They need not initialize in numeric VC ID order (that is to say, VC1 initializes before VC2 initializes before VC3, and so on) nor does one channel's initialization need to complete before another can begin (aside from VC0, which must be initialized before the link is considered active). Additionally, since VC0 is active prior to the initialization of any other virtual channels, there may already be TLP traffic flowing across that virtual channel. Such traffic has no direct impact on the initialization procedures for other virtual channels. Additional details on virtual channel and flow control initialization are contained later in this chapter.

Flow Control Credits

As discussed previously, there are six types of flow control credits: PH, PD, NPH, NPD, CplH, and CplD. Initialization takes care of providing the initial values for each of these credit types. This is accomplished via the Init_FC1 and Init_FC2 DLLPs. During this initialization, receivers must initially advertise virtual channel credit values equal to or greater than those shown in Table 9.3.

Table 9.3   Minimum Initial Flow Control Credit Advertisements

Credit Type	Minimum Advertisement
PH	1 unit – credit value of 01h
PD	Largest possible setting of the Max_Payload_Size for the component divided by the FC unit size (16 bytes)
	For example, if the Max_Data_Payload size is 1024 bytes, the smallest permissible initial credit value would be 040h (64 decimal)
NPH	1 unit – credit value of 01h
NPD	1 unit – credit value of 01h
CplH	Switch: 1 unit – credit value of 01h
	Root complex and endpoint: infinite FC units – initial credit value of all 0s – this is interpreted by the transmitter as infinite, which allows it to never throttle
CplD	Switch: Largest possible setting of the Max_Payload_Size for the component divided by the FC unit size (16 bytes), or the largest read request the unit will ever generate (whichever is smaller)
	Root complex and endpoint: infinite FC units – initial credit value of all 0s – this is interpreted by the transmitter as infinite, which allows it to never throttle

If an infinite credit advertisement is made during initialization, no flow control updates (UpdateFC DLLPs) are required following initialization. Since InitFC and UpdateFC DLLPs contain the credits for both header and data credits for a given type, this really only holds true if both the header and data are advertised as infinite. In the case where only one, for example NPD, is advertised as infinite, UpdateFCs are still required for NPH values. In this example, UpdateFC-NP packets always need to have a value of zero (infinite) for the NP data credits.

For devices that are likely to receive streams of TLPs, it is desirable to implement receive buffers larger than the minimum required. This should help to avoid throttling due to lack of available credits. Likewise, UpdateFC packets need to be passed from receiver to transmitter in a timely fashion.

Flow Control at the Transmitter

For each credit type, there are two quantities that the transmit side of the Transaction Layer must check to properly implement flow control: Credits_Consumed and Credit_Limit. Credits_Consumed, which is initially set to 0 after initialization, tracks the total number of flow control credits that have been consumed by TLPs. Credit_Limit indicates the most recent number of flow control units legally advertised by a link mate. This value is first set during flow control initialization and may be updated via UpdateFC packets.

Prior to transmitting any TLP, the Transaction Layer must first determine if there are sufficient outstanding credits for that TLP. If the transmitter does not have enough credits, it must block the transmission of that TLP. This may stall other TLPs that use that same virtual channel. The transmitter must follow the ordering and deadlock avoidance rules detailed earlier in this chapter to allow certain types of TLPs to bypass others if the latter are blocked. As mentioned previously, there are no ordering or blocking relationships between traffic on different virtual channels. If there are not enough flow control credits for transmission of a given transaction, transactions that use other traffic classes/virtual channels are not impacted.

A Quick Example of Flow Control Credits

At initialization, Device B indicates that it has 04h PH credits and 040h PD credits. Device A logs those in its PH and PD Credit_Limit counters/registers. After initialization, Device A has set its PH and PD Credits_Consumed counters/registers to zero.

Device A then sends out two P requests (sequence numbers #1 and #2) that each utilizes a single PH unit and 10h PD units. It therefore updates its PH and PD Credits_Consumed counters/registers to 02h and 20h, respectively.

Device A now wants to send out another P request (sequence #3) that uses a single PH unit and 30h PD units. In this example, however, the Transaction Layer of Device A must gate that TLP and not transmit it just yet. For while it has the necessary PH credits for this transaction, it does not have the proper number of PD credits left. Device B originally advertised support for 040h PD units and Device A has already sent out packets that consumed 020h of that. That leaves only 020h credits available, not enough to cover the 030h that TLP #3 requires.

Device A must gate this TLP and, based on the transaction ordering rules discussed previously, potentially stall other TLPs on the same virtual channel. Once Device B issues an UpdateFC-P packet that indicates that one or both of the outstanding TLPs (sequence #'s 1 and/or 2) has been cleared from its queues, Device A can release TLP #3 and transmit it as appropriate.

It should be noted that return of flow control credits does not necessarily mean that the TLP has reached its final destination or that the associated request/completion has been processed. It simply means that the buffer or queue space allocated to that TLP at the receiver has been cleared. In Figure 9.1, the upstream port of the switch may send an UpdateFC that indicates it has freed up the buffer space from a given TLP that is destined for the endpoint. The root complex should not imply that this has any meaning other than that the TLP has been cleared from the upstream receive buffers of the switch. That TLP may be progressing through the core logic of the switch, may be in the outgoing queue on the downstream port, or may be already received down at the endpoint.

Flow Control at the Receiver

For each credit type, there is one quantity that the receiver side of the Transaction Layer must check to properly implement flow control, Credits_Allocated. The Transaction Layer may optionally implement a Credits_Received register/counter. Credits_Allocated is initially set according to the buffer size and allocation policies of the receiver. This value is included in the InitFC and Update FC packets that are sent across to a link mate. This value is incremented as the receiver side of the Transaction Layer frees up additional buffer space by processing received TLPs. Credits_Received is an optional error-checking register or counter. Here, the Transaction Layer simply counts up all the credits (of a given type) that have been successfully received. If the receiver implements this option, it can check for receiver overflow errors (TLPs that exceeded the Credits_Allocated limit).

For finite NPH, NPD, PH, and CplH credit types, an UpdateFC packet must be scheduled for transmission if all advertised flow control units for a particular type are consumed by received TLPs. Additionally, for all finite credit types, UpdateFC packets are required if one or more units of that type are made available by processing received TLPs. When the link is in the L0 or L0s state, UpdateFC packets for all (enabled and finite) credit types must be scheduled for transmission at least every 30 microseconds. UpdateFC packets may be scheduled for transmission more often than required.

For a given implementation, it is possible that queues need not be physically implemented for all credit types on all virtual channels. For example, since non-posted writes are required to be on VC0, there is no need to implement an NPD queue on virtual channels other than VC0. For unimplemented queues, the receiver can advertise infinite flow control during initialization to eliminate the appearance of tracking flow control credits for that type.

Virtual Channels and Traffic Classes

PCI Express provides a virtual channel mechanism that, along with traffic class designations, serves to facilitate traffic flow throughout the system. The basic idea behind virtual channels is to provide independent resources (queues, buffers, and so on) that allow fully independent flow control between different virtual channels. Conceptually, traffic that flows through multiple virtual channels is multiplexed onto a single physical link, and then de-multiplexed on the receiver side.

System traffic is broken down into a variety of traffic classes (TCs). In the traffic example from earlier in the chapter, the traffic classes would consist of carpoolers, fast drivers, and slow drivers. PCI Express supports up to eight different traffic classes. Each traffic class can be assigned to a separate virtual channel (VC), which means that there can be at most eight virtual channels. Support for traffic classes and virtual channels beyond the defaults (TC0 and VC0) is optional. Each supported traffic class is assigned to a supported virtual channel for flow control purposes. TC0 is always associated with VC0, but beyond that, traffic class to virtual channel mapping is flexible and device-dependent. Although each traffic class may be mapped to a unique virtual channel, this is not a requirement. Multiple traffic classes can share a single virtual channel. However, multiple virtual channels cannot share a single traffic class, as a traffic class may only be assigned to a single virtual channel. Unlike drivers on a highway who may continually change lanes, once a TLP is assigned a traffic class it cannot change to another traffic class.

Virtual channels allow the finite physical link bandwidth to be divided up as appropriate. Each virtual channel has its own set of queues and buffers, control logic, and a credit-based mechanism to track how full or empty those buffers are on each side of the link. Thinking back to the highway example, in the real world those lanes can become congested. Some lanes may have more space for traffic to move than others. Likewise, if the receive queues and buffers for a virtual channel on one side of the link are full, then no further transactions can travel across that virtual channel until space is made available. One quick clarification at this point: unlike on a highway where a specific lane can be designated for a type of traffic (for example, a carpool lane), PCI Express traffic differentiation is entirely virtual. A x4 PCI Express interface does not identify one of its four physical lanes for high priority traffic and the other three for normal traffic. Instead, PCI Express virtual channels can be used to provide a portion (for example, 25 percent) of the total bandwidth across the whole link for a given type of traffic.

Figure 9.2 illustrates how PCI Express links can support multiple virtual channels. Each virtual channel can support one or multiple traffic classes. However, a single traffic class may not be mapped to multiple virtual channels. Again, recall that virtual channels are just that—virtual. They do not change the link width, nor do they add to the overall available bandwidth. They are simply a way to divide the total available bandwidth to help differentiate and prioritize traffic.

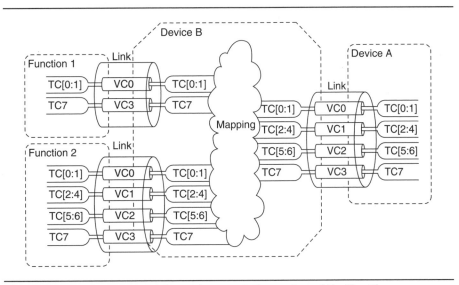

Figure 9.2 Flow Control through Virtual Channels and Traffic Classes

Since each device configures its ports independently, a device can support different numbers of virtual channels or apply different TC-to-VC mapping across its ports. This is seen quite easily in Figure 9.2. Device B has three separate ports, one upstream to the root complex, and two downstream ports to two separate functions. The link to function 1 supports only two virtual channels (VC0 and VC3) and three traffic classes (TC0, TC1 and TC7). The upstream port to the root complex and the other downstream port both support four virtual channels (VCs[0:3]) and all eight traffic classes (TCs[0:7]).

In this example, the system software has chosen to align the virtual channels and TC-to-VC mapping on the link between the switch and function 1 to line up with the mapping seen on the other ports. That alignment is not required, however, because independent TC-to-VC mapping is required on a per port basis. In fact, it would be just as likely that the system software would call the two virtual channels between the switch and function 1 as VC0 and VC1, and map traffic classes [0:6] to VC0 and TC7 to VC1. The switch's mapping logic would then need to take care of properly aligning that traffic to the appropriate virtual channel on the upstream link.

Traffic Class to Virtual Channel Mapping

Each TLP has a traffic class associated with it via the TC field (bits 6:4 of byte 1) in the header. However, there is never a specific virtual channel value associated with each TLP. The association (mapping) of a TLP to a virtual channel is not done at the TLP level. Rather, each port is responsible for mapping each TLP to the appropriate virtual channel on its link. During configuration, system software is responsible for determining and assigning the appropriate number of virtual channels per port. This is done through the examination of the VC capability registers within each device (refer to Chapter 10). The two ports that share a link need to be configured to use the same number of virtual channels as well as the same TC-to-VC mapping. Figure 9.3 illustrates an example of what two ports could look like prior to virtual channel and traffic class configuration.

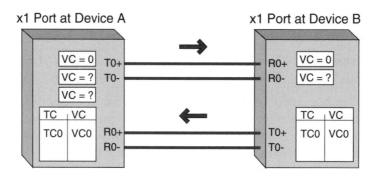

Figure 9.3   Virtual Channel and Traffic Class Setup Prior to Configuration

In the above example, the port on Device A advertises support for up to three virtual channels, while the port on Device B advertises support for two virtual channels. Since these two ports share a link, they need to have a common virtual channel and TC-to-VC mapping configuration. As such, Device A's port is only capable of utilizing two virtual channels and must use the same TC-to-VC mapping as Device B. An example of how these two ports could be configured is shown in Figure 9.4.

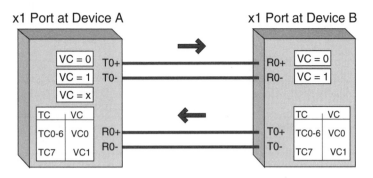

Figure 9.4   Virtual Channel and Traffic Class Setup after Configuration

The ports on both devices are configured to support two virtual channels, VC0 and VC1. Mapping TC0 to VC0 is required by the specification, but the rest of the mapping is specific to the system software. In the above example, traffic classes zero through six map to VC0, while TC7 maps to VC1. Again, note that there does not need to be a one to one relationship between traffic classes and virtual channels and that the mapping is quite flexible.

Aside from the requirement of TC0 on VC0, system software has a great amount of flexibility in implementing a variety of traffic class to virtual channel mapping options. In this example, system software seems to have identified TC7 as a high priority traffic class and allocated that traffic class its own virtual channel (just like a carpool lane). System software could have just as easily prioritized both traffic classes six and seven and allowed those two traffic classes to share their own virtual channel (for example, motorcyclists and carpoolers get to use the carpool lane).

There are some rules that system software must follow when mapping the various traffic classes to the supported virtual channels. First, every traffic class that is supported must be mapped to a virtual channel. Also, as previously mentioned, TC0 must be mapped to VC0. The other supported traffic classes have flexibility during their assignment to a virtual channel. Lastly, both ports that share a link must map their traffic classes to virtual channels in an identical fashion. Additional examples of traffic class to virtual channel mapping are shown in Table 9.4.

Table 9.4   Examples of Traffic Class to Virtual Channel Associations

Supported VCs	TC/VC Mapping Options
VC0	TC(0-7) mapped to VC0
VC0, VC1	TC(0-6) mapped to VC0, TC7 mapped to VC1
VC0 through VC3	TC(0-1) mapped to VC0, TC(2-4) mapped to VC1, TC(5-6) mapped to VC2, TC7 mapped to VC3
VC0 through VC7	TC0 mapped to VC0, TC1 mapped to VC1 … TC7 mapped to VC7

Again, these are example associations and not the only possible traffic class to virtual channel associations in these configurations.

There are several additional traffic class/virtual channel configuration details to make note of. As seen in Figure 9.3, all ports must support VC0 and map TC0 to that virtual channel by default. This allows traffic to flow across the link without (or prior to) any VC-specific hardware or software configuration. Secondly, implementations may adjust their buffering per virtual channel based on implementation-specific policies. For example, in Figure 9.4, the queues or buffers in Device A that are identified with a VC ID of x may be reassigned to provide additional buffering for VC0 or VC1, or they may be left unassigned and unused.

Virtual Channel Initialization

All virtual channels follow a similar initialization path, with the major exception being that VC0 goes through this process by default. There are two states in the initialization process, defined as FC_Init1 and FC_Init2. As such, there are two flow control DLLPs that are associated with these two stages, InitFC1 and InitFC2 (discussed in Chapter 7). Figure 9.5 shows the flowchart for flow control initialization state FC_Init1.

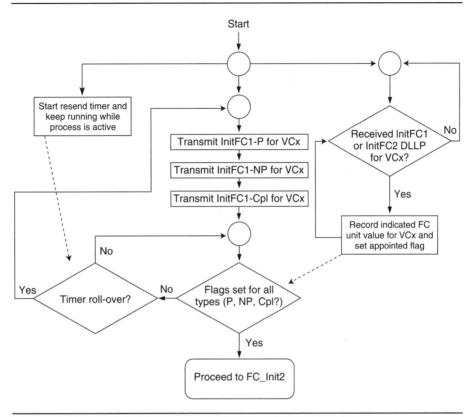

Figure 9.5   Flow Control Initialization State FC_Init1

Entrance to FC_Init1 occurs upon entrance to the DL_Init state (for VC0), or when software enables a virtual channel (for all other virtual channels). While in FC_Init1, the Transaction Layer must block transmission of all TLPs that utilize that virtual channel. While in this state, the device must first transmit the InitFC1-P DLLP, then InitFC1-NP, and then InitFC1-Cpl. This sequence must progress in this order and must not be interrupted. While in this state for VC0 no other traffic is possible. As such, this pattern should be retransmitted in this order continuously until exit into FC_Init2. For other virtual channels, this pattern is not repeated continuously. Since other traffic may wish to use the link during nonzero virtual channel initialization, this pattern does not need to be repeated continuously, but it does need to be repeated (uninterrupted) at least every 17 microseconds while in this initialization state.

While in this state, the FC logic also processes incoming InitFC1 (and InitFC2) DLLPs. Upon receipt of an InitFC DLLP, the device records the appropriate flow control unit value. Each InitFC packet contains a value for both the header units and data payload units. Once the device has recorded values for all types of credits for a given virtual channel (P, NP and Cpl, both header and data), it sets a flag (FI1) to indicate that the virtual channel has successfully completed FC_Init1. As long as a trio of InitFC1 packets are not in the process of being transmitted, the device proceeds to the FC_Init2 stage. Figure 9.6 shows the flowchart for flow control initialization state FC_Init2.

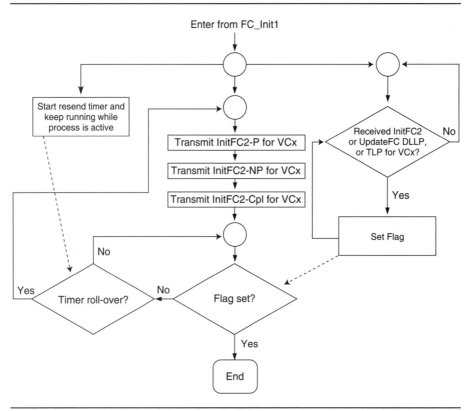

Figure 9.6   Flow Control Initialization State FC_Init2

For all virtual channels, the entrance to FC_Init2 occurs after successful completion of the FC_Init1 stage. While in FC_Init2, the Transaction Layer no longer needs to block transmission of TLPs that use that virtual channel. While in this state, the device must first transmit InitFC2-P, then InitFC2-NP, and then InitFC2-Cpl. This sequence must progress in this order and must not be interrupted. While in this state for VC0, this pattern should be retransmitted in this order continuously until successful completion of FC_Init2. For other virtual channels, this pattern is not repeated continuously, but is repeated uninterrupted at least every 17 microseconds until FC_Init2 is completed.

While in this state, it is also necessary to process incoming InitFC2 DLLPs. The values contained in the DLLP can be ignored, and InitFC1 packets are ignored entirely. Receiving any InitFC2 DLLP for a given virtual channel should set a flag (FI2) that terminates FC_Init2 and the flow control initialization process. The FI2 flag is dependent on receipt of a single Init_FC2 DLLP, and not all three (P, NP and Cpl). Additionally, the FC_Init2 flag may also be set upon receipt of any TLP or UpdateFC DLLP that uses that virtual channel.

What exactly is the purpose of this FC_Init2 state? It seems as if it is just retransmitting the same flow control DLLPs, but with a single bit flipped to indicate that it is in a new state. The purpose for this state is to ensure that both devices on a link can successfully complete the flow control initialization process. Without it, it could be possible for one device to make it through flow control while its link mate had not. For example, say that there is no FC_Init2 state and a device can proceed directly from FC_Init1 to normal operation mode. While in FC_Init1, Device A transmits its three InitFC1 DLLPs to Device B and vice versa. Device B successfully receives all three DLLPs and proceeds on to normal operation. Unfortunately, one of Device B's flow control DLLPs gets lost on its way to Device A. Since Device A has not received all three types of flow control DLLPs, it stays in FC_Init1 and continues to transmit flow control DLLPs. Device B is no longer transmitting flow control initialization packets, so Device A never gets out of FC_Init1 and all traffic from Device A to B is blocked.

Including the FC_Init2 state ensures that both devices can successfully complete the flow control initialization process. In the above example, Device B would transfer into the FC_Init2 state and could begin to transmit TLPs and other DLLPs. However, Device B still needs to periodically transmit FC2 DLLPs for all three flow control types (P, NP, Cpl). If Device A does not see the three original FC1 DLLPs, it can still eventually complete FC_Init1 since it periodically receives FC2 packets that contain the needed flow control configuration information.

Tying this all together, what would a real flow control initialization look like? Figure 9.7 illustrates the first step in an example flow control initialization.

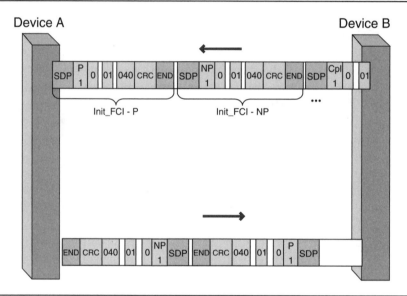

Figure 9.7   Flow Control Initialization Example: Step 1

Devices A and B exit out of reset and begin the default initialization of VC0. In this example, Device B happens to begin the initialization first, so it begins to transmit Init_FC1 packets before Device A does. It starts with an SDP symbol (Start DLLP Packet—refer to Chapter 8 for additional details on framing) and then begins to transmit the DLLP itself. The first packet that Device B must transmit is Init_FC1 for type P. It does so, differentiating it as an FC1 initialization packet for credit type P in the first four bits of the DLLP (refer to Chapter 7 for more details on the format of these DLLPs). Device B then indicates that this packet pertains to VC0 by placing a 0 in the DLLP's VC ID field. The next portions of the packet identify that Device B can support 01h (one decimal) posted header request units and 040h (64 decimal) posted request data units. At 16 bytes per unit, this equates to a maximum of 1024 bytes of data payload. Following this information is the CRC that is associated with this DLLP. The Init_FC1-P DLLP then completes with the END framing symbol. Device B continues on with the transmission of the Init_FC1-NP and Init_FC1-Cpl DLLPs.

Device A also begins transmitting Init_FC1 DLLPs, but does so just a little later than Device B. At the point in time of this example, Device A has just completed the transmission of the second initialization packet, Init_FC1-NP DLLP, whereas Device B is already well into the transmission of the third packet, Init_FC1-Cpl DLLP. Nonetheless, Device A identifies its flow control capabilities in the specified manner. Like Device B, Device A advertises support for just a single PH and NPH unit, and 40h PD and NPD units. Recall that these values are the minimum permitted values for each of these types of flow control credit (as shown in Table 9.3).

Now that each device has started to transmit its InitFC1 DLLPs properly, what happens once these packets make it to the device on the other side? Figure 9.8 demonstrates what occurs once these packets start to be processed.

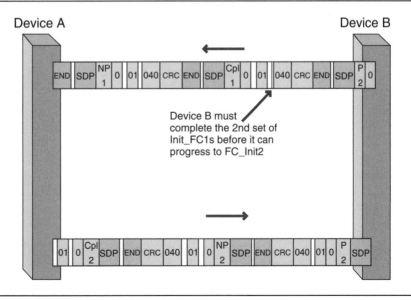

Figure 9.8   Flow Control Initialization Example: Step 2

Device B has sent out all three Init_FC1 packets (P, NP, and Cpl), but has not yet received all three Init_FC1 packets from Device A. This means that Device B cannot yet exit from the FC_Init1 state and must therefore retransmit all three Init_FC1 packets. Device A, on the other hand, has already received all three Init_FC1 packets by the time it completes transmitting its own Init_FC1 packets. This means that Device A can exit from the FC_Init1 state after only one pass and proceed on to FC_Init2.

In Figure 9.8, Device A has begun to send out Init_FC2 packets. It begins, as required, with the P type. Only this time, it is identified as an Init_FC2 packet and not an Init_FC1. It proceeds to send out the Init_FC2 packet for NP and has started to send out the Init_FC2 packet for Cpl at the time of this example.

Device B, on the other hand, has had to continue through the second transmission of Init_FC1 packets. Once it completes the set of three, it can transition to FC_Init2 and begin to transmit Init_FC2 packets. In this example, Device B has just started to send out an Init_FC2 packet for type P.

Now that each device has entered into the FC_Init2 stage, what do things look like as they exit the flow control initialization and enter into normal link operation? Figure 9.9 illustrates the completion of the flow control initialization process.

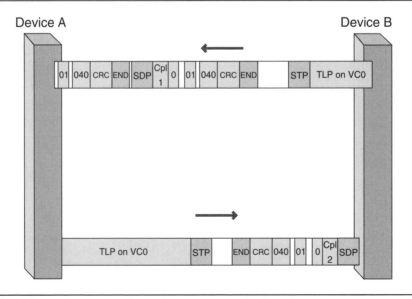

Figure 9.9   Flow Control Initialization Example: Step 3

Device A has sent out all three Init_FC2 packets (P, NP, and Cpl), but has not yet received all three Init_FC2 packets from Device B. As discussed previously, however, exit from FC_Init2 is not dependent on receiving all three Init_FC2 packets. Receipt of any Init_FC2 DLLP allows that device to exit from the FC_Init2 state (as long as it does not interrupt the transmission of a trio of its Init_FC2 DLLPs). As such, Device A does not need to retransmit its Init_FC2 packets and has completed the flow control initialization. If it had not successfully received and processed the first Init_FC2 DLLP from Device B by the time the transmission of its Init_FC2-Cpl was complete, Device A would have needed to retransmit all three Init_FC2 DLLPs. That was not the case in this example, and Device A begins to transmit a TLP.

Device B has already received an Init_FC2 DLLP, but must complete transmission of all three of its own Init_FC2 DLLPs. It does so, and then exits the FC_Init2 stage and begins to transmit a TLP. Please note that this entire example only demonstrates the flow control initialization for a single channel (VC0 in this example). This procedure occurs on every PCI Express link in a system, and for all virtual channels on each of those links. To keep things simple, this example did not include other traffic jumping in between the various flow control initialization procedures (as it may for nonzero VCs), nor did it include any data integrity errors within the DLLPs. A receiver ignores initialization attempts (InitFC DLLPs) for a virtual channel that has not been enabled. However, if a TLP is received that uses a TC that is not mapped to any initialized virtual channel, the receiver must report that as an error condition.

Isochronous Support

Servicing isochronous traffic requires a system to not only provide guaranteed data bandwidth, but also specified service latency. PCI Express is designed to meet the needs of isochronous traffic while assuring that other traffic is not starved for support. Isochronous support may be realized through the use of the standard flow control mechanisms described above: traffic class traffic labeling, virtual channel data transfer protocol and TC-to-VC mapping. End-to-end isochronous support also requires the support of software, since the paths between isochronous requester and completer must be configured appropriately.

Software must configure all virtual channel resources used to support the isochronous traffic to have the appropriate bandwidth and latency. For example, isochronous traffic should be allocated a traffic class and virtual channel of its own to ensure proper prioritization of this type of traffic. However, software cannot set up the virtual channel arbitration model to only service isochronous virtual channel/traffic class traffic since this would prohibit the forward progress of other packets.

There are two types of isochronous communication pathways within a PCI Express system: endpoint to root complex, and endpoint to endpoint (peer to peer). Figure 9.10 demonstrates these two models.

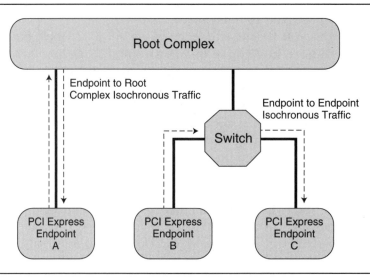

Figure 9.10   Isochronous Pathways

In this example, Device A exchanges isochronous traffic with the root complex. Peer-to-peer isochronous traffic is shown between endpoint B and endpoint C. In order to guarantee that the appropriate bandwidth and latency exists between devices supporting isochronous traffic flows, an isochronous contract must be established between the requester and completer of this type of traffic. This contract enforces both resource reservation and traffic regulation for isochronous traffic. This is necessary to solve several isochrony-related problems. First, if link bandwidth is oversubscribed, isochronous traffic may not be transmitted within an appropriate timeframe. Conversely, if there are too many isochronous transfers within a given time period, other traffic may be starved and/or isochronous flow control credits may not be returned in an appropriate timeframe. The isochronous contract is set up based upon the desired packet sizes, latencies, and period of isochronous traffic. When allocating bandwidth for isochronous traffic, only a portion of the total available bandwidth should be used, because sufficient bandwidth needs to remain available for other traffic. Additional details on the isochronous contract variables and their impact on virtual channel and traffic class configurations are contained in the *PCI Express Base Specification*.

Generally speaking, isochronous transactions follow the same rules that have been discussed in this chapter. Software just uses the mechanisms described to ensure that the isochronous traffic receives the bandwidth and latencies needed. Since isochronous traffic should be differentiated by traffic class and virtual channel, there are no direct ordering relationships between isochronous and other types of transactions. Devices that may see an isochronous traffic flow should implement proper buffer sizes to ensure that normal, uniform isochronous traffic does not get backed up and require throttling. If the isochronous traffic flow is bursty (lots of isochronous traffic at once), throttling may occur, so long as the acceptance of the traffic is uniform (and according to the isochronous contract). Chapter 10 gives additional explanations of the software setup for isochronous traffic.

Chapter 10

PCI Express Software Overview

Those parts of the system that you can hit with a hammer are called hardware; those program instructions that you can only curse at are called software.

—Anonymous

This chapter introduces the PCI Express software architecture. It starts off with an explanation of device and system configuration. This addresses the basics of how PCI Express devices can live within the existing PCI configuration environment, as well as how PCI Express allows for additional configuration capabilities. Next, the chapter goes into the baseline and advanced error reporting capabilities offered by the architecture. Finally, the chapter contains a discussion of how the software architecture supports some of the newer features, such as power management, hot plug, and isochrony.

Software Initialization and Configuration

The *PCI Express Base Specification* defines two models for configuration space access. The first is a PCI-compatible configuration mechanism that supports 100 percent binary compatibility with operating systems that support the *PCI Local Bus Specification, Revision 2.3* configuration model. Support for this model should ease the adoption of PCI Express because it removes the dependency on operating system support for PCI Express to have baseline functionality. The second PCI Express configuration model is referred to as the enhanced mechanism. The enhanced mechanism increases the size of available configuration space and provides some optimizations for access to that space.

Refresher on PCI Configuration

To maintain compatibility with the existing PCI software configuration mechanisms, all PCI Express devices have a PCI compatible configuration space representation. Recall that all PCI device functions reside on a PCI bus and respond to a specified device and function number. A single physical PCI device may consist of and respond to multiple (up to eight) logical functions. All configuration requests are routed and accepted based on these three variables: PCI bus number, device number, and function number. Within each logical PCI function there are configuration registers that are accessed based on the register address. For each logical function, PCI provides support for 256 bytes of configuration space. A portion of the configuration space is set aside for a configuration header.

The PCI configuration model begins with a host/PCI bridge that connects the host bus to PCI bus number zero. PCI devices may directly reside on that PCI bus. Alternatively, PCI can be "fanned out" through the use of PCI-PCI bridges. These bridges act as the intermediary between a primary PCI bus (the PCI bus closer to the host bus) and a secondary PCI bus (further away from the host bus). PCI-PCI bridges may be cascaded, which is to say that the secondary bus of one PCI-PCI bridge may be the primary bus of another PCI-PCI bridge. During configuration, system software "walks" the PCI bus to determine which logical busses, devices, and functions are present. Each PCI bridge (including the host/PCI bridge) must keep track of its assigned primary bus number and secondary bus number. Additionally, each bridge must keep track of the subordinate bus associated with that bridge in order to properly route traffic to devices behind PCI-PCI bridges.

The *PCI Local Bus Specification, Revision 2.3* differentiates between two different configuration types, Type 0 and Type 1. Type 0 configuration transactions are destined for a target that resides on that given PCI bus. If the configuration target resides behind a PCI-PCI bridge (or multiple PCI-PCI bridges), the configuration transaction passes through the PCI bus hierarchy as a Type 1 transaction. A configuration transaction of this type indicates that only the PCI-PCI bridges on that bus need to pay attention to the configuration transaction. If the target PCI bus for the configuration is a bridge's subordinate but not secondary bus, the bridge claims the transaction from its primary bus and forwards it along to its secondary bus (still as a Type 1). If the target PCI bus for the configuration is a bridge's secondary bus, the bridge claims the transaction from its primary bus and forwards it along to its secondary bus, but only after modifying it to a Type 0 configuration transaction. This indicates that the devices on that bus need to determine whether they should claim that transaction. Please refer to the *PCI Local Bus Specification, Revision 2.3* for additional details on PCI configuration.

For PCI Express, each link within the system originates from a *virtual* PCI-PCI bridge and is mapped as the secondary side of that bridge. Figure 10.1 shows an example of how this configuration mechanism applies to a PCI Express switch. In this example, the upstream PCI Express link that feeds the primary side of the upstream bridge originates from the secondary side of a virtual PCI bridge (either from the root complex or another switch). A PCI Express endpoint is represented as a single logical device with one or more functions.

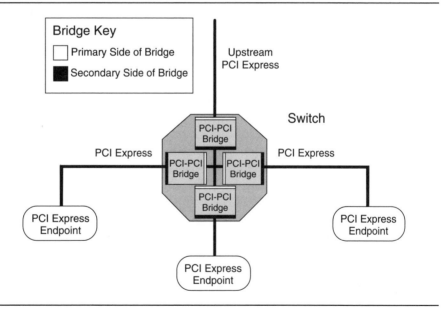

Figure 10.1   PCI Configuration Representation of a PCI Express Switch

Recall that Type 1 configuration transactions are intended for PCI bridges, and must be turned into Type 0 configuration transactions when they reach the appropriate PCI logical bus. If an endpoint sees a Type 1 configuration request, it handles the request as an unsupported request. Additionally, the only Type 0 configuration requests that an endpoint receives should be for a valid local configuration space. This does not mean, however, that endpoints can assume that all Type 0 transactions seen are valid and intended for their configuration space. The endpoint still must check the bus, device, function, register, and extended register addresses associated with the configuration request. If the request is not valid, the device should not process the transaction and handle it as an unsupported request.

Configuration Mechanisms

PCI allows 256 bytes of configuration space for each device function within the system. PCI Express extends the allowable configuration space to 4096 bytes per device function, but does so in a way that maintains compatibility with existing PCI enumeration and configuration software. This is accomplished by dividing the PCI Express configuration space into two regions, the PCI compatible region and the extended region.

The PCI compatible region is made up of the first 256 bytes of a device's configuration space. This area can be accessed via the traditional configuration mechanism (as defined in the *PCI Local Bus Specification, Revision 2.3*) or the new PCI Express enhanced mechanism. The extended region of configuration space consists of the configuration space between 256 and 4096 bytes. This area can be accessed only through the enhanced PCI Express mechanism, and not via the traditional PCI access mechanism. This is shown in Figure 10.2. The extension of the configuration space is useful for complex devices that require large amounts of registers to control and monitor the device (for example, a Memory Controller Hub). With only 256 bytes of configuration space offered by PCI, these devices may need to be implemented as multiple device or multifunctional devices, just to have enough configuration space.

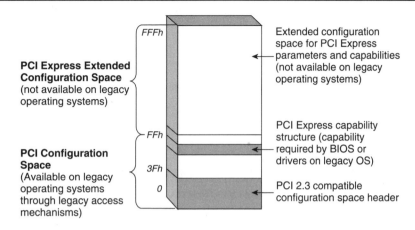

Figure 10.2   PCI Express Configuration Space Layout

PCI Compatible Configuration Mechanism

The PCI compatible configuration mechanism follows the configuration space programming model defined in the *PCI Local Bus Specification, Revision 2.3*. By supporting this model, PCI Express devices are compliant with existing bus enumeration and configuration software. As mentioned previously, support for this model should ease the adoption of PCI Express, as it removes the dependency on new operating system support for baseline functionality.

PCI Express devices are required to implement a configuration register space similar to PCI 2.3 devices. There are some differences in this space (which are detailed in the *PCI Express Base Specification*), but PCI Express configuration registers are generally organized to follow the format and behavior identified in the *PCI Local Bus Specification, Revision 2.3* for the first 256 bytes.

Both the legacy PCI configuration access mechanism and the enhanced PCI Express configuration access mechanism use a similar request format. The main difference between the two is that accesses that use the PCI configuration access model must fill the Extended Register Address field with all 0s.

PCI Express Enhanced Configuration Mechanism

The enhanced PCI Express configuration access mechanism uses a flat memory-mapped address space to access device configuration registers. For these transactions, the memory address determines the configuration register that is being addressed. The memory data contains the contents for the configuration register being accessed. The mapping from memory address A[27:0] to PCI Express configuration space is shown in Table 10.1.

Table 10.1   Enhanced Configuration Address Mapping

Memory Address	PCI Express Configuration Space
A [27:20]	Bus Number
A [19:15]	Device Number
A [14:12]	Function Number
A [11:8]	Extended Register Number
A [7:2]	Register Number
A [1:0]	Along with size of access, used to generate Byte Enables

Again, both the enhanced PCI Express and the PCI compatible access mechanisms use this request format. PCI compatible configuration requests must fill the Extended Register Address field with all 0s.

The PCI Express host bridge is required to translate the memory-mapped PCI Express configuration accesses from the host processor to legitimate PCI Express configuration transactions. Refer to Chapter 6 for additional details on how configuration transactions are communicated through PCI Express.

Error Reporting

This section explains the error signaling and logging requirements for PCI Express. PCI Express defines two error reporting mechanisms. The first is referred to as baseline and defines the minimum error reporting capabilities required by all PCI Express devices. The second is referred to as advanced error reporting and allows for more robust error reporting. Advanced error reporting requires specific capability structures within the configuration space. This is touched upon briefly in this section, but not to the same level of detail as in the *PCI Express Base Specification*.

In order to maintain compatibility with existing software that is not aware of PCI Express, PCI Express errors are mapped to existing PCI reporting mechanisms. Naturally, this legacy software would not have access to the advanced error reporting capabilities offered by PCI Express.

Error Classification

There are two types of PCI Express errors: uncorrectable errors and correctable errors. Uncorrectable errors are further classified as either fatal or nonfatal. Specifying these error types provides the platform with a method for dealing with the error in a suitable fashion. For instance, if a correctable error such as a bad TLP (due to an LCRC error) is reported, the platform may respond with some monitoring software to determine the frequency of the TLP errors. If the errors become frequent enough, the software may initiate a link specific reset (such as retraining the link). Conversely, if a fatal error is detected, the platform may initiate a system-wide reset. These responses are presented as examples. It is up to platform designers to determine appropriate platform responses to error conditions.

Correctable errors are errors where the PCI Express protocol can recover without any loss of information. Hardware corrects these errors (for example, through a Data Link Layer initiated retry attempt for a bad LCRC on a TLP). As mentioned previously, logging the frequency of these types of errors may be useful for understanding the overall health of a link.

Uncorrectable errors are identified as errors that impact the functionality of the interface. Fatal errors are uncorrectable errors that render a given link unreliable. Handling of fatal errors is platform-specific, and may require a link reset to return to a reliable condition. Nonfatal errors are uncorrectable errors that render a given transaction unreliable, but do not otherwise impact the reliability of the link. Differentiating between fatal and nonfatal errors allows system software greater flexibility when dealing with uncorrectable errors. For example, if an error is deemed to be nonfatal, system software can react in a manner that does not upset (or reset) the link and other transactions already in progress. Table 10.2 shows the various PCI Express errors.

Table 10.2   Error Types

	Error Name	Default Severity	Detecting Agent Action
Physical Layer	Receive Error	Correctable	*Receiver (if checking):* Send ERR_COR to root complex
	Training Error	Uncorrectable (Fatal)	If checking, send ERR_FATAL to root complex
Data Link Layer	Bad TLP	Correctable	*Receiver:* Send ERR_COR to root complex
	Bad DLLP		*Receiver:* Send ERR_COR to root complex
	Replay Timeout		*Transmitter:* Send ERR_COR to root complex
	Replay Num Rollover		*Transmitter:* Send ERR_COR to root complex
	Data Link Layer Protocol Error	Uncorrectable (Fatal)	If checking, send ERR_FATAL to root complex
Transaction Layer	Poisoned TLP Received	Uncorrectable (Nonfatal)	*Receiver (if data poisoning is supported):* Send ERR_NONFATAL to root complex Log the header of the poisoned TLP
	ECRC Check Failed		*Receiver:* Send ERR_NONFATAL to root complex Log the header of the TLP that encountered the ECRC error
	Unsupported Request		*Request Receiver:* Send ERR_NONFATAL to root complex Log the header of the TLP that caused the error
	Completion Timeout		*Requester:* Send ERR_NONFATAL to root complex Log the header of the completion that encountered the error

Table 10.3   Error Types (continued)

	Error Name	Default Severity	Detecting Agent Action
Transaction Layer (continued)	Completer Abort	Uncorrectable (Nonfatal) (continued)	*Completer:*
			Send ERR_NONFATAL to root complex
			Log the header of the completion that encountered the error
	Unexpected Completion		*Receiver:*
			Send ERR_NONFATAL to root complex
			Log the header of the completion that encountered the error
			This error is a result of misrouting
	Receiver Overflow	Uncorrectable (Fatal)	*Receiver (if checking):*
			Send ERR_FATAL to root complex
	Flow Control Protocol Error		*Receiver (if checking):*
			Send ERR_FATAL to root complex
	Malformed TLP		*Receiver:*
			Send ERR_FATAL to root complex
			Log the header of the TLP that encountered the error

Error Signaling

The PCI Express device that detects an error is responsible for the appropriate signaling of that error. PCI Express provides two mechanisms for devices to alert the system or the initiating device that an error has occurred. The first mechanism is through the Completion Status field in the completion header. As discussed in Chapter 6, the completion packet indicates if the request has been completed successfully. Signaling an error in this manner allows the requester to associate that error with a specific request.

The second method for error signaling is through in-band error messages. These messages are sent to the root complex in order to "advertise" that an error of a particular severity has occurred. These messages are routed up to the root complex and indicate the severity of the error (correctable versus fatal versus nonfatal) as well as the ID of the initiator of the error message. If multiple error messages of the same type are detected, the corresponding error messages may be merged into a single error message. Error messages of differing severity (or from differing initiators) may not be merged together. Refer to Chapter 6 for additional details on the format and details of error messages. Once the root complex receives the error message, it is responsible for translating the error into the appropriate system event.

Baseline error handling does not allow for severity programming, but advanced error reporting allows a device to identify each uncorrectable error as either fatal or nonfatal. This is accomplished via the Uncorrectable Errors Severity register that is implemented if a device supports advanced error reporting.

Error messages may be blocked through the use of error masking. When an error is masked, the status bit for that type of error is still affected by an error detection, but no message is sent out to the root complex. Devices with advanced error reporting capabilities can independently mask or transmit different error conditions.

Advanced Error Capabilities Configuration

Devices that implement advanced error reporting need to implement an advanced error reporting capability structure within their configuration space. Figure 10.3 shows the basic format for this capability structure. Please note that some registers are only required for ports within a root complex.

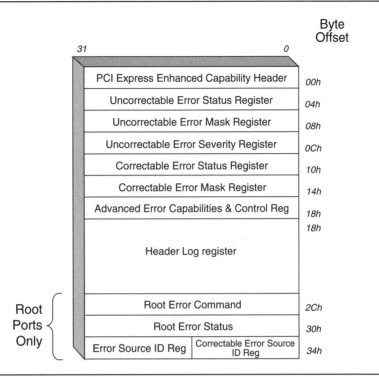

Figure 10.3   PCI Express Advanced Error Reporting Extended Capability
Structure

The PCI Express Enhanced Capability header is detailed in the specification and uses a Capability ID of 0001h to indicate it as an advanced
error reporting structure. The error status registers (Uncorrectable Error
Status register and Correctable Error Status register) indicate if a particular type of error has occurred. The mask registers (Uncorrectable Error
Mask register and Correctable Error Mask register) control whether that
particular type of error is reported. The Uncorrectable Error Severity register identifies if an uncorrectable error is reported as fatal or nonfatal. All
of these registers call out the error types shown in Table 10.2 (that is to
say, all of the uncorrectable errors shown in that table have a bit associated with them in each of the uncorrectable error registers).

The Advanced Error Capabilities and Control register takes care of some of the housekeeping associated with advanced error reporting. It contains a pointer to the first error reported (since the error status registers may have more than one error logged at a time). It also details the ECRC capabilities of the device. The Header Log register captures the header for the TLP that encounters an error. Table 10.2 identifies the errors that make use of this register.

Root complexes that support advanced error reporting must implement several additional registers. Among them is the Root Error Command and Root Error Status registers that allow the root complex to differentiate the system response to a given error severity. Finally, if supporting advanced error reporting, the root complex also implements registers to log the Requester ID if either a correctable or uncorrectable error is received.

Error Logging

Figure 10.4 shows the sequence for signaling and logging a PCI Express error. The boxes shaded in gray are only for advanced error handling and not required for baseline error handling.

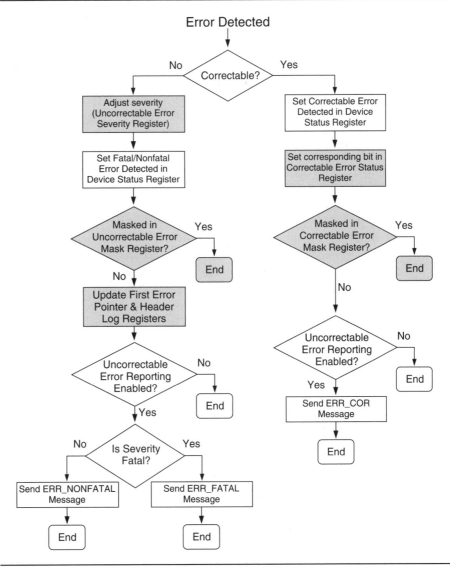

Figure 10.4   PCI Express Error Handling Sequence

Devices that do not support the advanced error handling ignore the boxes shaded in gray and only follow the flow shown in the white boxes. Some errors are also reported using the PCI compatible configuration registers, using the parity error and system error status bits (refer to the *PCI Express Base Specification* for full details on this topic).

Software Particulars for Key PCI Express Features

Like the features of any new interconnect, most of the new features of PCI Express require some level of software involvement in order to configure and/or sustain the feature functionality. The introduction of these key features depends on the level of software support available at technology introduction. For the purpose of this discussion, two levels of software support are discussed. The first level is associated with features that can be enabled by means of new drivers and BIOS code working in legacy operating systems, or in other words operating systems that are unaware of PCI Express. The second level is associated with features that require operating systems that support the PCI Express enhanced configuration mechanism. For the most part, the line between these two levels of support is drawn between where the PCI compatible configuration space ends and the PCI Express expanded configuration space begins. In other words, which features are accessible through the PCI compatible configuration mechanism and which are accessible only through the PCI Express enhanced configuration mechanism.

PCI Express Power Management

PCI Express power management can be supported directly by operating systems that are unaware of PCI Express. All of the status and configuration registers for PCI Express power management are located within the first 256 bytes of configuration space for each PCI Express device function in the system (PCI compatible region). Since PCI Express power management is compatible with the *PCI Bus Power Management (PCI-PM) Specification Revision 1.1*, no new drivers or BIOS code is required to support the legacy PCI software-based power management functionality.

PCI Express power management introduces a new hardware-based power saving feature that is not PCI-PM compatible called *Active State Power Management* or ASPM for short. This power management capability is totally transparent to PCI power management software and uses hardware to auto-transition into various power savings states. The status and configuration registers for this feature exist within the first 256 bytes of configuration space for each PCI Express device function within the system. However, operating systems unaware of PCI Express do not have mechanisms to configure and enable this feature. ASPM can be supported on legacy operating systems through updated BIOS or drivers.

The specifics of PCI Express power management are covered in detail in Chapter 11 and therefore are not included here.

PCI Express Hot Plug

PCI Express Hot Plug is supported within the first 256 bytes of configuration space for each PCI Express device function in the system (PCI compatible region). Within this configuration space reside registers that provide the status and availability of the primary elements of the standard Hot Plug usage model defined in the *PCI Standard Hot-Plug Controller and Subsystem Specification, Rev 1.0* (see Table 10.3). For a full description of each element please refer to the *PCI Express Base Specification.*

Table 10.4   Primary Elements of the Standard Hot Plug Usage Model

Primary Element	Objective
Indicators	Reveal the power and attention state of the slot
Manually Operated Retention Latches (MRLs)	Hold add-in cards in place
MRL Sensor	Allows the port and system software to detect a change in the MRL state
Electromechanical Interlock	Prevents add-in cards from being removed while the slot is powered
Attention Button	Notifies the system that a Hot Plug event is desired
Software User Interface	Notifies the system that a Hot Plug event is desired
Slot Numbering	Provides visual identification of slots

PCI Express adopts the standard usage model for several reasons. One of the primary reasons, unrelated to software, is the ability to preserve the existing dominant Hot Plug usage model that many customers have become used to. Another reason is the ability to reuse software infrastructure and flow processes already defined for legacy Hot Plug implementations with PCI-X.

Software Considerations for Hot Plug Configurations and Event Management

PCI Express-aware operating systems will likely include support for Hot Plug. However, BIOS/firmware code and device drivers on legacy ACPI-capable operating systems can be updated to configure and comprehend Hot Plug events. In order to properly configure and enable PCI Express Hot Plug, a BIOS/Firmware or device driver must query each PCI Express device to understand whether or not Hot Plug is supported and what elements are available. Software achieves this by examining the Slot Capabilities register (offset 14h) which is part of the PCI Express Capabilities Structure (see Figure 10.2). The key Hot Plug abilities reported through this register are as follows:

1. Whether or not the slot supports Hot Plug

2. Whether or not the device supports removal without any prior notification

3. What indicators, controllers, sensors, and buttons are present

Software uses the information gathered from the Slot Capabilities register to configure the Slot Control register (offset 18h), which is also located in the PCI Express Capabilities Structure. Software configures this register to allow Hot Plug operations such as attention buttons and sensor status changes to cause Hot Plug interrupts and other Hot Plug events.

PCI Express switches and root ports use this register to configure Hot Plug operations and control Hot Plug sequences through the use of Hot Plug messages. The Slot Control register is also found in endpoint devices and is queried to determine the status of Hot Plug events.

Table 10.5 Hot Plug Signaling Messages

Message	Issued By	Description
Attention_Indicator_On	Switch/ Root Port	Sent when the Attention Indicator Control bits (7:6 of the Slot Control register) are set to 01b. The receiving endpoint device terminates the message and initiates the appropriate action, which causes the Attention Indicator located on the card to turn on.
Attention_Indicator_Off	Switch/ Root Port	Sent when the Attention Indicator Control bits (7:6 of the Slot Control register) are set to 11b. The receiving endpoint device terminates the message and initiates the appropriate action, which causes the Attention Indicator located on the card to turn off.

Table 10.6   Hot Plug Signaling Messages (continued)

Message	Issued By	Description
Attention_Indicator_Blink	Switch/ Root Port	Sent when the Attention Indicator Control bits (7:6 of the Slot Control register) are set to 10b. The receiving endpoint device terminates the message and initiates the appropriate action, which causes the Attention Indicator located on the card to blink.
Power_Indicator_On	Switch/ Root Port	Sent when the Power Indicator Control bits (9:8 of the Slot Control register) are set to 01b. The receiving endpoint device terminates the message and initiates the appropriate action, which causes the Power Indicator located on the card to turn on.
Power_Indicator_Off	Switch/ Root Port	Sent when the Power Indicator Control bits (9:8 of the Slot Control register) are set to 11b. The receiving endpoint device terminates the message and initiates the appropriate action, which causes the Power Indicator located on the card to turn off.
Power_Indicator_Blink	Switch/ Root Port	Sent when the Power Indicator Control bits (9:8 of the Slot Control register) are set to 10b. The receiving endpoint device terminates the message and initiates the appropriate action, which causes the Power Indicator located on the card to blink.
Attention_Button_Pressed	Add-in Slot Device	Sent by a device in an add-in slot that implements an Attention Button on the card to signal the Switch/Root Port to generate the Attention Button Pressed Event. The Switch Switch/Root Port terminates the message and sets the Attention Button Pressed register to 1b, which may result in an interrupt being generated.

Note: If no indicators are present on the card, the message is ignored.

If a device supports Hot Plug functionality, system interrupts and power management events are generated based upon Hot Plug activity (attention buttons being pressed, power faults, manual retention latches opening/closing) once software has enabled and configured the PCI Express device. When PCI Express Hot Plug events generate interrupts, the system Hot Plug mechanism services those interrupts. The Hot Plug mechanism is dependent upon the operating system. Legacy operating systems will likely use an ACPI implementation with vendor specific filter drivers. A contrast between a PCI Express aware and a legacy ACPI-capable operating system Hot Plug service model is provided in Figure 10.5. For additional information on ACPI refer to the *Advanced Configuration and Power Interface, Specification Revision 2.0b*.

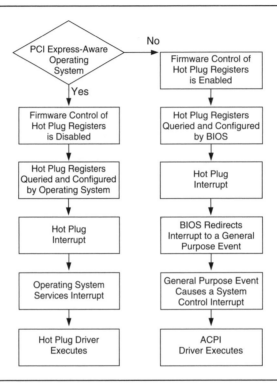

Figure 10.5   Generic Hot Plug Service Model for PCI Express Hot Plug

PCI Express Differentiated Traffic Support

PCI Express differentiated traffic capabilities are supported through each PCI Express device function's extended configuration space (beyond the 256-byte limit for PCI compatible configuration space). The PCI Express enhanced configuration mechanism is required to access this feature space. This means that differentiated traffic services, such as traffic class/virtual channel mapping for priority servicing (and used for isochronous data streams), cannot be supported by legacy operating systems. The following discussion assumes that software supports the PCI Express enhanced configuration mechanism.

Virtual Channel Capabilities Configuration

A device that supports more than the default virtual channel (VC0) and the default traffic class (TC0) needs to implement the PCI Express Virtual Channel Extended Capability Structure within its configuration space. Figure 10.6 shows the basic format for this capability structure.

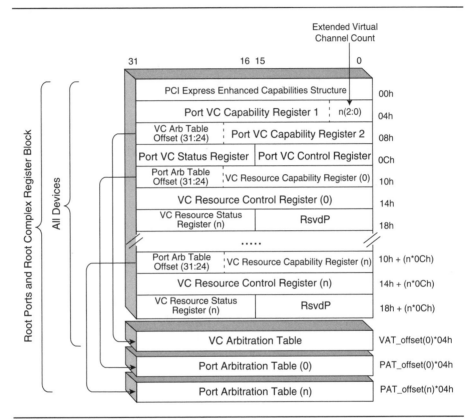

Figure 10.6   PCI Express Virtual Channel Extended Capability Structure

The PCI Express Enhanced Capability Header is detailed in the specification and uses a Capability ID of 0002h to indicate it as a virtual channel structure. The Port Virtual Channel Capabilities registers (Port VC Capability 1 register and Port VC Capability 2 register) indicate the number of other virtual channels (VC[7:1]) that a device supports in addition to the default virtual channel VC0. These registers also contain arbitration support information and the offset location of the actual Virtual Channel Arbitration Table. The capability and status registers (Port VC Status register and VC Resource Capability [n:0] registers) report the Virtual Channel Arbitration Table status, the types of port arbitration supported by the available virtual channels (also referred to as resources) and the offset location of the Port Arbitration Table for each virtual channel. The Port VC Control register allows software to select, configure and load an available virtual channel arbitration scheme. The VC Resource Control [n:0] registers are used to enable and configure each available virtual channel as well as map which particular traffic classes use that virtual channel. The VC Resource Status [n:0] registers are used to report the status of the Port Arbitration Table associated with each individual virtual channel as well as report whether or not a virtual channel is currently in the process of negotiating for port access.

Available Arbitration Mechanisms

The *PCI Express Base Specification* defines three virtual channel arbitration mechanisms for virtual channel arbitration and three port arbitration mechanisms for arbitrating between traffic that is mapped to the same virtual channel but coming from different ports (such as a switch). No one mechanism is necessarily better than the other; it is all a matter of the requirements of the target applications. The *PCI Express Base Specification* defines three key objectives of virtual channel arbitration:

1. Prevent false transaction timeouts and guarantee data flow forward progress.

2. Provide differentiated services between traffic flows within the PCI Express fabric.

3. Provide guaranteed bandwidth with deterministic (and reasonably small) end-to-end latency between components.

Virtual Channel Arbitration Mechanisms

The three available virtual channel arbitration mechanisms that software must choose from (assuming the device supports the arbitration mechanism) are *Strict Priority, Round Robin*, and *Weighted Round Robin*. Strict Priority arbitration is based on strict prioritization of the virtual channels. In other words, VC0 would get the lowest priority and VC7 would get the highest priority. This arbitration mechanism is the default arbitration mechanism for PCI Express virtual channel arbitration. The use of this arbitration scheme does require some amount of software regulation in order to prevent potential starvation of low priority devices. Round Robin arbitration is a common technique that allows equal access opportunities to all virtual channel traffic. This method does not guarantee that all virtual channels are given equal bandwidth usage, only the opportunity to use some of the available bandwidth. Weighted Round Robin arbitration is a cross between Strict Priority and Round Robin. This mechanism provides fairness during times of traffic contention by allowing lower priority devices at least one arbitration win per arbitration loop. The latency of a particular virtual channel is bounded by a minimum and maximum amount. This is where the term "weighted" comes in. Weights can be fixed through hardware, or preferably, programmable by software. If configurable by software, the ability is reported through the PCI Express Virtual Channel Extended Capability Structure outlined in Figure 10.6.

Port Arbitration Mechanisms

The three available port arbitration mechanisms that software must choose from (assuming the device supports the arbitration mechanism) are *Hardware-fixed, Programmable Round Robin* and *Programmable Time-based* Round Robin. Hardware-fixed arbitration is the simplest port arbitration mechanism since it does not require any programming. This mechanism makes all ports equal in prioritization. This arbitration mechanism is the default port arbitration mechanism for PCI Express. Programmable Round Robin arbitration can be configured to regular Round Robin where equal opportunities are given to all ports or Weighted Round Robin where some ports may be given more opportunities (weighted) than others. Programmable Time-based Round Robin arbitration is a tightly controlled form of Programmable Round Robin. This mechanism is used to not only control the bandwidth allocation of a port, but to control the amount of traffic that is injected into the switch or root complex within a given amount of time. If configurable by software, the ability is reported through the PCI Express Virtual Channel Extended Capability Structure outlined in Figure 10.6.

The Virtual Channel Arbitration Table and the Port Arbitration Table

It can be a bit confusing, when mentioning the different arbitration tables, to understand what each table is used for. It is useful at this point to make some sort of distinction between the two. The Virtual Channel Arbitration Table contains the arbitration mechanism for prioritizing virtual channels competing for a single port. The Port Arbitration Table contains the arbitration mechanism for prioritizing traffic that is mapped onto the same virtual channel, but originates from multiple receiving (also called ingress) ports. Port Arbitration Tables are only found in switches and root complexes since they are the only devices that have multiple ingress ports. Figure 10.6 illustrates the arbitration structure that is configured through the PCI Express virtual channel structure. An example of port arbitration and virtual channel arbitration is illustrated in Figure 10.7.

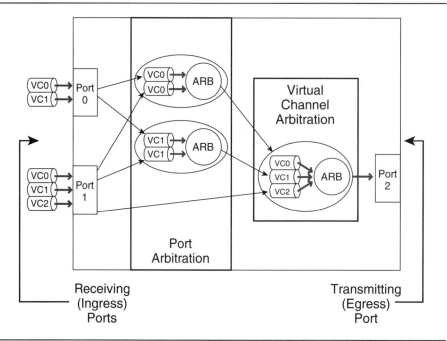

Figure 10.7   PCI Express Port and Virtual Channel Arbitration Example

Virtual Channel Arbitration Table Configuration

Before software can configure the Virtual Channel Arbitration Table, the arbitration mechanism must be chosen by software. The available options for each device are documented in the Port VC Capability 2 register (offset 08h), bits [7:0], as shown in Figure 10.6. Table 10.5 is an excerpt from this register as documented in the *PCI Express Base Specification*. Software can select an available arbitration option by setting bits in the Port VC Control register, as shown in Figure 10.6.

Table 10.5 Port VC Capability Register 2: VC Arbitration Capability

Bit Location	Description
0	Hardware fixed arbitration scheme
1	Weighted Round Robin arbitration with 32 phases
2	Weighted Round Robin arbitration with 64 phases
3	Weighted Round Robin arbitration with 128 phases
4–7	Reserved

These bits are read-only and typically hardwired by the device.

Suppose a device supported Weighted Round Robin arbitration with 128 phases and software selected that arbitration mechanism. Please note that the mechanism chosen is not arbitrary. Software selects a mechanism based on several factors. One of the key factors is the bandwidth available on the link and the maximum payload size that a device supports. The specific payload size of the device is documented in the Device Control register (offset 08h, bits [14:12]) of the PCI Express Capability Structure, shown in Figure 10.2. The default value for this register is set to 512 bytes.

The Virtual Channel Arbitration Table has a four-bit field for each phase that can be programmed with the identification of a particular virtual channel. The lower 3 bits (2:0) contain the virtual channel ID value. Bit 3 is currently reserved and may be used in the future to define other virtual channels. If software does not program the table, the table retains default values (VC0) for every phase. An example of a 128 phase Virtual Channel Arbitration Table can be found in Figure 10.8. Software programs each phase field with a virtual channel identification number. The example table in Figure 10.8 shows how software may have programmed each phase with one of three virtual channels (VC0, VC1, or VC2).

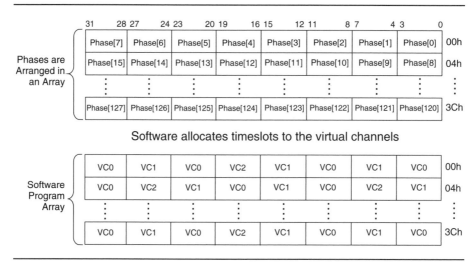

Figure 10.8 VC Arbitration Table Structure with 128 Phases Programmed by Software

Port Arbitration Table Configuration

Configuring the Port Arbitration Table is very similar to that of the Virtual Channel Arbitration Table. Before software can configure the Port Arbitration Table, the arbitration mechanism must also be chosen by software. The available options for each root complex or switch are documented in the VC Resource Capability register (shown in Figure 10.6). Software can select an available arbitration option by setting bits in the VC Resource Control register, shown in Figure 10.6. The Port Arbitration Table is not available for root ports or endpoint devices.

The phase field of the Port Arbitration Table is not set to four bits like the Virtual Channel Arbitration Table. Instead, the phase field can be programmed by software (through the Port VC Capability 1 register) to be 1, 2, 4, or 8 bits in length. The length of the phase field of the Port Arbitration Table is related to the number of ports that a switch has. For example, a switch that has four ports should set the phase field to be 2 bits in length. The Port Arbitration structure is similar to the Virtual Channel Arbitration structure, with the exception of programmable phase field widths. Software programs the phase fields of the Port Arbitration Table with receiving (ingress) port numbers instead of virtual channel identifiers. Please note that software does not have to alternate each phase with a different port. It is up to software to decide how to allocate phases to each available port. If the default port arbitration is selected instead of a programmable mechanism, the Port Arbitration Table default values contain an entry for each receiving (ingress) port.

Each *phase* represents a virtual time slot on the PCI Express link or more particularly, a time slot within an arbitration period. Currently the duration of a single phase is set to 100 nanoseconds (defined by the *PCI Express Base Specification*). The isochronous time period is the number of phases multiplied by the virtual timeslot. If a port arbitration table is set to 128 phases then the isochronous time period is 12.8 microseconds (100 nanoseconds × 128 phases).

Chapter 11

Power Management

He who has great power should use it lightly.

—Seneca

This chapter provides an overview of the power management capabilities and protocol associated with PCI Express. During this chapter the existing PCI power management model is discussed as a base for PCI Express power management. The chapter expands on this base to define the new power management capabilities of PCI Express such as *Link State Power Management* and *Active State Power Management* (ASPM). The chapter also discusses the impact of PCI Express power management on current software models as well as the general flow that new software must take to enable the new power management capabilities.

Building on PCI Power Management

Prior to PCI power management, power management was platform-unique and defined by the specific system hardware, the system BIOS, and the System Management Mode (SMM) code. This power management technique worked reasonably well for fixed configuration systems until the concept of the add-in card was defined. Several years after the standardization of general I/O through PCI adoption, it became apparent that a system-independent power management standard was needed to address PCI based add-in cards. In June of 1997 the PCI-SIG released the *PCI Bus Power Management Interface Specification Revision 1.0* to standardize PCI-based system power management.

Though not specifically required to do so, each PCI and PCI Express device is capable of hosting multiple functions. The *PCI Bus Power Management Specification Revision 1.1*, which PCI Express is compatible with, defines four function-based power management states, D0 through D3. Functions within a single device can occupy any of the supported function states as dictated by the systems power management policy. In fact, since each function represents an independent entity to the operating system, each function can occupy a unique function-based power management state within a singular device independent of the other functions within the device (with the exception of Power Off), as shown in Figure 11.1. PCI Express power management supports and defines the same function states as PCI power management.

Table 11.1   PCI/PCI Express Power Management Function State Summary

Device State	Characterization	Function Context	Exit Latency	Required/ Optional
D0	Full Device Power	Preserved	n/a	Required
D1	Light Sleep State	Preserved	0	Optional
D2	Deep Sleep State	Preserved	200µS	Optional
D3$_{HOT}$	Software Accessible	Not Maintained	10ms	Required
D3$_{COLD}$	Device Power Off	Not Maintained	n/a	Required

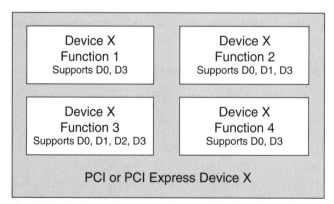

Each function of Device X may support a unique combination of the optional function power management states.

Figure 11.1   Example of a Multi-Function PCI or PCI Express Device

PCI Power Management Software Base Operations

PCI Power Management defines four base operations to allow the system to report, utilize, and transition to and from power management states. PCI Express supports these base operations as defined in the *PCI Bus Power Management Specification Revision 1.1*. Legacy operating systems can utilize these base operations to manage PCI Express devices in accordance with the system power management policy. These capabilities are defined as the Get Capabilities operation, the Set Power State operation, the Get Power States operation and the Wakeup operation. With the exception of the Wakeup Operation, all PCI and PCI Express functions are required to support each capability.

The operating system performs the Get Capabilities operation during device enumeration. The Get Capabilities operation also informs the operating system of the power management capability of a particular function. The Set Power State operation places a function in one of its supported power states. This operation is performed when called upon by the power management policy that the system has defined. The Get Power States operation is an informative operation that reports a function's current power state. The optional Wakeup operation causes a function to wake the system from a sleep state based on the occurrence of a defined event such as a "Wake on LAN" or "Wake on Ring" event.

Table 11.2   PCI/PCI Express Base Operating System Operations Summary

Operation	Characterization	Required/Optional
Get Capabilities	Informs the operating system of a function's power management capabilities	Required
Set Power State	Places a function in one of its supported power states	Required
Get Power States	Reports a function's current power state	Required
Wakeup	Wakes the system from a sleep state	Optional

Each PCI and PCI Express device function maintains 256 bytes of configuration space. PCI Express extends the configuration space to 4096 bytes per device function; however, only the first 256 bytes of the configuration space is *PCI Local Bus Specification Revision 2.3*-compatible and therefore compatible with PCI power management software stacks. Additionally the first 256 bytes of the extended PCI Express configuration space is all that is visible to current (Microsoft Windows XP) and legacy operating systems. Refer to Chapter 10 for additional information.

The base power management operations are supported through specific registers and offsets within the 256 bytes of *PCI Local Bus Specification Revision 2.3*-compatible configuration space. The two key registers of concern are the Status register and the Capabilities Pointer register. The Status register, located at offset 04h, has a single bit (bit 4) that reports whether the device supports PCI power management extended capabilities. Extended power management capabilities, not to be confused with the extended configuration space of PCI Express, can be described as the function states D1, D2 and $D3_{HOT}$. The function states D0 and $D3_{COLD}$ are naturally supported by every function since they correspond to the function being fully on or powered off, respectively. For example, an unplugged hair dryer supports $D3_{COLD}$ because it does not have any power.

During device enumeration the operating system uses the Get Capabilities operation to poll the status register of each function to determine whether any extended power management capabilities are supported. If bit 4 (capabilities bit) of the Status register is set, the operating system knows that the function supports extended power management capabilities. As a result, the operating system routines reads the offset value contained in the Capabilities Pointer register at offset 34h, which points to the location of the registers that inform the operating system of the specific extended power management capabilities, as shown in Figure 11.2.

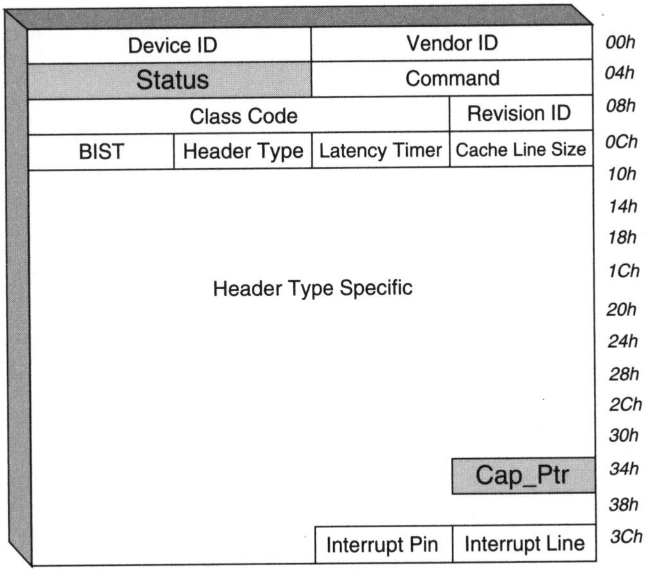

Device ID		Vendor ID	00h
Status		Command	04h
Class Code		Revision ID	08h
BIST	Header Type	Latency Timer	Cache Line Size	0Ch
			10h
			14h
			18h
			1Ch
Header Type Specific			20h
			24h
			28h
			2Ch
			30h
		Cap_Ptr	34h
			38h
	Interrupt Pin	Interrupt Line	3Ch

Figure 11.2   Common PCI/PCI Express Configuration Space Header

The offset value in the Capabilities Pointer register corresponds to a specific location within the 256 bytes of configuration space that contains the capabilities linked list, which is 64 bits or two DWords long, as shown in Figure 11.3. There are six PCI Power Management registers located at the offset value indicated by the capabilities register. A short description of each registers power management role is given below. For the specific contents of each of the six PCI Power Management registers, refer to the *PCI Bus Power Management Interface Specification Revision 1.1*.

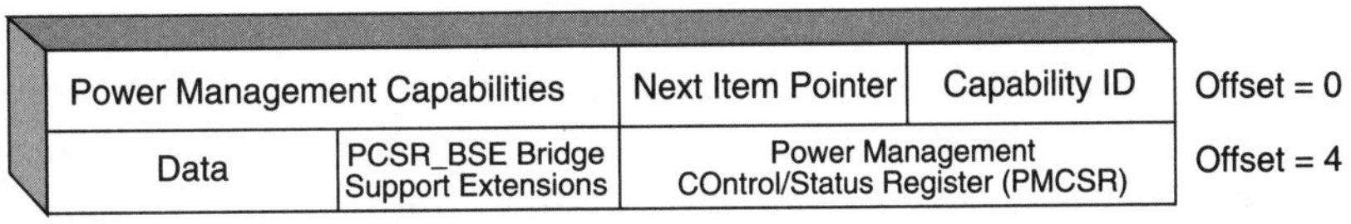

| Power Management Capabilities | | Next Item Pointer | Capability ID | Offset = 0 |
| Data | PCSR_BSE Bridge Support Extensions | Power Management COntrol/Status Register (PMCSR) | | Offset = 4 |

Figure 11.3   PCI Power Management Register Block

The base power management operations (executed by software) read and write data from and/or into the PCI Power Management registers to obtain specific function capabilities, to obtain current function power states, and to cause transitions into and out of the supported function power management states. The Capability ID field identifies the register block as the PCI Power Management registers. The Next Item Pointer identifies the location of the next available register in the functions capability list. The Power Management Capabilities register (a read-only register) provides information to the operating system such as which function power management states are supported. This register is queried when the Get Capabilities base operation is executed by the operating system. The Power Management Control/Status register manages the function's power management state and is used by the operating system during Set Power State, Get Power State and Wakeup base operations. The Power Management Control/Status register for Bridge Support Extensions (a read-only register) provides information to the operating system regarding a PCI/PCI Express bridge's ability to control the power state of a secondary bus (downstream link in the case of PCI Express) based upon the originating device's power state, as shown in Figure 11.4. The Data register (also a read-only register) provides state-dependent data to the operating system such as the amount of power consumed.

PCI Express devices maintain a power management register block that provides the same functionality as the PCI power management register block. The base power management operations utilized by operating systems that are not PCI Express-aware will continue to function since the PCI Express device looks just like a PCI device in this configuration space.

PCI Bus States versus PCI Express Link States

The *PCI Bus Power Management Specification Revision 1.1* defines four bus power management states, B0 through B3. Similar to the defined function based power states, the bus power management states are characterized by the ability to move traffic across the bus. In the bus state B0 the bus is fully on; in the bus state B3 the bus is fully off, and states B1 and B2 are in-between sleep states. PCI Express replaces the Bus states defined by the PCI power management specification with a similar set of states called Link states, as shown in Table 11.5. As with PCI, legacy software does not directly read the Bus (PCI) or link state (PCI Express) from a given register location. Instead the Bus or Link state is derived from reading the state of the primary bridge in the case of PCI or both devices on the link in the case of PCI Express.

The bus states of PCI are controlled indirectly through software by means of manipulating the originating or primary PCI bridge's power management state (this feature must be enabled in the PMCSR Bridge Support Extensions register in the power management register block). In other words, as software sets the function power management state of a primary bridge, the bus state of the secondary bus behind the primary bridge is also set, as illustrated in Figure 11.4. Likewise software can determine the bus state of a secondary PCI bus by examining the power management state of the primary PCI bridge.

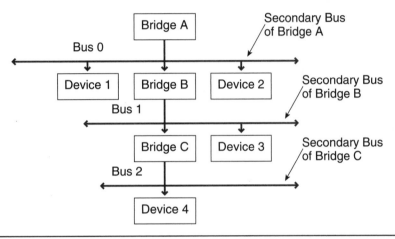

Figure 11.4   Secondary Bus Relationship

As mentioned before, the PCI Express link states replace the bus states defined by the *PCI Bus Power Management Specification Revision 1.1*. The newly defined link states are not a radical departure from the PCI bus states. These link states have been defined to support the new advanced power management concepts and clock architecture of PCI Express. For the most part, the general functionality of the PCI Express link states parallels the bus states of PCI with the exception of a couple of new states added by PCI Express. PCI Express defines the following link states: L0, L0s, L1, L2/L3 Ready, L2, and L3. Similar to the PCI bus states, in the L0 state, the link is fully on, in the link state L3 the link is fully off, and L0s, L1, L2/L3 Ready, and L2 are in-between sleep states, as shown in Figure 11.5 and Table 11.3. Of the above PCI Express link states, the only state that has no functional equivalent in PCI is the L0s state. This state is part of the advanced power management features of PCI Express and is transparent to PCI power management.

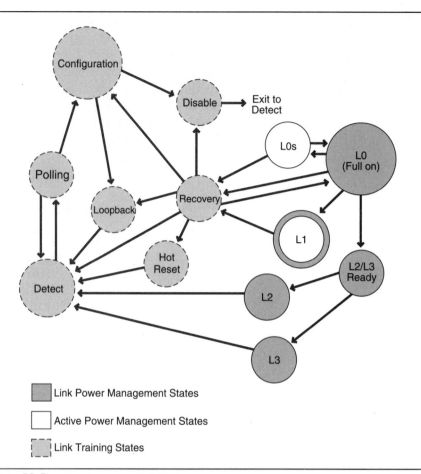

Figure 11.5   PCI Express Link States

Table 11.3   PCI Express Link State Summary

Link State	PCI Compatible Power Management	PCI Express Advanced Power Management
L0	Required	Required
L0S	Not Applicable	Required
L1	Required	Optional
L2/L3 Ready	Required	Not Applicable
L2	Required if Vaux is on the platform)	Not Applicable
L3	Required	Not Applicable

PCI Express Link State L0 and PCI Bus State B0

The L0 state of PCI Express parallels the B0 state of PCI power management and represents a fully functioning link in the case of PCI Express or a fully functioning bus in the case of PCI. As with PCI power management, all PCI Express devices must support the L0 state. Since the clock architectures differ between the technologies, there is also a level of detail that defines the clock status of this particular Link state.

In PCI power management the clocks are either on or off at the external clock source level. This statement is too generic for PCI Express clocking architecture. Since PCI Express uses an embedded clocking architecture there are multiples levels at which the clocks can be controlled. Each device has a 100-megahertz differential clock input from an external clock source. Internal to the device may be a phase locked loop circuit (recall from Chapter 8) that takes an input, the 100 megahertz clock signal, and converts it into a 2.5-gigahertz reference clock signal that is used to drive serial shift registers of the transmitter output stages. As a result the clocks can be shut off at the phase locked loop level or the clock source level, as shown in Figure 11.6. PCI Express defines fully functioning or fully on to mean that the reference clock (input clock to the device) is active and the phase locked loop circuit, or similar circuit, is functioning.

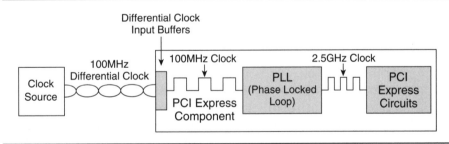

Figure 11.6   PCI Express Device Clock Path

PCI Express Link State L0s

PCI Express defines a sub-state of the L0 state called L0s, or in other words, L0 standby. The L0s state is a required low resume latency standby or idle state that appears to be similar to the optional B1 Bus state of PCI power management. The L0s Link state, however, is part of the advanced power management capabilities of PCI Express called Active State Power Management (ASPM) and as such has no functional equivalent to PCI power management. PCI Express ASPM is discussed in more detail in the next section; however, as touched upon in Chapter 8, PCI Express ASPM is a hardware-based power management mechanism, not a software-based mechanism like PCI power management. This means that the L0s state is transparent to PCI power management. The L0s Link state is a fully powered state with all clocks running (the reference clock input to the device is active and a phase locked loop or similar circuit is functioning). The L0s Link state does not allow the communication of Transaction Layer Packets or Data Link Layer Packets over the link. L0s is an *electrical idle* state where differential signals are in a terminated state (that is, no transitions take place).

PCI Express Link States L1, L2, and PCI Bus State B2

PCI Express defines two link states that are similar to the optional PCI power management bus state B2. At a high level, the similarity between these PCI Express link states and the B2 PCI power management bus state is an idle bus and the absence of a clock. In terms of PCI Express, the link states L1 and L2 correspond to a medium latency low power state and a higher latency deep sleep state.

The L1 Link State

The L1 link state is an idle state with the internal phase lock loop circuit or equivalent turned off. PCI Express devices must support the L1 Link state for PCI compatible power management. The L1 link state is also used for ASPM; however, the support of the L1 link state by PCI Express ASPM is optional.

At a device level this link state looks similar to the PCI power management bus state B1, since the source clock is still feeding a 100-megahertz differential clock signal to the PCI Express device. The resume latency for this state would be larger in relative magnitude than the PCI power management bus state B1, since the internal phase locked loop or equivalent circuit of the device must be turned back on and stabilized before the link can begin to function again.

The L2 Link State

The L2 link state is an optional auxiliary idle state with the internal phase lock loop or equivalent circuit, the external clock source and the main device power turned off (auxiliary power remains on to keep enough circuitry alive to generate wake-up event). The L2 link state provides the highest level of power savings, aside from powering the system down, at the cost of high resume latency. Resuming from the L2 link state requires that main power be applied to the device, the source clock must be turned back on, and the phase locked loop or equivalent must be turned on and stabilized.

PCI Express Link State L3 and PCI Bus State B3

PCI Express defines the L3 link state, which is similar to the PCI power management bus state B3. Since this link state is simply power off, there is not much of interest to discuss this state any further. The support of this link state is required to maintain PCI power management compatibility. Since all devices are capable of having power removed, support of this state is inherent.

PCI Express Link State L2/L3 Ready

The PCI Express link state L2/L3 Ready cannot be compared to any of the PCI bus states. The L2/L3 Ready state is a preparatory state prior to removing main power to the device or peripheral. A links transition to the L2/L3 Ready state does not immediately result in a transition to the L2 or L3 link state. The L2/L3 Ready state is a handshake transition state to determine the readiness before removing main power.

PCI Express Link Recovery State

The PCI Express Link Recovery state is really a training state but can be considered a sub-state of power management. There is no comparable PCI power management mechanism. Recovery is used by both PCI Express Link State Power Management and by PCI Express Active State Power Management to resynchronize and establish bit and symbol lock. This is typically the result of the internal phase locked loop being turned off (as in the L1 state) or if one or both of the devices require synchronization (L0 and L0s). During normal operation (L0), if a device receives TS1 or TS2 training ordered sets, the device must transition to the Recovery state. Software can also force the link to be retrained, which causes entry into the Recovery state. The link does not enter the Recovery state if main power has been removed from the system. In the case that main power has been removed the link must be entirely retrained.

PCI Express Link Training States

In the course of PCI Express power management it is sometimes necessary to retrain the PCI Express link. The PCI Express link training states Detect, Polling, Configuration, Hot Reset, and Recovery (mentioned above) are used to train the link. The Loopback state is called out as a training state. However, this state is only used in a lab/debug environment as a test state (refer to Chapter 8).

When main power and clocks are removed from the link, the link no longer retains any of the configuration information from a previous training sequence. As a result, all the key factors must be re-established such as bit rate, bit lock, symbol lock, and more (refer to Chapter 8 for specifics on PCI Express link training). As a refresher on what is accomplished through each of the training states see Table 11.4.

Table 11.4   PCI Express Link Training State Summary

Link Training State	Function
Detect	Detect whether or not a receiving device is present and powered
Polling	Establish bit and symbol lock, data rate, and lane polarity
Configuration	Configure link width, lane reversal, and lane-to-lane skew
Disable	Disables the link
Hot Reset	Reset a link without requiring a full system reset
Loopback	Test feature for the lab and debug environment
Recovery	Used to achieve bit and symbol level synchronization

Table 11.5 PCI Bus State and PCI Express Link State Comparison

PCI Bus State	Characterization	Device Power	PCI Express Link State	Characterization	Device Power
B0	Bus is fully on Free running bus clock	Vcc	L0	Link is fully on Device reference clock running Device PLL or equivalent is running	Vcc
B1	Bus idle state Free running bus clock	Vcc	L0s	No TLP or DLLP communication over link Device reference clock running component PLL or equivalent is running Signals are in an electrical idle state	Vcc
B2	Bus idle state Bus clock stopped	Vcc	L1	No TLP or DLLP communication over link Device reference clock running Device PLL or equivalent is shut off Signals are in an electrical idle state	Vcc
			L2	No TLP or DLLP communication over link Device reference clock input shut off Device PLL or equivalent is shut off Signals are in an electrical idle state	Vaux
			L2/L3 Ready	Staging point for removal of main power	Vcc
B3	Off (system unpowered)	Off	L3	Off (system unpowered)	Off

The Comparison of PCI power management bus state B1 to link state L0s is for a functionality comparison only

PCI Express Active State Power Management ASPM

A key difference in the power management capabilities of PCI and PCI Express is the concept of Active State Power Management (ASPM). ASPM is a hardware-autonomous mechanism to reduce PCI Express link power through hardware management rather than software management. This hardware-autonomous power management mechanism provides the system with a method to aggressively pursue the reduction of link power consumption. Since this mechanism is not software based, CPU cycles are also spared as a result and can be utilized by other system devices. As mentioned briefly in Chapter 8, ASPM utilizes two of the defined PCI Express link states, L0s and L1, to manage the link's power consumption.

Although hardware controls ASPM, software must still intervene to enable and configure it in a system. As a result, PCI Express ASPM does require new software to enable the capability. In this case the definition of new software does not mean a new operating system, but rather new BIOS code that works in conjunction with a legacy operating system. ASPM does not coincide with basic PCI power management software-compatible features.

ASPM capabilities are accessed through the PCI Express Capability Structure that exists within *PCI Local Bus Specification Revision 2.3*-compatible configuration space, as shown in Figure 11.7. ASPM is managed at each PCI Express port through registers in the PCI Express Capability Structure, as shown in Figure 11.8.

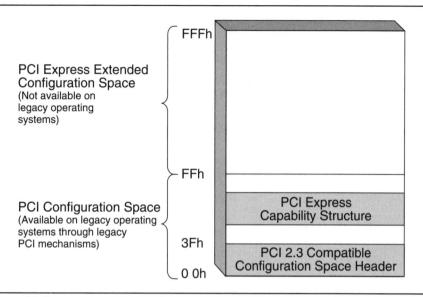

Figure 11.7   PCI Express Configuration Space Layout

Software Requirements for PCI Express Active State Power Management

The software procedure that configures and enables PCI Express ASPM can be broken into essentially five key steps. These steps can be completed by either a future operating system with support for ASPM or a new BIOS in a system running Microsoft Windows XP or earlier that support the PCI configuration mechanism. Software must read and write to specific registers, which are all located within the PCI Express Capability Structure outlined in Figure 11.7.

Step 1: Determining Whether or not Active State Power Management Is Supported

The first step that software must take is to determine whether the link supports ASPM, and if so, to what level. This is accomplished by querying the Link Capabilities register (offset 0Ch, bits 11:10) of the PCI Express Capability Structure, as shown in Figure 11.8. If the link does not support ASPM, the rest of the steps are not necessary. The available options for ASPM are no support, L0s support only, or both L0s and L1 support.

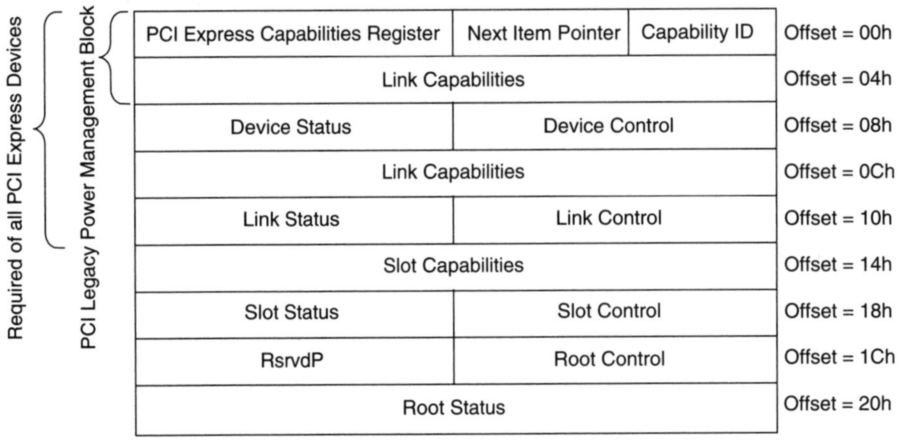

PCI Express Capabilities Register	Next Item Pointer	Capability ID	Offset = 00h
Link Capabilities			Offset = 04h
Device Status		Device Control	Offset = 08h
Link Capabilities			Offset = 0Ch
Link Status		Link Control	Offset = 10h
Slot Capabilities			Offset = 14h
Slot Status		Slot Control	Offset = 18h
RsrvdP		Root Control	Offset = 1Ch
Root Status			Offset = 20h

Left margin labels: *Required of all PCI Express Devices* / *PCI Legacy Power Management Block*

Figure 11.8 PCI Express Capability Structure

Step 2: Scanning and Updating the Slot Clock Configuration and Common Clock Configuration Registers

Software must determine whether or not both PCI Express devices on the link utilize the same clock. This step is aimed more at links that span a PCI Express connector. Software can scan the PCI Express Capabilities register at offset 02h, bit 8 of the PCI Express Capability Structure to determine whether the device is connected to a slot or an integrated device of the system. Typically all integrated devices use the same clock source. If the PCI Express device is a slot-based device, software must query the Link Status register (offset 12h, bit 12) of the PCI Express Capability Structure to determine whether the device utilizes the reference clock provided to the slot by the system or a clock provided on the add-in card itself. The results of the previous query are used to update the Link Control register located at offset 10h, bit 6 of the PCI Express Capability Structure. Bit 6 corresponds to the common clock configuration and when set causes the appropriate L0s and L1 exit latencies to be reported in the Link Capabilities register (offset 0Ch, bits 14:12). It is no surprise that exit latencies will vary dependent upon whether two PCI Express devices on a link utilize the same reference clock or different reference clocks. This is due to difference in how long it takes to recover the link synchronization.

Step 3: Determining State-Based Exit Latencies

Software must next query the Link Capabilities register for state-based exit latency information. Exit latency is considered to be the time required to transition back to the L0 state. If L0s ASPM is supported, software queries the Link Capabilities register (offset 0Ch, bits 14:12) of the PCI Express Capability Structure. If L0s and L1 ASPM is supported, software queries the Link Capabilities register (offset 0Ch, bits 17:12) of the PCI Express Capability Structure to determine the exit latency associated with a device. Table 11.6 shows the possible exit latency settings.

Table 11.6   L0s and L1 Exit Latency Settings

L0s (offset 0x0 Ch, bits 14:12)	L0s Available Exit Latency Settings	L1 (offset 0x0Ch, bits 17:15)	L1 Available Exit Latency Settings
000b	Less than 64 ns	000b	Less than 1 us
001b	64 ns to less than 128 ns	001b	1 us to less than 2 us
010b	128 ns to less than 256 ns	010b	2 us to less than 4 us
011b	256 ns to less than 512 ns	011b	4 us to less than 8 us
100b	512 ns to less than 1 us	100b	8 us to less than 16 us
101b	1 us to less than 2 us	101b	16 us to less than 32 us
110b	2 us to 4 us	110b	32 us to 64 us
111b	Reserved	111b	More than 64 us

Step 4: Determining Endpoint Exit Latency Tolerance

If a PCI Express device is identified as being an endpoint device through polling the PCI Express Capabilities register (offset 02h, bits 7:4) of the PCI Express Capability Structure, software must determine the device's exit latency tolerance for both L0s and L1. This is accomplished through polling the Device Capabilities register (offset 04h, bits 11:6) of the PCI Express Capability Structure. Software takes this information and compares it with the reported maximum exit latency for the link to determine what level of ASPM can be enabled without suffering performance loss and in some cases functionality loss through buffer overruns.

Step 5: Setting the Level of Active State Power Management Support

The final step that software must take is to set the actual bits that enable ASPM to function. This is accomplished through setting bits 1:0 of the Link Control register (offset 04h) of the PCI Express Capability Structure. The available switch options are disabled, L0s entry supported, and L0s and L1 entry supported. There is no option to only support L1 entry.

Prior to software setting up ASPM, the isochronous PCI Express Devices that exist in the platform should be considered. Turning on ASPM can possibly add latency that may be beyond the expected system limits. In other words, if an isochronous device in a system cannot tolerate the time it takes to transition out of an ASPM state, ASPM should not be enabled.

A Quick Example

Consider the following example. On a certain link there is a root complex and an endpoint device. Software determines that L0s ASPM is supported on the link. After polling the individual devices for L0s exit latency information it finds that the root complex has an exit latency of 256 nanoseconds and the endpoint device has an exit latency of 64 nanoseconds. Further investigation reveals that the endpoint can tolerate up to 512 nanoseconds of exit latency before risking, for example, the possibility of internal buffer overruns. Based upon this information software enables Active State Power Management on the link. If the endpoint device above was determined to be capable of tolerating only 128 nanoseconds of exit latency, then L0s ASPM should not be enabled.

L0s Active State Power Management

When the L0s state is enabled the link transitions to this state whenever the link is not in use. Because the link will likely transition into and out of this state often, the latencies associated with coming in and out of this state must be relatively small (several microseconds maximum). This power-saving state is managed on a per-direction basis. In other words, the transmit path from a port could be in the L0s state while the receive path to that port could remain in the fully functional L0 state.

L0s Active State Entry and Exit

Since L0s entry is managed on a per-direction basis, each device on the link is responsible for initiating entry into the L0s state by transmitting the electrical idle ordered set on all its lanes. The link transitions to the L0s state as a result of an absence of link activity such as TLPs and DLLPs. A PCI Express device exits from the L0s state when there is activity that must traverse the link.

L1 Active State Power Management

The L1 ASPM state allows for additional power savings over the L0s state but at the cost of higher exit latency. During this state the transmitter continues to drive the DC common mode voltage and all device on-chip clocks are turned off. The details of transitioning into and out of the L1 state are very similar to the L0s state.

L1 Active State Entry and Exit

Entry into the L1 ASPM state can be requested by PCI Express devices on both sides of the link. A device requests the L1 ASPM state by sending out a Data Link Layer Packet (PM_Active_State_Request_L1) to the other device. Table 11.8 gives a brief description of these types of packets. One major difference between a device-initiated L0s ASPM state entry and a device-initiated L1 ASPM state entry is that an L1 ASPM state entry is negotiated between both devices. If one of the devices denies the request then the L1 ASPM state is not entered into. Either device on the PCI Express link may initiate an exit from the L1 ASPM state without negotiation with the other PCI Express device. If a device denies a request to enter the L1 state it must enter the L0s state as soon as possible.

Power Management Messages and Packets

There are four specific Transaction Layer messages and four specific Data Link Layer Packets (DLLPs) that are used to initiate and acknowledge power management events and requests, as shown in Table 11.8. The Transaction Layer power management messages are Transaction Layer Packets (TLPs) containing no payload, with the type field set to message (MSG). PCI Express TLP messages are treated as posted transactions. In other words, TLP messages are serviced on a first-come first-serve basis.

Table 11.8 Power Management TLP Message and DLLP Summary

Packet	Type	Use	Function
PM_PME (Power Management Event)	TLP MSG	Software Directed PM	A message that is used to inform power management software which device is requesting a power management state change
PME_Turn_Off	TLP MSG	Software Directed PM	A message that is broadcast to all downstream devices in order to stop any subsequent PM_PME messages
PME_TO_Ack	TLP MSG	Software Directed PM	Response from downstream devices to the originator of the PME_Turn_Off message
PM_Active_State_Nak	TLP MSG	Active State PM	A rejection message sent by an upstream device in response to a downstream device's request to enter the L1 active state
PM_Enter_L1	DLLP	Software Directed PM	Used to transition the link to the L1 state
PM_Enter_L23	DLLP	Software Directed PM	Used to request a transition into the L2/L3 ready state
PM_Active_State_Request_L1	DLLP	Active State PM	Used by a device to request a transition to the L1 Active state
PM_Request_Ack	DLLP	Software Directed/ Active State PM	Completion response to a power management request

The PCI_PME (power management event) Transaction TLP message is software-compatible with the PME mechanism defined by the *PCI Power Management Specification Revision 1.1*. PCI Express devices use this power management event to request a change in their power management state. In most cases, the PCI_PME event is used to revive the system from a previously injected lower power state (L1). If a link is in the L2 state, an out-of-band mechanism must be used to revive the system since the link is no longer communicating. The out-of-band signal takes the form of an optional *WAKE#* pin defined in the *PCI Express Card Electromechanical Specification*. A change in state on this pin generates a wake event on devices that implement it.

Root complexes and switches send the PME_Turn_Off TLP message to their downstream devices. This message informs each downstream device to discontinue the generation of subsequent PCI_PME messages and prepare for the removal of main power and the reference clocks (the message informs them to enter the L2/L3 Ready state). PCI Express devices are required to not only accept the PME_Turn_Off message, but also to acknowledge that the message was received. Downstream devices reply with the PME_TO_Ack TLP message to acknowledge the PME_Turn_Off TLP message from a root complex or a switch.

Downstream devices send the PME_Enter_L23 DLLP to inform the root complex or switch that a downstream device has made all preparations for the removal of main power and clocks and is prepared to enter the L2 or L3 state. As soon as the root complex or switch receives the PME_Enter_L23 DLLP it responds back to the downstream device with the PM_Request_Ack DLLP, which acknowledges the devices preparation for the L2 or L3 state, whichever the case may be. After all downstream devices have reported their preparation for entry into L2 or L3 the main power and clocks for the system can be removed. A root complex or switch that sends the PME_Turn_Off TLP message to its downstream PCI Express devices must not initiate entry into the L2 or L3 state until each downstream device sends the PME_Enter_L23 DLLP.

Downstream devices also send the PME_Enter_L1 DLLP to inform the root complex or switch that a downstream device has made all preparations for turning off its internal phase lock loop circuit and is prepared to enter the L1 state (not the L1 ASPM state). Downstream devices send this packet in response to software programming the device to enter a lower power state. As soon as the root complex or switch receives the PME_Enter_L1 DLLP it responds back to the downstream device with the PM_Request_Ack DLLP, which acknowledges the devices preparation for the L1 state. At that point the link is fully transitioned to the L1 link state.

If ASPM is supported and enabled on a downstream device, the device may send the PM_Active_State_Request_L1 to inform the root complex or switch that it would like to enter the L1 ASPM state. If the root complex or switch is not able to support the L1 active state or software has previously disabled this ability in the root complex or switch, it responds back to the downstream device with a PM_Active_State_Nak DLLP. If the root complex or switch can support the L1 active state it responds back to the downstream device with a PM_Request_Ack DLLP.

Chapter 12

PCI Express Implementation

Our Age of Anxiety is, in great part, the result of trying to do today's jobs with yesterday's tools.

—Marshall McLuhan

This chapter touches on some of the basics for PCI Express implementation. It begins with some examples of chipset partitioning, explaining how PCI Express could be used in desktop, mobile, or server environments. The rest of the chapter identifies some of the ways that PCI Express lives within, or can expand, today's computer systems. This focuses on example connectors and add-in cards, revolutionary form factors, and system level implementation details such as routing constraints.

System Partitioning

PCI Express provides a great amount of flexibility in the ways that it can be used within a system. Rather than try to explain all the various ways that this architecture could be used, this section focuses on how the chipset may implement a PCI Express topology. Generically speaking, the chipset is the way that the CPU talks to the rest of the components within a system. It connects the CPU with memory, graphics, I/O components, and storage. A common chipset division is to have a (G)MCH and an ICH. The GMCH (Graphics & Memory Controller Hub) connects the CPU to system memory, graphics (optionally), and to the ICH. The ICH (I/O Controller Hub), then branches out to communicate with generic I/O devices, storage, and so on.

How exactly could a chipset like this make use of PCI Express? First, recall the generic PCI Express topology discussed in Chapter 5 and shown in Figure 12.1.

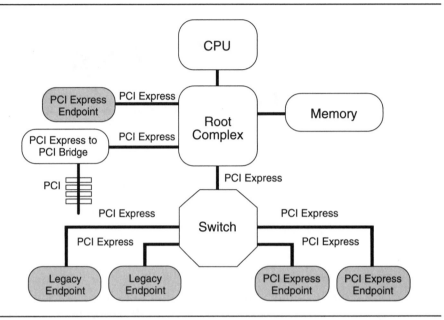

Figure 12.1 PCI Express Topology

Depending on the chipset partitioning, either the (G)MCH or the (G)MCH and ICH combined can be considered the root complex. If the GMCH and ICH communicate via a PCI Express link, then the GMCH would be the root complex and the ICH can act like a switch to fan out to multiple I/O devices. If the GMCH and ICH communicate using an interconnect other than PCI Express, both devices combined are considered the root complex. Keep in mind that proprietary implementations of interconnects based on PCI Express are likely to emerge, and may be used for the GMCH to ICH connection (among others).

When creating a PCI Express topology, there are a wide variety of options available. The next few sections discuss examples of how a topology may be set up for desktop, server, and mobile environments. These examples are just that, examples, and actual PCI Express designs may or may not be implemented as such.

Desktop Partitioning

Desktop chipsets generally follow the (G)MCH and ICH divisions discussed above. An example PCI Express topology in the desktop space is shown in Figure 12.2.

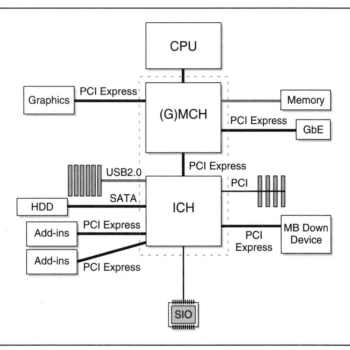

Figure 12.2   Example Desktop Topology

In the above hypothetical example, the GMCH acts as the root complex, interacting with the CPU and system memory and fanning out to three separate hierarchy domains. One goes to the graphics device or connector, the second domain goes to the GbE (Gigabit Ethernet) LAN device or connector, and the third domain goes to the ICH (domain identifying numbers are arbitrary). The connection to the ICH may occur via a direct connection on a motherboard or through several connectors or cables if the GMCH and ICH reside on separate boards or modules (more on this later in the chapter). Recall that this is a theoretical example only, and actual PCI Express products may or may not follow the topology breakdowns described here.

In this example, the chipset designers may have identified graphics and Gigabit Ethernet for direct attachment to the GMCH. By providing them with separate PCI Express domains off of the root complex, it may facilitate flow control load balancing throughout the system. Thanks to the traffic classes and virtual channels defined by the specification, it would be possible to place all these devices on a single domain and prioritize traffic via those specified means. However, if multiple bandwidth intensive applications are on the same domain, they may compete with each other for the available flow control credits and physical link transmission time. Separating these devices onto separate domains may facilitate bandwidth tuning on all domains.

Naturally, the downside to this possibility is that the GMCH/root complex is required to be slightly larger and more complex. Supporting multiple domains requires the GMCH to implement some arbitration mechanisms to efficiently handle traffic flow between all three PCI Express domains, the CPU and main memory interfaces. Additionally, the GMCH needs to physically support PCI Express logic, queues, TX and RX buffers, and package pins for all three domains. For these reasons, it may be just as likely that the Gigabit Ethernet connection, for example, is located off of the ICH instead of the GMCH.

Since graphics tends to be a bandwidth-intensive application, the GMCH may implement a x16 port for this connection. This allows for a maximum of 16×250 megabytes per second = 4 gigabytes per second in each direction. The graphics device may make use of this port via a direct connection down on the motherboard or, more likely, through the use of a x16 PCI Express connector (more on PCI Express connectors later in this chapter). Through this connector, a graphics path is provided that is very similar to today's AGP (Accelerated Graphics Port) environment, but provides additional bandwidth and architectural capabilities.

Gigabit Ethernet bandwidth requirements are much less than those for graphics, so the GMCH may only implement a x1 port for this connection. This allows for a maximum of 1×250 megabytes per second = 250 megabytes per second in each direction. The Gigabit Ethernet device may make use of this port via a x1 connector or may be placed down on the motherboard and tied to the GMCH directly.

The bandwidth requirements for the PCI Express connection between the GMCH and ICH depend mostly on the bandwidth requirements for the devices attached to the ICH. For this example, assume that the bandwidth needs of the ICH can be met via a x4 PCI Express connection. This allows for a maximum of 4×250 megabytes per second = 1 gigabyte per second in each direction. In order to prioritize and differentiate between the various types of traffic flowing between the GMCH and ICH, this interface likely includes support for multiple traffic classes and virtual channels.

This example GMCH identifies one of the benefits that PCI Express offers. There are three different PCI Express interfaces from the GMCH, one for graphics, one for Gigabit Ethernet, and one to connect to the I/O subsystem. Despite the varying needs of these applications, PCI Express is flexible enough to effectively span all of them. Can today's graphics interface handle the needs of Gigabit Ethernet? Can today's LAN interface handle the needs of a GMCH to ICH hub interconnect? Can today's hub interconnect handle the bandwidth needs for graphics? They *might* be able to, but certainly not very efficiently and certainly not in a manner that scales to meet the needs of future bandwidth requirements.

The ICH in this hypothetical example essentially acts as a switch that fans out the third PCI Express domain. Internal to the ICH may be what amounts to a PCI Express switch that has the PCI Express connection to the GMCH as its upstream port. The downstream portions of that switch include the three PCI Express ports shown on the ICH. That internal switch also connects to an internal PCI Express to PCI bridge, which then connects to the PCI interface shown on the ICH. Finally, the internal switch also interacts with the ICH core, which translates and arbitrates traffic between PCI Express and USB2, Serial ATA, Super I/O, and any other interfaces attached to the ICH.

The three (downstream) PCI Express ports shown on the ICH are likely x1 ports. These provide high speed (250 megabytes per second per direction) connections to generic I/O functions. In the example shown in Figure 12.2, one of those generic I/O functions is located on the motherboard, while the other two ports are accessed via x1 connectors. Please note that in this example the PCI Express connectors do not completely replace the PCI connectors found in a desktop system. Since the ICH has integrated a PCI Express to PCI bridge, it concurrently supports both PCI and PCI Express. The motherboard that implements this example likely has a mixture of PCI Express and PCI connectors. If the GMCH does not supply a x1 port for Gigabit Ethernet, that functionality could just as easily be located on one of the ICH's x1 ports. This holds true as long as there is appropriate bandwidth and access to the GMCH through either a standard x4 PCI Express GMCH-ICH interconnect, or a proprietary version with similar features.

What sort of PCI Express to PCI Express traffic is likely to occur in this system? Recall from Chapter 5 that a root complex is not required to implement peer-to-peer traffic across hierarchy domains. A switch, however, does support peer-to-peer traffic between downstream links. As such, the GMCH (acting as the root complex) may not support accesses between its Gigabit Ethernet, ICH and graphics PCI Express links. It is likely that some traffic would be supported, though, to enable common usage models (for example, to allow a USB video camera connected to the ICH to write to the PCI Express graphics device). On the other hand, if the ICH is implemented as a switch it supports peer-to-peer transactions amongst the various PCI Express devices attached to it.

Mobile Partitioning

Mobile chipsets also tend to follow the (G)MCH and ICH divisions discussed above. An example PCI Express topology in the mobile space is shown in Figure 12.3. Again, this is a hypothetical example only, and actual PCI Express products may or may not follow the topology breakdowns described here.

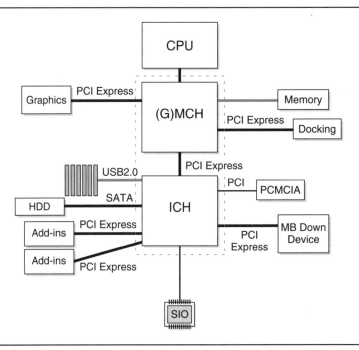

Figure 12.3   Example Mobile Topology

This example looks remarkably similar to the desktop model just discussed. The GMCH still acts as the root complex, interacting with the CPU and system memory, and fanning out to three separate hierarchy domains. One still goes to the graphics device or connector and another still goes to the ICH. The only noticeable difference between Figure 12.2 and Figure 12.3 is that the mobile platform has identified one of the GMCH/root complex's domains for docking, whereas the desktop model had identified it for Gigabit Ethernet. If the GMCH does not supply a x1 for Gigabit Ethernet (desktop) or docking (mobile), that functionality would likely be located on the ICH.

Just like on the desktop model, mobile graphics tends to be a bandwidth intensive application so the GMCH may implement a x16 port for this connection (with a maximum of 4 gigabytes per second in each direction). The graphics device may make use of this port via a mobile-specific x16 connector, or more likely, through a direct connection if it is placed on the motherboard. Alternatively, a mobile platform may not need a graphics interface that is as high-performance as the desktop. This interface could only run as a x8 interface (if the port supports downshifting to a x8) to save on the amount of power that the GMCH and graphics device use. Docking bandwidth requirements are much less than those for graphics, so the GMCH may only implement a x1 port for this connection (with a maximum of 250 megabytes per second in each direction). PCI Express allows for a variety of docking options due to its hot-plug and low-power capabilities.

As on the desktop model, the bandwidth requirements for the PCI Express connection between the GMCH and ICH depend mostly on the bandwidth requirements for the devices attached to the ICH. For this example, assume that the bandwidth needs of the ICH can still be met via a x4 PCI Express connection (with a maximum of 1 gigabyte per second in each direction). In order to prioritize and differentiate between the various types of traffic flowing between the GMCH and ICH, this interface likely includes support for multiple traffic classes and virtual channels.

The ICH in this example is also almost identical to that in the desktop model. It continues to act as a switch that fans out the third PCI Express domain. The three (downstream) PCI Express ports shown on the ICH are likely x1 ports. These provide high speed (250 megabytes per second maximum each way) connections to generic I/O functions. In the example shown in Figure 12.3, one of those generic I/O functions is located on the motherboard, while the other two ports are accessed via x1 connectors. The x1 connectors used for a mobile system are obviously not going to be the same as those used in a desktop system. There are specifications under development that define mobile specific add-in cards, similar to mini-PCI (from PCI SIG) and the PC Card (from PCMCIA) in existing systems. The PCI Express specification provides a great amount of flexibility in the types of supported connectors and daughter cards that it can support. For example, the power and voltage requirements in a mobile system and for a mobile x1 PCI Express connector likely need to meet much different standards than those used in a desktop environment. Since PCI Express is AC coupled, this allows a wide range of options for the common mode voltages used by a PCI Express device.

This example demonstrates another of the benefits of PCI Express— functionality across multiple segment types. The GMCH and ICH used in the desktop model could, in fact, be directly reused for this mobile model. Even though the x1 port off the GMCH is intended as a Gigabit Ethernet port for desktops, it could just as easily be a x1 docking port for mobile systems. Since PCI Express accounts for cross-segment features such as hot-plugging and reduced power capabilities, it can span a wide variety of platforms.

Server Partitioning

Server chipsets generally follow the MCH and ICH divisions discussed above, with the difference being that the MCH generally has more I/O functionality than a desktop or mobile MCH. An example PCI Express topology in the server space is shown in Figure 12.4.

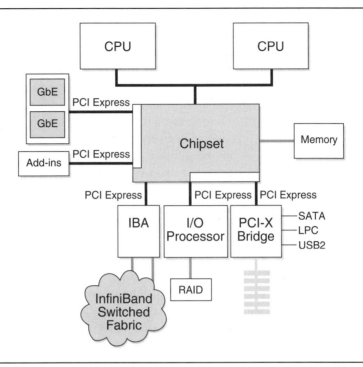

Figure 12.4   Example Server Topology

In the above example, the MCH acts as the root complex, interacting with the CPU and system memory, and fanning out to multiple hierarchy domains. In this example, the MCH has implemented three x8 interfaces, but supports each as two separate x4 ports. In this example, the MCH is running one interface as a x8 port and is running the other two as x4 ports, providing a total of five PCI Express ports (four x4 ports and a x8 port). The full x8 port is connected to an InfiniBand Host Controller Adapter device. The second x8 port splits into two x4 ports, with one x4 port connected to a PCI Express to PCI-X bridge and the other x4 port connected to an I/O Processor (RAID: Redundant Array of Independent Disks controller). The third x8 port is also split into two x4 ports, with one x4 port going to a dual Gigabit Ethernet part and the other x4 port going to a connector.

In this example, the dual Gigabit Ethernet, RAID controller, PCI Express to PCI-X bridge, and generic add-in connector are each provided a x4 port (with a maximum of 1 gigabyte per second in each direction). If a function, such as the PCI Express to PCI-X bridge, requires more bandwidth, this platform is flexible enough to accommodate that need. The system designer could provide that function with a full x8 connection (with a maximum of 2 gigabytes per second in each direction) if they were willing to sacrifice one of the other x4 ports (for example, the generic add-in x4 port). The example shown here has prioritized the Infini-Band Host Controller Adapter device by providing it with a full x8 port, rather than providing an additional x4 port.

This example further demonstrates the great flexibility that PCI Express offers. The chipset designers have simply provided three x8 PCI Express interfaces, but have allowed a wide variety of implementation options. Depending on the platform's needs, those x8 interfaces could be configured as identified here or in a much different manner. If a system does not need to provide PCI Express or PCI-X connectors, this same chip could be used to provide three full x8 interfaces to RAID, Gigabit Ethernet, and InfiniBand. Nor do the chip designers need to identify ahead of time if the port is used on the motherboard, through a single connector on the main board, or through a riser connector in addition to the card connector. PCI Express inherently allows for all of those options. In the above example, any one of the identified functions could be located directly down on the main board, through a connector on the main board, up on a riser, or through a connector located on a riser.

One important item to note at this point is that PCI Express does not require larger interfaces to be able to be divided and run as multiple smaller ports. The chipset designers in this example could have simply implemented three x8 ports and not supported the bifurcation into multiple x4 ports. Each PCI Express port must be able to "downshift" and run as a x1 port, but that does not mean that a x8 port needs to run as 8 separate x1 ports. Implementing multiple port options as discussed here is an option left to the chip designers.

Impact on System Architecture

PCI Express is flexible enough to live within today's computer systems while at the same time expanding system architecture capabilities. As discussed in Chapter 3, one of the goals of PCI Express is to exist within the conventional PCI system environment. This includes leveraging existing operating system support, form factor infrastructure, connector and motherboard manufacturing technologies. The rest of this chapter focuses on how PCI Express impacts the various aspects of system architecture (software implications, however, are covered in Chapter 10).

Form Factors

PCI Express can be used in a variety of form factors and can leverage existing infrastructure. Motherboards, connectors, and cards can be designed to incorporate existing form factors such as ATX/µATX in the desktop space, or rack mount chassis in the server space. This is shown in Figure 12.5.

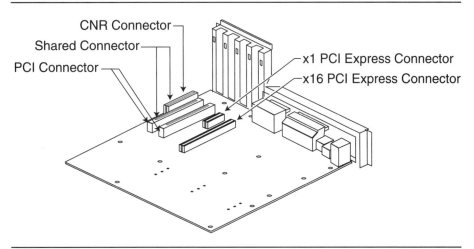

Figure 12.5   PCI Express in µATX Form Factor

In the example shown in Figure 12.5, the µATX motherboard has incorporated five connectors using a total of four expansion slots in the chassis. This design incorporates two PCI slots, one of which shares an expansion slot with the CNR (Communication and Networking Riser) connector. In addition to these three connectors, there is also a x1 PCI Express connector along with a x16 PCI Express connector. The PCI Express connectors are offset (from the back edge of the chassis) by a different amount than CNR, PCI or AGP connectors. Additionally, PCI Express connectors and cards are keyed differently than other standards. Neither of these modifications inhibits PCI Express from properly meeting ATX/ µATX expansion slot specifications. Rather, these modifications are needed to prevent improper insertion of non-PCI Express cards into PCI Express connectors, and vice versa.

Similarly, PCI Express can meet existing form factor requirements in both the mobile and server space. The electrical specifications for the interface are designed to accommodate the high layer-count motherboards and multiple connectors that are often found in these environments.

Adaptation to the existing infrastructure should facilitate the adoption of PCI Express since it does not require a massive retooling effort to precede its arrival. This is also assisted by the ability of PCI Express to coexist with existing technologies on a single platform. As shown in Figure 12.5, PCI Express does not require a system to lose support for existing technologies and connectors. This is not to say that chip designers will not make an either/or tradeoff (for example, AGP8x *or* PCI Express x16), but rather that the technology itself does not force that tradeoff to be made.

Modular Designs

Because of PCI Express' flexibility, it is not necessarily contained to existing form factors. It can be used to help expand new concepts in form factors, and help in evolutionary and revolutionary system designs. For example, PCI Express can facilitate the use of modular or split-system designs. The system core can be separated from peripherals and add-in cards, and be connected through a PCI Express link. For the desktop chipset shown in Figure 12.2, there is no reason that the GMCH and ICH need to be located on the same motherboard. A system designer could decide to separate the ICH into a separate module, then connect that module back to the GMCH's module via a PCI Express connection. Naturally, PCI Express electrical and timing requirements would still need to be met, and the connectors and/or cables needed for such a design would need extensive simulation and validation. Example modular designs are shown in Figure 12.6.

Figure 12.6   Example Modular Designs

Connectors

In order to fit into existing form factors and chassis infrastructure, PCI Express connectors need to be designed to meet the needs of today's system environment. Since PCI Express is highly scalable, however, it also needs to have connectors flexible enough to meet the variety of functions that PCI Express can be used for. As such, PCI Express does not inherently require a single connector. Rather, connector standards are likely to emerge that define connectors and cards for a variety of different needs. There is already work being done on generic add-in cards for desktop, mini-PCI and PC Card replacements for communications and mobile, and modules for server systems. Generic add-in cards are likely to use the connector family shown in Figure 12.7.

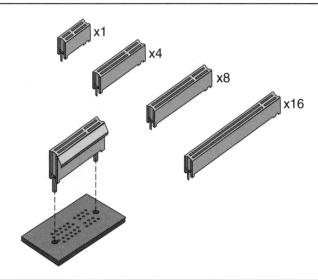

Figure 12.7   PCI Express Connectors

These connectors are simple through-hole designs that fit within the existing ATX/μATX form factor. The scalable design allows for connectors from x1 up to x16. The cards associated with these connectors use the existing PCI I/O bracket and follow PCI card form factor requirements for height (standard versus low profile) and length (half versus full). The connectors are designed in a modular manner such that each successively larger connector acts like the superset connector for its smaller brethren. For example, the x8 connector has all the same connections (in the same places) as the x4 connector, but then adds the four additional lanes to the "end" of the connector. This unique design allows PCI Express connectors to support multiple card sizes. For example, a x8 connector can support x1, x4 as well as x8 cards. This flexibility is shown in Table 12.1.

Table 12.1 PCI Express Card and Connector Plug-in Options

Slot Card	x1	x4	x8	x16
x1	Yes	Yes	Yes	Yes
x4	No	Yes	Yes	Yes
x8	No	No	Yes	Yes
x16	No	No	No	Yes

A system that implements a x16 connector can support all four card sizes, but this does not necessarily mean that the interface will run at all four port widths. If the motherboard uses a x16 connector, the chip attached to that connector is likely to support a port width of x16 (since it does not make much sense to use a connector larger than the port attached to it). Following the specification, that port needs to be able to downshift and run as a x1 port. Whether that port can also run as a x4 port and/or a x8 port is dependent on the implementation details of that chip.

The ability to support multiple connector sizes, as well as card sizes within each connector, poses some interesting problems for shock and vibration. In addition to the connector and card/module standards that are to emerge for PCI Express, there is a need for new retention mechanisms for those cards and connectors. The retention mechanisms currently in use (for example, with AGP) are not necessarily well suited for the shock and vibration issues that face PCI Express.

As mentioned in previous chapters, these connectors are very similar, in terms of materials and manufacturing methods, to those used for conventional PCI. By using the same contact style and through-hole design, the manufacturing costs are less than they would be for a completely new connector design. Additionally, the same processes for securing connectors to the printed circuit board can be reused.

Since PCI Express connectors vary in length (in relationship to the maximum supported link width), connector and card costs are also likely to vary. For generic add-in support, akin to the multiple PCI connectors found in existing desktop systems, system designers are likely to use a x1 connector (providing a maximum of 250 megabytes per second in each direction, or 500 megabytes per second of total theoretical bandwidth). Not only does this provide increased bandwidth capabilities (PCI provides a theoretical maximum of 132 megabytes per second in total bandwidth), but it uses a smaller connector as well. The smaller x1 PCI Express connector should help motherboard designs by freeing up additional real estate for component placement and routing. Since PCI Express requires a smaller connector than PCI, there are also some potential material savings from a manufacturing standpoint. Figure 12.8 shows the comparative size of a x8 PCI Express connector.

Figure 12.8   Sample x8 PCI Express Connector—Quarter is shown for size comparison, not cost comparison!

Presence Detection

The PCI Express connectors shown in Figures 12.7 and 12.8 provide support for presence detection. Specific presence detection pins, located throughout the connector, allow the motherboard to determine if and when a card is inserted or removed. This allows the motherboard to react properly to these types of events. For example, a motherboard may gate power delivery to the connector until it is sure that the card is fully plugged in. Alternatively, the presence detect functionality may be used to log an error event if a card is unexpectedly removed. This feature is optional to implement on the motherboard, as it may make sense for some applications but not for others. For example, does a desktop motherboard need to implement presence detection on a x16 connector that would be primarily used for graphics? Not likely, as having end users plug or unplug a graphics card while the system is still powered up is not a likely scenario.

Power Implications

The PCI Express connectors shown here only provide 3.3 volts and 12 volts to the add-in card (in addition to a 3.3-volt auxiliary supply). This provides some interesting benefits and issues that system designers need to make note of. By having so few voltage rails passed to the card, it eases the motherboard congestion that results from having to supply numerous voltage rails to each connector. The downside to this, however, is that the system needs to be able to supply all the power for PCI Express cards on these rails. Because of this, system designers should perform thorough analysis on power budgets. Confining PCI Express connector power delivery to these rails may require modifications to the silver box (power supply), compared to what may be used in a non-PCI Express system.

Additionally, PCI Express card designers should make note of the small number of power rails they are being provided. A graphics card, for example, will likely need a good deal of voltage regulation on the card that it may not have needed previously. For example, an AGP card could expect to receive 12 volts, 5 volts, 3.3 volts and Vddq (usually 1.5 volts) in addition to an auxiliary voltage. Having so many different voltage rails available limited the amount of local voltage regulation that the card required. PCI Express cards need to account for this and ensure that their power needs are properly considered in the design.

Routing Implications

Stackup

Advances in computer-based electronics, especially cutting edge advances, often require the advancement of printed circuit board (PCB) manufacturing capabilities. This is usually needed to accommodate new requirements for electrical characteristics and tolerances.

The printed circuit board industry uses a variety of glass laminates to manufacture PCBs for various industries. Each laminate exhibits different electrical characteristics and properties. The most common glass laminate used in the computer industry is FR4. This glass laminate is preferred because it has good electrical characteristics and can be used in a wide ˙variety of manufacturing processes. Processes that use FR4 have relatively uniform control of trace impedance, which allows the material to be used in systems that support high speed signaling. PCI Express does *not* require system designers to use specialized glass laminates for printed circuit boards. PCI Express can be implemented on FR4-based PCBs.

The majority of desktop motherboard and add-in card designs are based on a four-layer stackup to save money on system fabrication costs. A traditional four-layer stackup consists of a signal layer, a power layer, a ground layer, and another signal layer (see Figure 12.9). There is significant cost associated with adding additional signal layers (in multiples of two to maintain symmetry), which is usually highly undesirable from a desktop standpoint. Due to increased routing and component density, mobile and server systems typically require stackups with additional layers. In these designs, there are often signal layers in the interior portion of the board to alleviate much of the congestion on the outer signal layers. Signal routing on internal layers (referred to as stripline) have different electrical characteristics than those routed on external layers (referred to as micro-strip). PCI Express electrical requirements are specified in order to accommodate either type of routing.

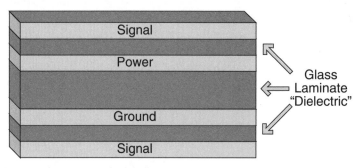

Four-layer stackups are used primarily in the desktop computer market, which equates to approximately 70 percent of overall computer sales.

Figure 12.9 Four Layer Stackup Example

Routing Requirements

As discussed in Chapter 8, PCI Express uses differential signaling. This requires that motherboards and cards use differential routing techniques. Routing should target 100 ohms differential impedance. The PCB stackup (micro-strip versus stripline, dielectric thickness, and so on) impacts what trace thickness and spacing meets that target. For micro-strip routing on a typical desktop stackup, 5-mil wide traces with 7-mil spacing to a differential partner and 20-mil spacing to other signals (5–7–20), meets the 100-ohm differential target.

From a length-matching perspective, PCI Express offers some nice advances over parallel busses such as conventional PCI. In many instances designers have to weave or "snake" traces across the platform in order to meet the length-matching requirement between the clock and data signals for a parallel bus. This is needed to ensure that all the data and clocks arrive at the receiver at the same time. The length-matching requirements of parallel busses, especially as bus speeds increase, come at a high cost to system designers. The snaking required to meet those requirements leads to extra design time as well as platform real estate, as shown on the left side of Figure 12.10. Since each PCI Express lane uses 8-bit/10-bit encoding with an embedded clock (refer to Chapter 8), the lanes' length-matching requirements are greatly relaxed. A PCI Express link can be routed without much consideration for length matching the individual lanes within the link (however, lengths within a differential pair must be closely matched). This is shown on the right side of Figure 12.10.

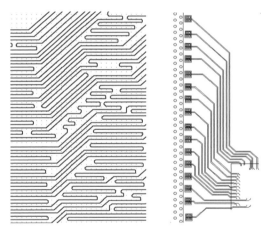

Left side shows a parallel bus routing example where the traces are "snaked" to length-match them to the clock in order to guarantee data and clock arrive simultaneously.

Right side shows a PCI Express routing solution. Note that the freedom from length matching frees up board space and simplifies the routing.

Figure 12.10 Simplified PCI Express Routing

Polarity Inversion

PCI Express offers several other interesting items to facilitate the routing. One example of this is the support for polarity inversion. PCI Express devices must be able to invert a signal after it has been received if its polarity has been reversed. This occurs if the TX+ pin of one device is connected to the RX- pin of its link mate. As discussed in Chapter 8, polarity inversion is determined during link initialization.

Polarity inversion may occur due to a routing error, or it may be deliberate to facilitate routing. For example, as shown in Figure 12.11, the natural alignment between these two devices has the TX+ of one device aligned with the RX- of its link mate. In this scenario, the system designer may want to purposely use polarity inversion to simplify the routing. Trying to force the TX+ of one device to connect to the RX+ of the other would force a crisscross of the signals. That crisscross would require an extra layer change and would force the routing to be non-differential for a time. Polarity inversion helps to simplify the routing.

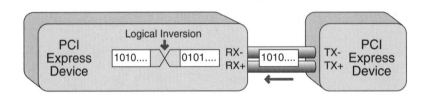

Figure 12.11 Polarity Inversion

Lane Reversal

Lane reversal is another technique that PCI Express offers to facilitate the routing. Lane reversal allows a port to essentially reverse the ordering of its lanes. For instance, if a port is a x2 port, lane 0 may be at the top of the device with lane 1 at the bottom, as shown on the left in Figure 12.12. If a device supports lane reversal, it can reverse its lane ordering and have lane 1 act like lane 0 and lane 0 act like lane 1.

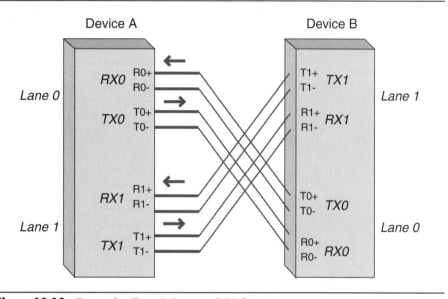

Figure 12.12   Example "Bowtie" on a x2 Link

Why would this be useful? As with polarity inversion, the natural alignment between devices may line up such that lane 0 of Device A does not always line up with lane 0 of Device B. Rather than force the connection of lane 0 to lane 0, forcing a complete crisscross of the interface (referred to as a "bowtie"), lane reversal allows for an easier and more natural routing. This is shown in Figure 12.13.

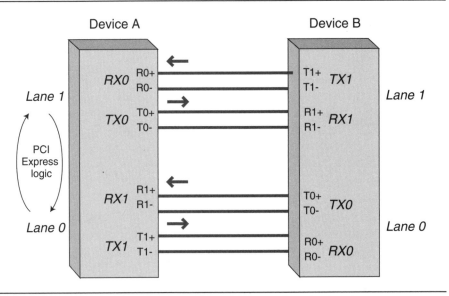

Figure 12.13 "Bowtie" Fixed through Lane Reversal on Device A

Lane reversal should not be considered a "lane anywhere" technique. This cannot be used to allow any pair from one PCI Express device to connect to any pair from its link-mate. For example, on a x8 link: lane reversal does not allow a system designer to arbitrarily decide to hook up Device A lane 0 to Device B lane 5, Device A lane 1 to Device B lane 2, and so on. Lane reversal only allows for normal lane ordering, or a *complete* reversal of the lane ordering: lane 7 becomes lane 0, lane 6 becomes lane 1, and so on.

Whereas polarity inversion is a required mechanism, lane reversal is an optional technique that may or may not be implemented by a PCI Express device. As such, a board designer should only make use of lane reversal if the device is known to support it.

AC Coupling

PCI Express signals are AC coupled to eliminate the DC common mode element. By removing the DC common mode element, the buffer design process for PCI Express becomes much simpler. Each PCI Express device can also have a unique DC common mode voltage element, eliminating the need to have all PCI Express devices and buffers share a common voltage.

This impacts the system in several ways. First, it requires AC coupling capacitors on all PCI Express traces to remove the common mode voltage element. As can be seen near the connector in Figure 12.10, each PCI Express signal has a discrete series AC capacitor on it (capacitor packs are not recommended). The range of AC capacitance that is permissible by the PCI Express specification is 75 to 200 nanofarads.

The removal of the DC common mode element should also facilitate power delivery. Since each PCI Express device can set the common mode voltage of its buffers to differing levels, there is no need to ensure that power delivery is common or shared amongst PCI Express devices. This is quite helpful, because it is difficult to ensure that a common voltage is identical at multiple devices, especially if those devices share a link through multiple connectors. Each PCI Express device can operate at independent and device-optimal voltages, and set the power delivery requirements for that supply accordingly. The dependency on the common mode voltage of its link mate is completely removed from the equation.

Chapter 13

PCI Express Timetable

An invasion of armies can be resisted, but not an idea whose time has come.

—Victor Hugo

This chapter looks more closely at the timeline for products based on PCI Express to enter the market. Several factors play a role in the introduction of applications. This chapter looks at the factors that affect adoption and discusses the profiles, benefits, challenges, and tools for early adopters as well as late adopters of the technology.

Anticipated Schedule

The applications that can take advantage of the benefits of PCI Express will be the first to enter the market. Graphics, Gigabit Ethernet, IEEE 1394, high-speed chip interconnects, and 10 Gigabit Ethernet are a few examples of the types of applications to adopt PCI Express.

Application Roll Out

One of the initial applications expected to make use of PCI Express is PC graphics. The steady demand for increased graphics capability makes PC graphics applications the first opportunity for widespread adoption of PCI Express. Products based on the PCI Express architecture are expected to become available in late 2003. From 1985 to 2002, graphics capabilities evolved from text-only displays to advanced 3D complex images. During the same time period, the graphics interconnect evolved from the 16 megabytes per second bandwidth of the ISA bus to more than 2,000 megabytes per second bandwidth of the AGP8X bus. The PC graphics market has a proven evolution to higher capabilities and PCI Express-based graphics will be among the first applications to take full advantage of the PCI Express interface performance for accesses to the processor and main system memory.

Gigabit Ethernet is expected to experience a rapid adoption, again due to the performance advantages of PCI Express. With the growing number of users browsing the World Wide Web, PCs connected to the Internet, and increased enterprise data usage requirements, Gigabit Ethernet is expected to be the dominant LAN connection by 2004. PCI Express is well suited to interface to Gigabit Ethernet components due to the high-performance attributes of the interface.

High-speed chip interconnects are evolving as building blocks for communications, desktop, mobile, and server applications. By the end of 2004, it is expected that there will be a large number of system designs that implement PCI Express technology. Although standard PCI Express interconnects will co-exist with proprietary chip-to-chip interconnects, the PCI Express technology will pave the wave for high-speed chip-to-chip interconnect technology development.

Several server I/O adapter technologies are expected to take advantage of PCI Express. Some examples are 10 Gigabit Ethernet, InfiniBand[†], and FibreChannel[†]. In the case of 10 Gigabit Ethernet, IEEE 802.3ae standard for 10,000 megabits per second data transfers, PCI Express offers some unique advantages for local area networking within networking equipment as well as storage area networking. PCI Express, through the low-pin count and high-bandwidth interface, removes bridging devices and latency to 10 Gigabit Ethernet adapters. 10 Gigabit Ethernet will likely be deployed to allow organizations to further scale the existing Ethernet packet-based network backbone, data centers and server farms.

Factors Affecting Adoption and Schedule

Several factors affect adoption timing, such as engineering resources within a company, market dynamics, and the industry efforts behind enabling a new technology.

Sufficient Resources

A few companies have sufficient resources to develop the necessary intellectual property and building blocks for a PCI Express interface internally. Larger companies can afford to absorb the development costs and time. For example, Intel is a large company that can afford to develop PCI Express building blocks to be used across multiple divisions and markets. Intel plans to offer a wide range of products and support across multiple market segments that use the PCI Express architecture. Through developing a core PCI Express block, the intellectual property can be reused for mobile, server, embedded, desktop, and communications products thereby spreading the development costs across multiple products and increasing the overall return on investment. Silicon building blocks are expected in 2003 with systems available in 2004.

A wide majority of companies rely on third-party intellectual property suppliers for portions of their design and do not elect to develop the technology internally. The intellectual property provider market supplies the necessary intellectual property building blocks to other companies to build products. In the case of PCI Express, this could be as simple as the design for the pad (electrical interconnect portion of the silicon design) or as complete as a full PCI Express core including Transaction Layer, Data Link Layer, and Physical Layer capabilities. For example, companies such as Cadence and Synopsis derive profits through selling cores to other companies. Under this business model, companies without the resources or desire to enter the market on the leading edge will wait for the availability of intellectual property cores. If the intellectual property supplier market is slow to adopt or develop PCI Express-based cores, the adoption of the PCI Express technology will be hindered for a significant amount of the market. Intellectual property providers must also ensure that the core intellectual property is validated and accurate to establish confidence to their potential customers. In order to prove that the intellectual property is robust, test chips are often developed for testing. The development cycle from specification to test chips can take anywhere from 9 to 18 months. Intellectual property providers typically announce interoperability with other vendors as well as develop hardware kits to ease compliance testing. Multiple intellectual property providers such as Synopsis (www.synopsis.com) have publicly announced implementation and verification cores for PCI Express available in 2003.

Market Dynamics

Market dynamics also play a major role in the adoption of PCI Express applications. Compare the differences between the graphics suppliers and analog modem suppliers. In the case of the graphics market, the end user and customers continually drive for greater performance. Due to the market demand, graphics suppliers capture additional value through higher average selling prices and providing the latest technology and performance over the existing technology. If a graphics supplier can show demonstrable performance gains with PCI Express over AGP8x, that supplier will likely capture more value and more revenue for their latest product as the older technology continues to experience price erosion. The immediate realization in revenue plays a major role in recouping the development costs. The analog modem market provides a very different picture and is indicative of a market with mature technology. Traditional analog modems (56 kilobits per second and below) that attach to the standard phone line are limited to a maximum connection rate on the line side. Migrating to PCI Express over PCI provides no noticeable difference in performance or usability. Today there exists an abundance of PCI-based modems simply due to the wide adoption and low cost of PCI interconnects. Modem suppliers will likely wait until the PCI Express technology ramps and the architecture is established prior to migrating to PCI Express. In theory, new product technologies follow the life cycle of Figure 13.1 (Glen L. Urban and John R. Hauser, *Design and Marketing of New Products* [1980], page 559).

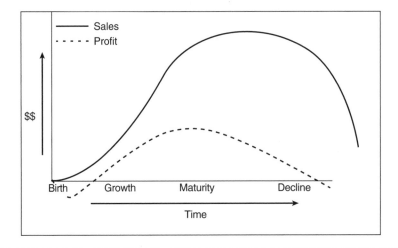

Figure 13.1　Theoretical Life Cycle Curve

When new products enter the market, it takes some time before sales and profits ramp. As products near the growth stage, sales result in profits as the volumes start to become the largest contributing factor. After achieving a peak volume, products eventually enter the decline stage where the profits and sales decline. The challenge a business faces is determining where the industry is on the ideal curve.

Industry Enabling

Industry enabling and collaboration between companies and within SIGs (Special Interest Groups) such as the PCI-SIG will have a significant impact on the adoption of new technologies. As with many new technology transitions, both challenges and opportunities exist. The challenge initial implementations face is the lack of a standard test environment or multiple devices in the market to test against for compliance. This manifests itself in two ways, the misinterpretation of the specification resulting in fundamental errors within the design, and the failure to optimize to vendor-specific implementations. On the flip side, opportunities abound for early adopters to get products to market quickly to establish the industry standard for performance.

The specification's goal is to adequately define a standard so that devices can interoperate yet allow enough range for specific vendors to optimize based on application requirements. In spite of every effort to make the specification clear, implementers are often forced to make assumptions and tradeoffs during the implementation. The risk of developing devices that do not operate grows as multiple vendors come to different conclusions and create incompatibilities that cause errors within the design. Another risk initial implementations face is fundamental errors in interpreting the specification. Over time, the compliance tests and verification programs within the PCI-SIG identify the common pitfalls and typically publish frequently asked questions (FAQs) or clarifications to the specification. The PCI SIG reduces risk of mistakes in later designs.

Another risk is that vendors may optimize within the range of the specification. If a supplier provides a portion of the solution (for instance, a graphics device) but did not make the same assumptions as the host, the overall system will not necessarily be optimized. In this example, although the implementation may not be a specification violation, the two parts may not operate very well with one another. One example left open in the specification is maximum packet size. The PCI Express specification allows for the maximum packet size in the range between 128 bytes and 4096 bytes supporting a wide variety of applications. If the host decided to support 128 bytes, but the attach point such as a Gigabit Ethernet controller or graphics device optimized for 4096 bytes, the performance of the overall system could be significantly less than optimal. Some companies may opt for a wait and see strategy rather than continually modify their design to achieve compatibility as new devices enter the market.

The PCI-SIG and technology leaders such as Intel play a key role in overcoming this obstacle through compliance workshops, co-validation, and developer forums. Intel as an example launched the Intel Developer Network for PCI Express (www.intel.com/technology/pciexpress/index.htm) as a means to provide multiple companies a means to work together to create compatible implementations and a common understanding of PCI Express. The Intel Developer Network for PCI Express is a website hosted by Intel which provides tools, white papers, and a means to contact Intel's experts contributing to the specification. For example, one of the tools available on the Intel Developer Network for PCI Express is the PCI Express Design Checklist. The PCI Express Design Checklist is a checklist of critical implementation specifics of Intel's core design allowing other companies to test pre-silicon design assumptions and check for a common understanding when it comes to implementation decisions. The PCI-SIG plays a larger role in developing compliance checklists, tools, and *plugfests,* where multiple companies collaborate to test and validate product compatibility. Companies that are not active in the PCI-SIG or directly with co-developers will often lose out on the benefits. Refer to the Appendix for more information on Compliance and Interoperability.

Profile of an Early Adopter

Early adopters have a business model that embraces the challenges of introducing new technology. This can be in the form of technology leadership to establish leading edge products or as a provider of the necessary tools and intellectual property to the broader industry. Early adopters usually enter the market to ensure that products are ready prior to the wide industry adoption.

Graphics vendors have established business models around developing the latest technology to maximize the user's experience. Next-generation PC games drive the market for new graphics. Each new generation of PC game is expected to be display-intensive with 3D realistic graphics that push the capabilities of the hardware and software graphics subsystem. PC enthusiasts require a high degree of realistic 3D graphics.

This creates demand for the latest high-end products since the enthusiasts are willing to pay for the experience. Although the PC enthusiasts represent a small segment of the overall market, the enthusiasts are influencers within the market and drive brand and technology leadership recognition for graphics suppliers. For example, current PC graphics suppliers have demonstrated strong execution ability by holding to a six-month product-introduction strategy and employing a multiple-design-team approach to accelerate the time to market. The PCI Express interface provides twice the bandwidth over existing AGP8x interfaces and is expected to be adopted by the graphics industry to deliver the next generation display capabilities.

Beyond graphics, several companies' business models rely on technology leadership. These companies must continue to stay ahead of the market to develop leading edge products. Technological leadership, such as first to market with PCI Express, is critical for brand and corporate image. Companies claiming to lead the technological revolution cannot afford to be caught without a flagship PCI Express product.

Other business models are established on the role of enabling the industry. Intellectual property providers offer core logic designs to PCI Express Physical Layer transceiver (PHY) designs to companies that would not otherwise decide to develop a PCI Express core internally. In this business model, the intellectual property provider develops the necessary cores and sells to other companies in exchange for upfront payments or royalty payments. As PCI Express proliferates and competition increases, the value of intellectual property offering declines with time. Intellectual property providers will therefore rush to be first to market.

Another example of an industry focused on solving early adoption problems are the suppliers of such tools as oscilloscopes, logic analyzers, and bus analyzers. Both Agilent and Tektronix for example have announced tools and capabilities to help the industry validate PCI Express implementations. The Tektronix AWG710[†], Arbitrary Waveform Generator shown in Figure 13.2 generates PCI Express waveforms to enable component suppliers to test, validate, and debug initial PCI Express implementations.

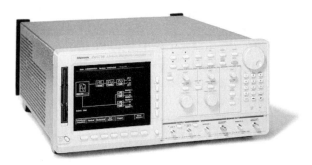

Figure 13.2   Tektronix AWG710, Example of a Tool for PCI Express
Developers

Challenges of Early Adoption

The obvious challenges of early adoption are overcoming the obstacles
and working through the issues that can hinder adoption. The largest
challenge is dealing with ambiguities or assumptions required to move
from the specification phase to actual implementation.

In addition to assumptions, initial specifications often do not adequately cover real world tradeoffs required to implement the design. A
hypothetical example would be that a designer might spend several iterations to achieve the required timing budget in the specification. If there
is enough lobbying to the SIG body that authored the specification, the
timing specification could potentially be modified to match real world
implementations. For the early adopter, this equates to additional resources, time, money, and effort to achieve a stringent specification.
Later adopters can take advantage of the practical knowledge gained
from the experience of earlier attempts and any potential modifications
or clarifications made to the specification. In the case of errata, or identified errors in the specification, the early adopter must navigate through
the issues and modify the design as the errata are published. This is an
unavoidable challenge for the early adopter and has occurred on specifications in the past from multiple standards bodies.

Benefits of Early Adoption

A key benefit to early adoption is to be first to market with a product. In some markets, such as PC graphics, companies gain market share and higher average selling prices for delivering cutting edge products. In these markets, the ability to repeatedly roll out the latest technology leads to revenue growth as users are willing to pay for the experience. As average selling prices face rapid erosion due to multiple suppliers entering the market, being first reduces a company's exposure to average selling price erosion. For the intellectual property provider market, first to market is critical for providing key intellectual property building blocks and establishing brand recognition.

Another benefit is being further down the learning curve. Some technology transitions are inevitable and PCI Express is expected to be one of them due to the wide market segment support and unique benefits covered in Chapter 4. A benefit to adopting earlier versus later is that companies are in a position to optimize prior to the market growing to large volumes. For example, if a component supplier elects to wait instead of developing an early PCI Express device, that component supplier may be faced with a competitor who is further along in development. The competitor may have gained practical knowledge from the early stages of development towards cost optimization. As the market enters heavy competition, the supplier who took advantage of this practical knowledge would potentially be able to gain market share and profit over the supplier late to production who is still working through bugs and defects. The learning curve also applies to market understanding in addition to design optimization. Another scenario would be that the early adopter has a better understanding of how to make the best trade-offs. For example, the market may place a premium of power consumption over performance. Through initial implementations and direct customer feedback, the early adopter would be armed with the information to optimize for performance over power. Direct customer engagement and experience can make the difference in several markets. Through bringing initial products to market, companies develop a good understanding of the market and can ensure follow on product success.

Technology transitions are a unique opportunity when the barrier to entry for a market is lower than normal and provide a benefit to emerging companies. A company may elect to enter a market as an early adopter. With a technology or time-to-market advantage, a company may be able to win key designs if the competitors are slow to adopt. In a stable market without the technology disruption, entrenched players with a strong customer base make it difficult to enter a particular market segment.

Tools for Early Adopters

The standards body behind the specification often provides a means to have access to the specification writers or a means for members to get questions answered. For PCI Express this standards body is the PCI-SIG. The PCI-SIG is the special interest group that owns and manages PCI specifications as open industry standards. The organization defines and implements new industry standard I/O specifications as the industry's local I/O needs evolve. The PCI Special Interest Group was formed in 1992, and the organization became a nonprofit corporation, officially named PCI-SIG in the year 2000. Currently, more than 800 industry-leading companies are active PCI-SIG members. The PCI-SIG, for example, often supports design conferences to members, provides frequently asked questions, a question submission capability, compliance testing workshops and plugfests. Figure 13.3 indicates the types of programs the PCI-SIG provides.

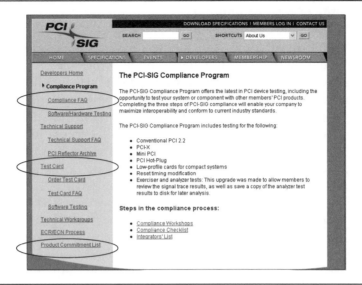

Figure 13.3   Example of PCI-SIG Supported Tools

The intellectual property provider market also provides key tools for developing products for emerging technologies. Companies exploring new product plans perform cost/benefit analysis of making versus buying for the PCI Express block. The benefit of purchasing the PCI Express Physical Layer transceiver (PCI Express PHY) for example, is that purchasing enables the component manufacturer to expedite product development on the core of the device and not spend time and resources on the PCI Express interface. Intellectual property providers typically provide tools for testing, debug, and designing with the core block. In this example, the intellectual property providers are a tool early adopters can use.

Profile of a Later Adopter

Unlike early adopters, late adopters have a business model that demands entering the market after the technology has matured. Some companies look to optimize for cost over time to market. Where cost is the key factor, companies will likely wait for technology maturity rather than spend resources on developing initial products. Until the intellectual property providers, tools, and industry deploy PCI Express in volume, there will be an initial cost impact relative to PCI. The later adopter must overcome the advances the early adopters have made on being further down the learning cure and usually these companies have a fundamental difference in their operating model to support a lower cost structure.

Applications that show little difference in migrating from PCI to PCI Express will transition later, or potentially never. For example, 10/100 Ethernet Network Interface Cards (NICs) are in abundance on PCI today. Migrating from PCI (133 megabytes per second) to PCI Express (250 megabytes per second per direction) for a maximum line connection of 100 megabits per second (12.5 megabytes per second) would give few performance gains because the performance today on PCI is sufficient. The LAN market is quickly adopting Gigabit Ethernet as the desired networking standard, and it is unlikely that 10/100 NIC cards will migrate to PCI Express rapidly, if ever.

Challenges of Late Adoption

Challenges of later adoption are more business risk than technology risk. Entering a market too late may leave the company fighting on razor-thin margins against competitors who have optimized the design and captured a significant portion of the market. The key for entering the market is to enter when the technological risk is low, but the market is still growing. In this case, the late adopter can benefit from the technology challenges resolved by the early adopters while not losing out on the business opportunity. Comparing two hypothetical scenarios highlights the challenge. Figure 13.4 depicts two such scenarios. Scenario 1 indicates a rapid ramp of the technology and scenario 2 shows a slower ramp of the technology.

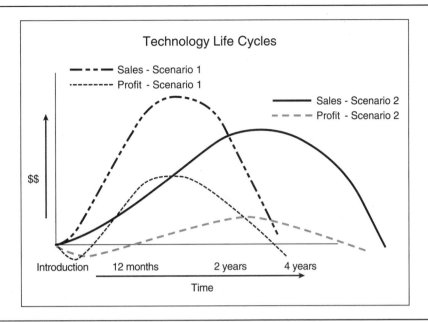

Figure 13.4   Technology Life Cycle Examples

Late adopters must decide when to enter the market. As most new architectures take 12 to 18 months to develop, this means companies must predict accurately or possibly miss the opportunity. For example in scenario 1 of Figure 13.4, products should enter the market prior to 12 months after introduction prior to the peak volume opportunity. This allows the intellectual property providers and the industry to work through some initial iterations while not burdening the late adopter with additional costs. The challenge comes in that, if the company believes the ramp will follow scenario 2, they will develop product plans and resources plans later than required. The end result is that the company enters the market later than anticipated and misses the peak profit opportunity. As mentioned previously, late adopters also need to time the market correctly to overcome the benefits of the learning curve and brand awareness the early adopter has established.

Benefits and Tools for Later Adopters

Benefits of late adoption are avoiding the issues and pitfalls associated with the factors that hinder technology adoption. By waiting, companies avoid the potential multiple design iterations with any new technology. If a change is made to the specification, early adopters will need to spend time and money on updating products to be compliant with the specification. The mask costs alone (the amount required to send a chip off to production) for 300-millimeter wafers is reaching as high as $1 million to $1.5 million for 90 nanometer technology. At 130 nanometers, masks currently cost about $600,000 a set (Clendenin, *EE Times*, September 23, 2002, "The 300-millimeter transition looks tougher for foundries.") Initial implementations may experience multiple design iterations costing several millions of dollars. For the later adopter, there is a wide variety of tools available to thoroughly validate and verify prior to releasing the design for manufacturing and purchasing the mask.

Late adopters also benefit from reduced technology risk. The intellectual property providers and tool providers have had adequate time to develop test silicon and test kits to demonstrate intellectual property compliance to the specification and expanded product portfolios. The late adopter has the ability to test vendors' claims with actual silicon and negotiate among several suppliers. Additionally, the SIG programs are in full steam with a wide variety of programs and tools.

Chapter 14

PCI Express
Product Definition
and Planning

*Setting a goal is not the main thing. It is deciding how you
will go about achieving it and staying with the plan.*

—Tom Landry

This chapter looks more closely at the aspects behind planning and
defining PCI Express-based products from two different perspectives.
The first example represents the challenges and decisions a component
manufacturer must make in developing a PCI Express based device.
There are some unique aspects PCI Express presents to silicon device
manufacturers. The second example takes a look at the challenges and
decisions a motherboard manufacturer must make in using PCI Express
devices.

PC Graphics Components as an Example

The first example presents a PC graphics manufacturer as a case study.
This section of the chapter covers the decisions implementers must make
and the tradeoffs they are faced with in developing new products. This
section highlights some of the unique challenges PCI Express poses beyond historical graphics evolution.

Market Assessment

As covered in Chapter 4, graphics is a unique application that has continuously evolved with faster and faster interfaces. Figure 14.1 shows the bandwidth evolution as discussed in Chapter 4 (Note the PCI Express bandwidth is shown for one direction in Figure 14.1). PC graphics is an application where suppliers can achieve higher prices on initial implementations to recoup the development costs associated with new development.

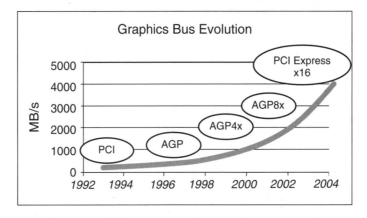

Figure 14.1 PC Graphics Bandwidth Evolution

Design Tradeoffs and Key Decisions

Several factors affect the decision-making process for implementers. The decision of whether to buy or make the new building blocks for PCI Express is tightly coupled with the device manufacturing and testing choices. The criteria for making decisions are time to market, cost, and strategic relevance. The first decision to explore is "buy" versus "make."

Buy versus Make

The graphics component supplier must consider whether to buy or make the necessary building blocks for PCI Express (such as the Physical Layer, Transaction Layer, and so on). Manufacturing and testing decisions are linked to this decision. This section takes three hypothetical scenarios and discusses the relevant topics in buy versus make for:

■ Using an ASIC Manufacturing and Design Flow

■ Using a Foundry Manufacturing and Design Flow

■ Using Internal Manufacturing and Design Flow

The three scenarios are listed in Figure 14.2.

Option	PROs	CONs
ASIC Flow "Vendor A"	• Frees up design resources for other activities • Partner for manufacturing core competency • Use ASIC IP technology	• Design limitations of ASIC process flow • Reliance on 3rd party for manufacturing • Limited to ASIC IP library
Foundry "Vendor B"	• Potentially frees up design resources for other activities • Partner for manufacturing core competency • Wide availability of IP providers	• Design limitations of foundry process flow • Reliance on 3rd party for manufacturing
Internal Fabrication "Vendor C"	• IP in house • IP used across multiple products • Manufacturing as a core competency	• Large capital expenditure for manufacturing • Design limitations of internal fabrication ability • Reliance on internal IP development

Increasing Reliance on 3rd Party (vertical arrow, pointing up)

Figure 14.2   Design Tradeoffs and Key Decisions

The first scenario is Vendor A utilizing an ASIC flow. In this model, the vendor typically partners with an ASIC supplier who provides manufacturing capability as well as access to leading edge intellectual property developed for the specific ASIC fabrication facility (fab). The graphics vendor submits the design to an outsourced manufacturer who owns and operates the fab. What is unique with the ASIC flow is the ability to use the vendor's intellectual property in conjunction with the ASIC manufacturing process for PCI Express building blocks. In this case, Vendor A may elect to use the ASIC's intellectual property library for the physical layer interconnect and bolt up to the internally developed graphics core logic such as DX9 shaders. The advantage for a resource-constrained company is the ability to focus on the core competency (that is, the graphics engine) while outsourcing the necessary but still critical pieces of the design. Key factors to consider in this scenario are costs, which are typically on a per-unit basis and include an upfront payment, and the long term strategic impact. Typically, ASIC flows do not offer multiple sources of intellectual property from other suppliers. ASIC flows become difficult for multiple product SKUs and multiple product generations due to the generally limited flexibility. ASIC flows usually encompass wafer and final component testing. The graphics vendor receives the finished product that is ready to ship.

The other category of silicon graphics suppliers who do not operate fabrication facilities use a fabless semiconductor business model or foundry flow. Here the tradeoffs are still to "buy" versus "make" the necessary building blocks, but the differences vary significantly. Vendor B for example operates a fabless business model and partners with foundries such as TSMC and UMC. In this business model, the graphics vendor pays for the mask set for the specific foundry's fab. The mask is used in the production facility to create wafers that contain multiple chips. At the end of the process flow, the vendor receives untested raw wafers. The foundry typically does not provide intellectual property, but provides the core libraries necessary to design the end product. Unlike the ASIC flow, there is a wide availability of intellectual property building blocks from multiple intellectual property suppliers.

However, the decision to make in this scenario is whether or not to buy intellectual property from the intellectual property suppliers targeted at a specific foundry or to develop the necessary building blocks internally. This decision boils down to time to market, cost, and strategic relevance. For example, if the company can expedite product development by several months at the expense of a million dollars in fees to the intellectual property provider for the Physical Layer core, this may be a worthwhile tradeoff to gain market segment share and several months of profits. Alternatively, if the vendor determines the PCI Express core is critical to their future and want to own the rights to the intellectual property outright, they may opt to develop the PCI Express building blocks internally. The graphics vendors typically partner with one fabless semiconductor supplier to attempt to gain the largest bargaining position on wafer costs. Unlike the ASIC flow, the foundry model still requires the vendor to determine packaging and testing options for the end device.

Finally, Vendor C is a vertically integrated company and has an established manufacturing process capability (such as Intel and SiS). The decision of "buy" versus "make" is significantly altered if the vendor has internal fabrication facilities. In this scenario, the process manufacturing capability (ability to build chips) is likely to be protected. The vendor may determine that gaining contract workers or entering a license agreement with an intellectual property provider to develop fab- or vendor-specific cores may free up critical resources, enabling the product to come to market quickly. The tradeoffs to determine are cost, impact to product schedule, and long-term strategic impact. If entering a license agreement only gains a month in development time versus designing the device from the ground up, the supplier will likely opt to develop the necessary cores in house to retain the skills, retain the acquired knowledge, and protect the intellectual property. However, given resource constraints in the design team, this decision will get more difficult as partnering with an intellectual property provider pulls in the product schedule. If partnering saves months of time, the increase in revenue and profits from entering the market early may justify the cost and risk. The strategic relevance the vendor must assess is long term availability of the intellectual property to future products.

Key Challenges of PCI Express

Unique to PCI Express in the "buy" versus "make" decision is the transition from parallel to serial technology. Comparing clocking implementations of the transition from AGP4x to AGP8x to PCI Express demonstrates the major shift in technology. Previous AGP evolutions introduced a change in the strobe or data sampling rate, but maintained the same underlying clocking implementation. AGP4x and AGP8x both relied on a 66 megahertz clock to drive the necessary logic. The strobe signals inform the necessary circuitry to sample all 32 bits of data on a parallel data bus. Figure 14.3 highlights the underlying clocking technology used in both AGP4x and AGP8x. For the graphics suppliers to accommodate the technology migration from AGP4x to AGP8x, graphics suppliers were required to modify the data recover circuitry on the 32-bit bus interface and add some additional logic. Relative to the PCI Express transition, this is a natural evolutionary transition, albeit with challenges.

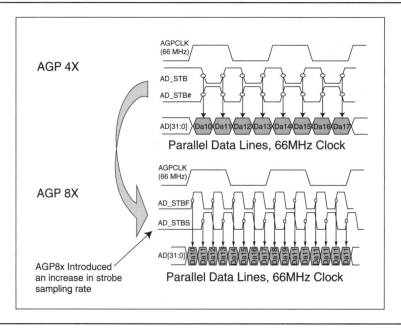

Figure 14.3   AGP4x to AGP8x Evolution

As the processor and main memory bandwidth continues to increase in capability, the graphics interface must also scale. AGP8x represents the end of the line for the practical limits of cost and performance for parallel graphics interconnects. The parallel data transfer cannot be easily scaled up in frequency and performance. The signal skew requirements to maintain accurate sampling of the entire 32-bit bus limit the ability to push the frequency higher. These factors limit the ability to continue developing cost-effective parallel interconnects. The advantages of high-speed, point to point, low-pin count in PCI Express solves the timing and skew problems while still providing the ability to transfer greater amounts of data across the interface. However, analog circuits that can handle the high-speed data transfer can be extremely difficult to design and introduce a new dynamic for suppliers. For example, with AGP8x, circuit designers dealt with sampling data 8 times in a given 66 megahertz clock cycle as shown in Figure 14.3, or approximately every 1.9 nanoseconds. In comparison, PCI Express is signaling at 2,500 megabits per second, or approximately every 0.4 nanoseconds. This is almost five times more often! Figure 14.4 shows the major shift in technology from the previous parallel data transfer to the serial PCI Express technology.

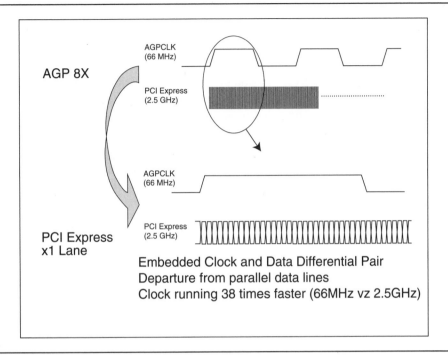

Figure 14.4   AGP8x to PCI Express Evolution

Along with the new high-speed challenges are device testing trade-offs. Graphics suppliers will want to ensure the product that leaves their factory is of a high standard of quality such that OEMs and end-users will not experience field failures. The objective of product test programs is to ensure that the products leaving the factory are of a high enough standard of quality to reduce return and failure costs. Quality is typically measured in the Defects per Million or DPM. To achieve these standards, the industry has embraced two methodologies, at-speed testing and structural testing. The objective of structural testing is to catch manufacturing defects. If the device has a damaged transistor, the functional test should identify the failure by detecting that the transistor did not turn on. Structural tests typically implement a scan chain, where a scan of 0s and 1s are inserted serially into the device and the tester captures a chain of output values that gets compared with the expected outcome. In the damaged transistor example where the transistor failed to turn on, the tester detects an error in the output.

The objective of at-speed testing is to ensure that the device operates as expected under "real world conditions." In this scenario, the transistor may have turned on as expected in the functional test, but the at-speed testing ensures that the transistor turned on in the right amount of time. The departure from the 66 megahertz clocking domain to the 2.5 gigahertz clocking capability will provide substantial initial challenges for at-speed testing. Although these speeds are not beyond the capabilities of some of the testers currently on the market, the cost of developing an entire test floor with at-speed testers would be prohibitive. Vendors must balance cost and risk in developing sufficient test coverage plans.

Key Challenges of Specification to Product

Challenges always exist when attempting to develop devices from concept and specification into reality. Although all the possible trade-offs and decisions could constitute a book on its own, this section discusses an example to highlight the difficulty of some of the implementation choices vendors are forced to make. Recall the PCI Express specification allows for packet payload (data portion of the packet) sizes between 128 bytes and 4096 bytes. Taking a simplified analysis of this decision highlights the tradeoffs implementers are forced to make.

Recall from Chapter 5, PCI Express uses Transaction Layer Packets (TLPs) to generate packets to convey a request or completion of a transaction and cover functionality from I/O and memory reads to flow control and configuration requests. Figure 14.5 (also Figure 5.5) describes the key pieces to build a TLP. The data payload portion is specified in the Max_Payload_Size field of the Link Command Register in the PCI configuration space.

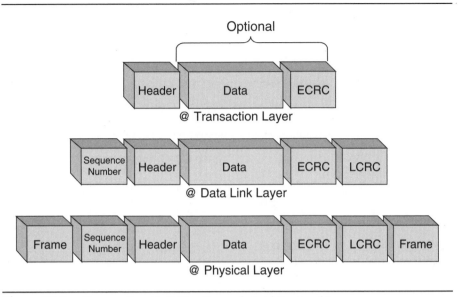

Figure 14.5 Transaction Build-Up through Architectural Layers

Analyzing a hypothetical example highlights the issues of transforming a specification into a product. Assuming a generic case of reading from memory, the maximum data payload of Figure 14.5 may vary from 128 bytes to 4096 bytes depending on the device configuration for Max_Payload_Size. However, the header remains at 16 bytes, the sequence Number at 2 bytes, the ECRC at 4 bytes, and the LCRC at 4 bytes (refer to Chapters 6 and 7). Choosing the maximum payload size to optimize the internal architecture becomes one of many challenges. Several factors impact link efficiency such as latency, configuration cycles, number of DLLPs used for link management, 8-bit/10-bit encoding, other TLP activity such as I/O packets, and so on. However, the data payload size alone has an impact on the per-packet efficiency. Figure 14.6 indicates the packet efficiency based on the data payload size setting for the allowable range and ignores the Framing sequence for simplicity. Note that the chart in Figure 14.6 assumes a worst case size for the header by assuming a 64-bit address field and is on a per-packet basis and not indicative of link efficiency. The values would be slightly better if a header with a 32-bit address field were used. For larger data payload sizes, the packet delivers more data content in relation to the total packet size (Data + Header + ECRC + LCRC + Sequence). This is what you would expect since the larger data payload configuration contains significantly more data than the framing and control information. The data packet density percentages shown in Figure 14.6 indicate the percentage of data characters per packet (minus framing). Actual link efficiency and "real" data throughput is impacted by link management functions (for example, DLLPs) and 8-bit/10-bit encoding (which reduces the "real" data throughput to 80 percent of the theoretical link transfer rate).

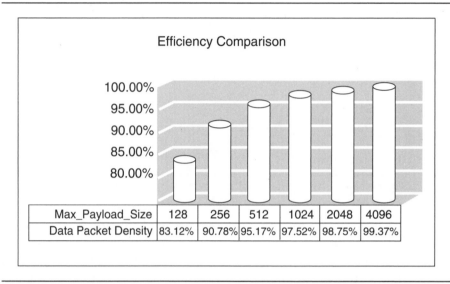

Max_Payload_Size	128	256	512	1024	2048	4096
Data Packet Density	83.12%	90.78%	95.17%	97.52%	98.75%	99.37%

Figure 14.6   Packet Efficiency as a Function of Max_Payload_Size

Implementing an architecture that is optimized for a 4096-byte payload size would improve the link efficiency for large data transfers because it provides close to 100 percent data content versus the overhead in a per packet basis. For a graphics device that needs to pull large amounts of display data from main memory, the implementation that uses the largest data payload whenever possible is the most efficient at the PCI Express interconnect level. So choose 4096 bytes and be done, right?

However, there are several other factors to take into consideration. The complete system architecture needs to be comprehended. Figure 14.7 is the main graphics subsystem of the PC today. It comprises of the processor, memory controller, main system memory, the graphics controller, and the local graphics memory.

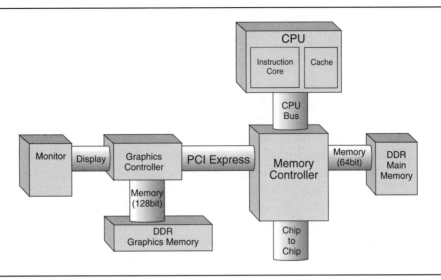

Figure 14.7   PC Graphics Subsystem

All these subsystems need to be considered before optimizing the graphics controller's PCI Express interface. The processors in the majority of today's systems implement a 64-byte cache line. Given that the majority of the memory controller's time is spent loading data and code from main memory to the processor, cache line sizes are a determining factor in developing the memory controller architecture. The other determining factor is the memory architecture. Figure 14.7 shows a 64-bit DDR interface. Also, DDR SDRAM can only transfer a limited amount of data at the peak rate. SDRAM devices transfer data from what are called open pages at the maximum rate and have a limited number of pages that can be open at one time. For example, most systems can only support up to 16 open pages at any one time. For large data transfers from main memory, there are typically not enough open pages to transfer data from main memory at the peak rate. In this event, the SDRAM devices need to be activated and allowed time to close the open pages and open new ones, which limits the effective data transfer rate. Given these two factors, the internal memory controller architecture will likely be optimized for smaller data transfers to align to the processor cache line size and optimized for the current memory technology. A graphics device connecting to the memory controller may not see a benefit or even support for a 4096-byte data payload size configuration. Additionally, the system design will require larger buffers, or on-chip memory, to temporarily store the packet. The larger on-chip memory in turn increases product cost.

The memory interface to the graphics local memory also introduces limitations as the graphics DDR SDRAM faces the same limitations as the main memory system experiences. Given all these factors, the graphics device needs to balance the internal architecture to maximize data transfer from local memory as well as across the PCI Express interface. Why optimize for a large data payload if the other connection does not support it and it costs more?

Actual product design implementations can create much more complex problems. Recall from Chapter 8, the Physical Layer contains all the necessary digital and analog circuits required to configure and maintain the link. For multiple lane configurations, such as a PCI Express graphics x16 connection, the individual links must train to the framing sequence to identify the start of the packet in the electrical sub-block. In addition to the parallel-to-serial conversion in the electrical sub-block, the receive buffer is responsible for recovering the link clock that has been embedded in the data. With every incoming bit transition, the receive side PLL circuits are resynchronized to maintain bit and symbol (10 bits) lock. The tradeoffs on implementation can be overwhelming in determining the accuracy versus the cost of implementing multiple PLLs (Phased Locked Loops).

Implementers must wade through a host of tradeoffs and decisions to ensure the product arrives on time with sufficient performance and adequate cost structure.

Motherboard Vendors as an Example

The second case study explores the challenges and factors a motherboard manufacturer will encounter in using PCI Express-based products. The decisions and tradeoffs are different from the ones silicon device manufacturers face. This section looks primarily at the market and cost impact of introducing products with PCI Express.

Market Assessment versus Cost

The challenges a motherboard vendor faces are different than the component vendors. Technology and market transition always cause chaos. The motherboard vendor must assess both market demand and cost in comparing the old and the new technology. Market demand comes back to end-user impact and willingness to pay for performance and features. To take advantage of the greater performance for Gigabit Ethernet and the new graphics cards, board vendors will likely pursue chipsets with the latest PCI Express interfaces. Motherboard vendor decisions will be heavily weighted by the choices component suppliers offer. For example, if Intel's latest chipset supports PCI Express x16 and AGP8x on the memory controller, the motherboard vendor is faced with less risk and can populate the necessary connectors and devices according to the market. However, if the chipset is a hard transition (supports PCI Express only), this forces the issue of which chipset to pursue, older AGP8x or newer PCI Express. Along with the market demand, cost during technology transition plays a critical role.

Prices typically fall with volume. Figure 14.8 below is a theoretical cost-volume curve. Due to the new connectors required for PCI Express, the initial lower volume from manufactures will present an initial cost impact until the volume ramps.

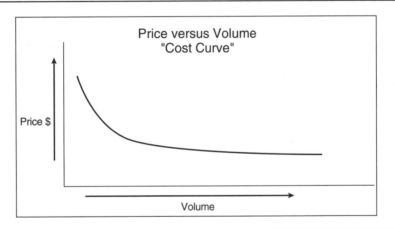

Figure 14.8   Cost Curve: Price as a Function of Volume

For example, the motherboard vendor is likely purchasing hundreds of thousands of PCI connectors for the existing inventory. To negotiate the best price, vendors typically place large orders. The price per connector on a 100 piece order will be higher than the price on a 100,000 piece order. This is expected to be a transitional problem only and should be ratified once the volume begins to ship. Recall from Chapter 3, one of the main objectives of PCI Express is to achieve system cost parity with existing implementations while providing significantly greater performance. Comparing the connectors for both PCI and PCI Express clearly indicates that in the long run, PCI Express will succeed in being the lower cost solution. The PCI connector consumes 120 pins and is roughly 84 millimeters long. The PCI Express x1 connector is much smaller at 25 millimeters long with 36 pins. Refer to Figure 14.9 for comparison of the various connectors. Although the cost parity will likely be achieved over time, the initial higher cost for the necessary components (silicon, connectors, and so on) may delay adoption in the most price-sensitive markets.

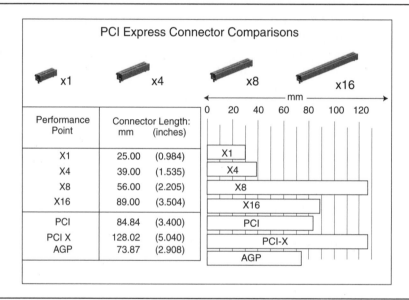

Figure 14.9　PCI Express Connector Comparisons

A potential solution would be to work directly with the component suppliers to ensure both interfaces are supported. Recall from Chapter 3, one of the key benefits of PCI Express is the high bandwidth and low pin count. PCI for example consumes 84 pins on an I/O controller to support up to six connections (Note: the pin count on the I/O controller is not the same as the connector due to auxiliary and power signals). A single x1 configuration only requires six pins. For the I/O controller to hypothetically support two x1 configurations in addition to the PCI interface only costs 12 more pins and the die area. This will likely be an acceptable tradeoff for both the board manufacturer and the component supplier. The graphics interface requires more consideration due to the large pin count. The memory controller today requires 63 pins to support AGP8x. To also supply PCI Express graphics in a x16 configuration requires another 96 pins and more die area.

The new features and performance of PCI Express will be the driving factor in pushing the adoption of PCI Express. The short term market transitional issues should be resolved with time.

Design Tradeoffs and Key Decisions

The largest challenge of using PCI Express is the significant shift in technology. PCI has operated well for the last ten years as a common clock implementation. A PCI clock is routed to a transmitter and the receivers of each device. Data is transmitted on a clock edge and captured at the receiver on the following edge. As discussed previously, the common clock implementation limits the frequency to less than 200 megahertz due to skew between components and the time it takes for the electrical signals to propagate from the transmitter to the receiver. Motherboard manufactures have experienced minimal signal integrity difficulties with the current PCI 33 megahertz clock. PCI Express is a major shift in focus and represents a signaling rate 75 times faster than PCI. Motherboard vendors will need to adhere to strict guidelines and follow high-speed design practices to develop a robust motherboard design. PCI Express inherently reduces some of the issues with high-speed signaling due to the embedded clock, differential pairs, and point-to-point topology, but still presents a significant challenge.

One of the key decisions due to the faster signaling is whether or not to perform simulations of the motherboard layout. Simulations allow the vendor to predict how the system will operate prior to manufacturing. Modeling signal integrity, via HSPCIE or IBIS, is an excellent tool to analyze the board and repair potentially fatal mistakes prior to manufacturing. Given the fact that PCI Express is up to five times faster than anything on the current PC, vendors need to consider expanding their simulation capabilities and factor in variables currently not accounted for. For example, PCB traces account for the majority of signal degradation in most cases. At the PCI Express signaling rate, traces look less and less like a connection between two devices and more like a transmission line with significant capacitance and inductance. The PCI Express specification defines the channel from the device package to the connector, so everything in between must be considered. Previous technologies did not require this level of signal analysis. Figure 14.10 is a diagram of a side view of a 4-layer motherboard to highlight all the potential causes for signal deformation that are trivial for most PCI implementations. Unlike previous technologies, vendors can no longer ignore the affects of vias, capacitive parasitics, and connectors.

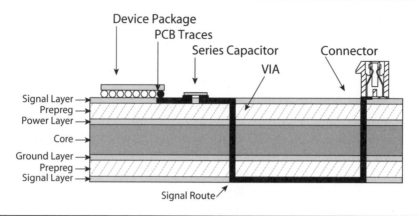

Figure 14.10 Side View of a 4-layer Motherboard

Technology transitions create both the opportunity and the necessity to revisit all of the previous operating assumptions. Vendors should revisit their test, debug, and manufacturing capabilities in light of a new technology. Refer to Chapter 12 for implementation specifics.

Conclusion

Hopefully, this book has helped show that PCI Express is an exciting new architecture that will help move both the computing and communications industries forward through the next ten years. The technology is flexible enough to span computing platforms from servers to laptops to desktop PCs, and serve as the interconnect for Gigabit Ethernet, graphics, as well as numerous other generic I/O devices.

This flexibility is afforded by PCI Express's layered architecture. The three architectural layers offer increased error detection and handling capabilities, flexible traffic prioritization and flow control policies, and the modularity to scale into the future. Additionally, PCI Express provides revolutionary capabilities for streaming media, hot plugging, and advanced power management.

PCI Express does this while maintaining compatibility with much of the existing hardware and software infrastructure to enable a smooth transition. At the same time, it offers exciting new opportunities to develop new form factors, cards and modules, and entirely new usage models.

For all these reasons, PCI Express truly offers an inflection point that will help computer and communication platforms evolve over the next decade. As a result, those that understand and embrace this technology now have the opportunity to help steer the direction of those industries through their evolution.

Appendix

PCI Express Compliance & Interoperability

Any technology, especially when it is new, requires careful nurturing and more importantly needs a set of well defined criteria by which implementations can be judged against the technology's relevant specifications. There have been such criteria for other PCI technologies in the past and efforts are underway to do the same for PCI Express. These criteria essentially address two aspects of a PCI Express device or function—Compliance and Interoperability (C&I). A function here refers to a component like BIOS and not a PCI Express function. It is worth noting that while compliance and interoperability are necessary, neither alone is sufficient by itself. A product must be both compliant and interoperable. This section is intended to show how the C&I criteria as well as the tools and mechanisms to test for adherence to that criteria are developed. It is highly recommended that readers of this book go to the PCI-SIG website to get the latest details on the recommended procedures. In particular, every vendor contemplating a PCI Express product is encouraged to pay special attention to the compliance and interoperability requirements. If the compliance and interoperability requirements are not satisfied, they could become a stumbling block in getting products to market.

Compliance and Interoperability Terminology

Assertion—Defines design requirements in terms of testable Boolean operations, mapping test pass/fail criteria directly back to design requirements and the related design specification(s). Each item in a checklist may be broken into and tested via one or more assertions.

C&I—Compliance and Interoperability. Taken together, these form the basis for measuring a device or function against related design requirements.

Checklists—A set of design requirements for each class of PCI Express devices and functions: root complex (RC), switches, endpoints, bridges, and so on. It is important to note that in some cases a checklist item may be the same as an assertion.

Compliance—Design conformance to the requirements detailed in the PCI Express Specifications.

DUT—Device Under Test.

Interoperability—Ability to coexist, function and interact as needed with other (compliant) PCI Express devices and functions within an operational domain (such as a computer system, operating system environment, application software, and so on).

Test Description—Consists of an algorithm to test an assertion, pass/fail criteria and topology recommendations for the test setup.

Compliance Development Process

Testing for compliance involves architecture specifications, checklists, assertions, test specifications, test tools and results. The relationship between each is shown in Figure A.1.

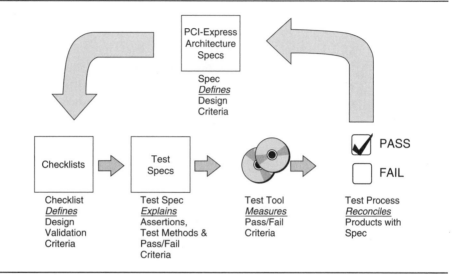

Figure A.1   Compliance Testing

The checklist documents are organized on the basis of classes of devices: root complex, endpoint, switches and bridges and so on. Inside each of these documents, there will be applicable checklist items defined at each layer (Physical Layer, Transaction Layer, and Data Link Layer) and at functional aspects (configuration, hot-plug, power management, and so on.). The test specifications break the checklist items into assertions as needed and specify the topology requirements and the algorithms to test those assertions. Test descriptions are the basis for guiding the process of either performing manual testing or developing automated test procedures for verifying compliance and interoperability of devices and functions.

In order to verify that a device or function meets a checklist item's requirements all the relevant tests (covering assertions for that checklist item and as defined in the related Test Specifications) must be executed successfully. It is imperative that all device and function vendors make every attempt to understand and fulfill the checklist requirements for the device and/or function they are building.

Compliance Testing

It is expected that all major test equipment vendors will provide compliance test tools applicable at various layers. In addition the PCI-SIG is likely to identify a set of equipment for the compliance testing process. A PCI Express product vendor should check the websites listed later in the Appendix to see what test equipment is relevant to their product and obtain them to test on their premises before going to a plugfest. Figures A.2 and A.3 show example topologies that may be used for testing at the platform (BIOS and root complex) and at the add-in device (endpoints, switches, bridges) levels. The actual test topologies employed in compliance testing may be different from what is shown here but are expected to be functionally equivalent. The Functional Compliance Test (FCT) card or an entity providing a similar function is intended to test at the link and above layers (including BIOS). A separate electrical tester card is intended to verify electrical compliance at multiple link widths. In all cases it is expected that the tests executed employing such cards will clearly map the test results to one or a set of assertions. In addition, test equipment, such as protocol analyzers or oscilloscopes, are expected to provide support for automatic checking of the results as much as possible thus reducing human intervention and any associated errors. It is worth noting that compliance testing is no substitute for product validation and vendors should make compliance checking as just one of many aspects of validation.

Platform Components

The example topology shown in Figure A.2 is suited to test the platform. The test confirms the BIOS's ability to configure PCI Express and PCI devices properly, program resources for supporting power management and hot-plug, the root complex's ability to handle messages, legacy interrupts, error conditions on the root ports' links, and so on. For electrical testing the electrical tester card is inserted into an appropriate slot (at the width the slot supports) and root ports' transmitter and receiver capabilities (like jitter and voltage levels) will be measured via oscilloscopes and analysis software.

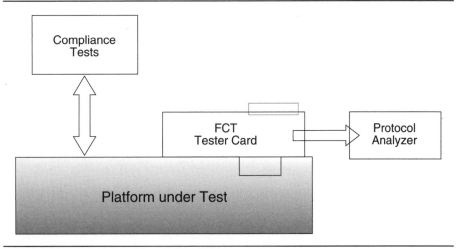

Figure A.2   Example Platform Compliance Test Topology

Add-in Card Components

This example topology is suited to test an add-in card based on endpoint, switch and/or bridge components. In this configuration it is expected that the component is operational and running any software application it supports, thus creating bidirectional traffic between itself and the root complex. Depending upon the final topology these components may be tested in x1 mode and xN mode (N > 1). The testing is expected to test the component configuration space, ability to handle different power management states, robustness of its link and so on.

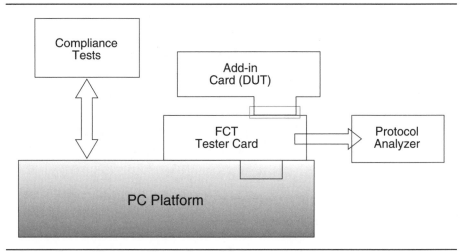

Figure A.3   Example Add-in Card Compliance Test Topology

Interoperability Testing

Compliance is a prerequisite to interoperability testing. Once compliance is established, it is necessary to verify that the device or function in question works with other devices and functions in a system. A typical way to test for this is to introduce the device into a well known operating environment and run applications that will measure the electrical characteristics of the link to which it is connected, power consumptions in the various power management states it supports, and functional characteristics like interrupts. A xN device will be tested in its natural xN mode and thus expose any issues with multi-link functioning like skews and link reversals. The test is repeated by using the devices and functions in as many platforms as applicable.

Plugfests

The PCI-SIG periodically arranges plugfests (multi-day events) where multiple PCI Express product vendors bring their products and participate in a structured testing environment. While it is expected that vendors will have tested their products to a good extent on their premises, early plugfest events provide a great venue to test against other implementations that otherwise may not be accessible. If necessary, there are usually opportunities to test and debug informally outside the established process. For these reasons it is recommended that vendors plan on sending a mix of developers and test engineers to these events. The bottom line is that vendors should take advantage of these events to refine their products and gain a time-to-market advantage.

Useful References

These links provide a starting point for finding the latest information on the C&I Test Specifications and events, architecture specifications, and tools:

- *www.agilent.com*
- *www.catc.com*
- *www.nital.com*
- *developer.intel.com/technology/pciexpress/devnet/*
- *www.pcisig.com/home*
- *www.tektronix.com/*

Glossary

8-bit/10-bit encoding Process of transmitting an 8-bit data value as a 10-bit character. Encoding scheme serves to maximize the number of bit transitions to facilitate clock recovery at the receiver.

AC coupling The process of adding series capacitance to a transmission line to remove DC elements.

Active State Power Management A hardware-autonomous power management mechanism to reduce PCI Express link power through hardware management rather than software management.

AGP Accelerated Graphics Port. Interface used to provide high-speed access to and from a graphics device. Consists of a variety of speeds, including AGP1X, AGP2X, AGP4X, and AGP8X.

ASIC Application Specific Integrated Circuit. Microchip designed for a specific application with a dedicated use.

assertion (Compliance and Interoperability) Defines design requirements in terms of testable Boolean operations, mapping test pass/fail criteria directly back to design requirements and the related design specification(s). Each item in a checklist may be broken into and tested via one or more assertions.

buffered isolation Isolation of peripherals and devices from each other by means of providing a mechanism to shield one device from the other.

bus mastering A mechanism that allows peripherals and devices requiring service to gain immediate and direct control of the bus through an arbitration process. This allows individual devices to master a transaction directly instead of waiting for the host bridge to service the device.

C&I Compliance and Interoperability. Taken together, these form the basis for measuring a device or function against related design requirements.

CardBus CardBus is a 32-bit bus architecture for PC Cards (also known as PCMCIA cards) standardized by the PCMCIA industry association. CardBus refers to the specification of the 32-bit electrical bus.

checklists Within the context of C&I, a set of design requirements for each class of PCI Express devices and functions: root complex (RC), switches, endpoints, bridges, and so on. It is important to note that in some cases a checklist item may be the same as an assertion.

clock extraction The process of extracting a clock signal which has been embedded into a data stream.

completer The device addressed by a request.

completion A packet that terminates (or partially terminates) a previously issued request transaction.

compliance Design conformance to the requirements detailed in the PCI Express Specifications.

concurrent data transmission Transmitting data while simultaneously receiving data.

CRC cyclic redundancy check. A 16-bit value used by the Data Link Layer to check for errors in DLLPs.

Data Link Layer Middle PCI Express architectural layer. Ensures the reliability of packets as they cross a link.

data scrambling A process of systematically scrambling data to avoid repeated data patterns.

DC balance Maintaining the balance of transmitted 1s and 0s from an electrical perspective.

de-emphasis A process used to reduce inter-symbol interference by reducing the transmission strength of subsequent same polarity bit transmissions by 3.5 decibels.

delayed transaction A protocol defined by PCI to address transactions that cannot be immediately serviced. During a delayed transaction the target device issues a retry, instructing the requesting device (master device) to try the transaction once again. This process is repeated until the target device can service the transaction.

deterministic transactions Transactions that are extremely time-critical. Bandwidth must be guaranteed for these types of transactions, which are very sensitive to system latencies. An example of a deterministic transaction is an audio stream that is synchronized to a video feed.

differential serial pathway A pathway where all data is sent and received through a single logical connection between two devices.

differential signaling Logical bits are defined based on a relative difference between two different signals referred to as a differential pair.

DLLP Data Link Layer Packet. A packet generated at the Data Link Layer to support link management functions (for example: flow control, TLP acknowledgment, power management, and so on).

downstream Used to describe a port or link that is farther from the root complex than another related port or link (for example, on a switch). Also describes the direction traffic is flowing when it is going away from the root complex.

dual uni-directional path A combination of two simplex paths going in different directions.

DUT Device Under Test for C&I.

DWord Double Word. Four bytes (32 bits) of data.

DX9 Microsoft DirectX is a group of technologies designed to make Windows-based computers an ideal platform for running and displaying applications rich in multimedia elements such as full-color graphics, video, 3D animation, and rich audio

ECRC End-to-end CRC. A 32-bit value used by the Transaction Layer to check for end-to-end errors in TLPs.

embedded clocking Placing a clock signal into a data stream by means of forcing multiple bit transitions. These multiple bit transitions facilitate clock recovery at the receiver.

endpoint A device that can request and complete PCI Express transactions for itself or on behalf of a non-PCI Express device.

FibreChannel FibreChannel refers to the name of a set of standards defining a high-performance, full duplex interface scaling from 1 gigabit per second and higher used in storage area networks.

GHz Gigahertz. One billion cycles per second.

header Set of fields contained at the front of a packet. Consist of the identifying characteristics and information for that packet.

hot plug The ability to swap I/O cards in a powered system through software intervention.

hot swap The ability to swap I/O cards in a powered system without software interaction.

HSPICE A high accuracy simulation environment used for integrated circuit emulation.

IBIS Input/Output Buffer Information Specification. Specification that describes a modeling technique providing a simple table-based buffer model of a semiconductor device.

InfiniBand A specification defined by the InfiniBand Trade Association that describes a channel-based, switched fabric architecture with performance from 500 megabytes per second to 6 gigabytes per second.

interoperability The ability to coexist, function, and interact as needed with other (compliant) PCI Express devices and functions within an operational domain (such as a computer system, operating system environment, application software, and so on).

I/O Input/Output.

IP Intellectual Property

isochrony The ability to support isochronous data transfers.

isochronous data transfers Time sensitive data transfers. Also known as deterministic transactions.

lane Unit of width for PCI Express interfaces. A single lane contains a dual unidirectional path between two devices.

lane-to-lane skew The difference between the time data is sent across a link, which comprises multiple lanes, to when it is received.

latencies Delays that prohibit a transaction from completing immediately.

LCRC Link CRC. A 32-bit value used by the Data Link Layer to check for link-specific errors in TLPs.

link A collection of lanes forming a communication path between two PCI Express devices.

MHz Megahertz. One million cycles per second.

MSI Message Signaled Interrupt. Mechanism that delivers interrupts via memory write transactions.

packet The fundamental unit for data transfer. Consists of a header and an optional data payload.

PCI Peripheral Component Interconnect. An open, versatile I/O technology originally developed by Intel in the early 1990s capable of theoretically transferring up to 133 megabytes of data per second. PCI is now owned and maintained by the Peripheral Component Interconnect Special Interest Group.

PCI Express to PCI (or PCI-X) bridge A device that has one PCI Express port and one or more PCI/PCI-X interfaces.

PCI-SIG Peripheral Component Interconnect Special Interest Group. Organized by Intel in 1992 as a body of key industry players united in the goal of developing and promoting PCI as an open free specification.

phase A single virtual timeslot on a PCI Express Link.

Physical Layer Lowest PCI Express architectural layer. Transmits and receives all PCI Express packets.

port A collection of transmitters and receivers that exist on a singular device.

QoS Quality of Service. QoS refers to the performance properties of a transaction protocol, which can include throughput, latency, and priority.

receive unit The *PCI Express Base Specification* does not define this as a term. However, for the purpose of this book this term is used to identify the logic in the logical sub-block of the physical layer which takes the deserialized physical packet, taken off the wire by the electrical sub-block, and prepares it to be passed up to the Data Link Layer.

request A packet that initiates a transaction sequence. A request may or may not require a completion.

requester A device that first introduces a PCI Express transaction sequence.

root complex The head (or root) of the connection from the PCI Express I/O system to the CPU and memory.

split transaction A protocol defined by PCI-X and PCI Express to address transactions that cannot be immediately serviced. During a split transaction the target device cues the request and automatically completes the transaction when able. A split transaction is broken into two parts: a request and a completion.

surprise insertion Inserting an unpowered device into a powered system without any advanced warning to the system.

surprise removal Removing a functioning device from a system without any advanced warning to the system.

switch A device that fans out a PCI Express hierarchy. Consists of a single upstream port and multiple downstream ports.

test description Within C&I, consists of an algorithm to test an assertion, pass/fail criteria and topology recommendations for the test setup.

theoretical bandwidth The bandwidth that, in theory, could be transferred between two separate devices. Typically the theoretical bandwidth is based upon the clock data rate and does not take into account design and protocol efficiencies.

TLP Transaction Layer Packet. A packet generated at the Transaction Layer to convey a request or completion.

traffic class Attribute associated with TLPs that identify the priority of that particular packet. Used in conjunction with virtual channels to provide efficient flow control policies.

Transaction Layer Uppermost PCI Express architectural layer. Begins the process of building a transaction.

transmit unit The *PCI Express Base Specification* does not define this as a term. However, for the purpose of this book this term is used to identify the logic in the logical sub-block of the Physical Layer that prepares data link packets received from the Data Link Layer for transmission.

TTM Time To Market. Measure of the time from product definition to entry into the market.

TCO Total Cost of Ownership. Measure of the total cost to own an item beyond the purchase price; includes maintenance cost, warranty costs, repair costs, and so on.

upstream Used to describe a port or link that is closer to the root complex than another related port or link (for example, on a switch). Also describes the direction traffic is flowing when it is going towards the root complex.

virtual channels Virtual connections between two PCI Express devices based upon priority-based servicing

Index